$S2.50$
a

13|22.

Strictly No!

For Vanessa, Phoebe and Amelia

Thanks to Claire Bowman, Lloyd Bradley, Bill Campbell, Kate Muir, Jasper Rees, Daniela Soave, Jim Taylor and Deborah Warner.

STRICTLY NO!

How We're Being Overrun by the Nanny State

Simon Hills

MAINSTREAM
PUBLISHING

EDINBURGH AND LONDON

First published in Great Britain in 2006 by
MAINSTREAM PUBLISHING COMPANY
(EDINBURGH) LTD
7 Albany Street
Edinburgh EH1 3UG

ISBN 978 1 84596 155 8 (from January 2007)
ISBN 1 84596 155 2

A catalogue record for this book is available
from the British Library

Typeset in Berkeley and Billboard

Printed in Great Britain by
Clays Ltd, St Ives plc

The whole aim of practical politics is to keep the populace alarmed – and hence clamorous to be led to safety – by menacing it with an endless series of hobgoblins, all of them imaginary.

H.L. Mencken

Contents

Contents

Introduction

It's coming up to nine-thirty on a Tuesday morning, and we're tramping down the steps from the platform of Shadwell Docklands Light Railway Station to ground level. Very slowly. A young woman is fiddling with her iPod, sauntering at the same speed as the person next to her, leaving no room for us to pass, and a swarm of people are huffing, puffing, shuffling behind them.

Even if you don't know Shadwell DLR, its Dickensian name gives you a fair impression of what you might encounter. It sits, plastic and steel canopies now somewhat tarnished, exposed atop a Victorian viaduct that otherwise hasn't had the benefit of the high-tech chrome makeovers some of our inner-city areas have enjoyed. Here in the East End of London, in the heart of Tower Hamlets, a borough awash with initiatives and outreach workers, litter collects in drifts across the streets and wrecked cars linger for weeks at the roadside. Green water overflows down the side of the viaduct and splashes onto the pavement. The bilious scent of last night's chips blows up the stairway. East End it might be, but Hoxton it ain't.

One of the passengers who has been stuck in the queue with us ambles out onto the road, which has a red-bricked speed bump the size of Snowdon, and is brushed aside by a cyclist.

'Thank you!' he shouts.

The cyclist, clad in black Lycra and a fluorescent-yellow spray top, stops and pulls down his pollution mask.

'What?' he cries. And again, louder, 'WHAT?'

The pedestrian, wearing the young non-suited professional uniform of Nike trainers, scruffy denims and baggy jacket, is sheepish, but he can't back down now, so he scowls at him. The two glare at each other in middle-class road rage for a few seconds, forming a drizzle-soaked cameo that might be called *The Good, The Bad and The Ugly Blue Crash Helmet*, before the cyclist pulls up his mask and pumps the pedals, all the while staring at his adversary behind him. A few furious revolutions send him tumbling into a parked-up plumber's van.

This rather delightful scene is not the most obvious place, I know, to start a book called *Strictly No!* It is not, after all, a book about angry young professionals crashing into vans, or the attire of early twenty-first-century man. But it is, in part, about the spores of self-righteousness that linger in the air after such contretemps and the state of mind that leads to them.

It is also about the ubiquitous crash helmet and the speed bump. These are totems of our age: symbols of an era in which we perceive ourselves constantly to be teetering on a dangerous path beyond which untold horrors wait to enfold us.

Strictly No!'s subject matter can be found, too, around the corner in Cable Street, site in 1936 of one of Britain's most infamous civic confrontations when Sir Oswald Mosley attempted to lead his Blackshirts through the East End. Today a rather more benign incident takes place when another of the throng held up on the station stairs marches straight onto a pedestrian crossing as if it were his garden path. A beaten-up Mercedes screeches to a halt, burying its wheels into the mudguards. The pedestrian ignores it. *Strictly No!* is about this, too: the counter-intuitive rules and regulations that mean that if the pedestrian ended up rolling off the bonnet of the car, it would be the driver who would automatically be in the wrong. It is about the prevalence of individuals, like this pedestrian, who exercise the common sense of a lobster and then clog up the legal system demanding compensation. And about the massed ranks of functionaries whose jobs depend on defending them.

It is also about Cable Street itself. It would take an act of spectacular stupidity – such as walking onto a zebra crossing just as a car was a yard away from it – to have an accident here. This is a thoroughfare laden with street furniture and signage to keep the wayward citizen on a safe, righteous civic path. Along with all the parking-permit signs and pavement build-outs, a huge lurid-green cycle lane stretches out for half a mile or so in both directions from Shadwell Underground station. Blue lollipop signs alert you to the fact that the cycle lane is for cyclists and the pavement for pedestrians. The message is reinforced with pictures of bicycles on the green asphalt just in case you thought it might be, say, a 6 ft by 3,000 ft tennis court. Bus stands and black railings, speed limits and 'CCTV in operation' signs complete the paraphernalia that dominates just one street in this impoverished borough.

At Cable Street's western end are traffic lights permanently on red for the few pedestrians in the area, although they have long since negotiated the crossroads – or indeed jaywalked through the traffic that often stretches for half a mile in a futile queue to cross this once bustling intersection.

Never has the outlook for our well-being been so secure, our life expectancy so high, but here we are, corralling cars into ever-smaller spaces, binding ourselves in reflective Lycra, smothering ourselves in factor 25 or 50, terrified of inhaling a whiff of someone else's cigarette smoke, and warned nightly by our weather forecasters to take extreme care in our cars because of the heavy rain, as if a journey up the M1 threatened hazards on a par with Shackleton's voyage from Elephant Island to South Georgia.

This book takes its cue from one of the most popular and widely disseminated global emails on the Internet. It goes under the title 'I Can't Believe You Made It!' and reads:

Looking back, it's hard to believe that we have lived as long as we have. As children, we would ride in cars with no seat belts or airbags. Riding in the back of a pick-up truck on a warm day was always a special treat.

Our cots were covered with bright-coloured lead-based paint. We had no childproof lids on medicine bottles, doors or cabinets, and when we rode our bikes, we had no helmets. (Not to mention hitchhiking to town as a teenager!)

We drank water from the garden hose and not from a bottle. Horrors.

We would spend hours building our go-karts out of scraps and then rode down the hill, only to find out we forgot the brakes. After running into the bushes a few times, we learnt to solve the problem.

We would leave home in the morning and play all day, as long as we were back when the streetlights came on. No one was able to reach us all day.

No mobile phones. Unthinkable. We played dodge-the-ball and sometimes the ball would really hurt. We got cut and broke bones and broke teeth, and there were no lawsuits from these accidents. They were accidents. No one was to blame but us. Remember accidents?

We had fights and punched each other and got black and blue and learnt to get over it.

We ate cupcakes, bread and butter, and drank sugary orange squash, but we were never overweight . . . we were always outside playing. We shared one lemonade from one bottle with four friends, and no one died from this.

We did not have PlayStations, Nintendo 64, Xbox, video games, 99 channels on cable, video-tape movies, surround sound, mobile phones, personal computers, Internet chat rooms . . . we had friends. We went outside and found them.

We rode bikes or walked to a friend's home and knocked on the door, or rang the bell, or just walked in and talked to them.

Imagine such a thing. Without asking a parent! By ourselves! Out there, in the cold cruel world! Without a guardian. How did we do it?

We made up games with sticks and tennis balls and ate worms and, although we were told it would happen, we did not put out very many eyes, nor did the worms live inside us for ever.

Football teams had trials and not everyone made the side. Those who didn't had to learn to deal with disappointment . . . Some pupils weren't as smart as others, so they failed a grade and were held back to repeat the test . . . Horrors. Tests were not adjusted for any reason.

Our actions were our own. Consequences were expected. No one to hide behind. The idea of a parent bailing us out if we broke a law was unheard of. They actually sided with the law!

This generation has produced some of the best risk-takers and problem solvers and inventors ever. The past 50 years have been an explosion of innovation and new ideas. We had freedom, failure, success and responsibility, and we learnt how to deal with it all.

Why does this strike such a chord with us now? Why is it that, for all the advantages of twenty-first-century living, a wistful air hangs over our centrally heated houses and air-conditioned cars? Maybe it's because we can't walk – let alone drive – down Cable Street without being harangued at every corner. No decision can be left safely to individuals lest we harm ourselves.

This is what we recognise as the nanny state. Political correctness has, over the past 20 years, crept up on us and unleashed a morality that no one particularly asked for, certainly no one voted for, but that dominates our lives with an ethical code that is becoming as all-pervasive as those of the religions of the past. Little additions to the legislature, rules and by-laws from local councils, nips and tucks to the English language – slowly and insidiously, we have been hectored by a ruling elite that has paradoxically got itself into power under the banner of equality. How has it come to dominate our lives so completely with so little resistance?

It is possibly because, although we use the term every day, political correctness is fiendishly difficult to define. It has no Bible. There is no New Testament, no Gideons edition over which to argue the boundaries of its influence. Political correctness is enshrined in the minutes and agendas of hundreds and thousands of conferences and summits, in initiatives and strategies formulated and chewed over in town halls and fluorescently lit community centres, fuelled by breaks for biscuits and tea. It is here that the nanny state was formed.

The nearest we can probably come to defining it would be to say it is a curious mixture of the two dominant intellectual themes of the twentieth century – Freudian individualism and Marxist social theory. Tower Hamlets' fussing over our welfare across its borough smacks of a paternalism worthy of Uncle Joe Stalin. No one's suggesting they're going to send us to the gulag if we cross the road while the red man's illuminated, but they certainly like bossing us about and – the cameras that line the streets are proof of this – like Stalin, keep a very keen eye on us.

On this socialist side of political correctness is an army of functionaries finding ever more dangers to warn us against and fuss over. In May 2005, the government warned of sizzling temperatures in July. No matter that the Met Office can just about predict the weather for the next 24 hours, £100,000 was spent on a leaflet that assumed no one had ever been in the sun before. 'Plan your day in a way that allows you to stay out of the heat,' was one tip. Another helpful piece of advice declared, 'If you must go out, stay in the shade. Wear a hat and light, loose-fitting clothes.' The pamphlet could almost have added, 'The sun's the big, yellow thing in the sky. Don't look at it or you'll go blind.'

Over there, with the Freudian individuals' team, is an army of lawyers poised to uphold our individual human rights, smacking their lips at the thought of suing the Government should one of its citizens get sunstroke. They're there to protect the rights of those like school cook Mary Watkins, who claimed in 2000 she was barely able to walk and had to sleep sitting up after contracting asthma from cooking every day since 1983. The reason for this crippling illness: an allergy to flour. You would have thought that being a professional cook wasn't perhaps the ideal occupation for a woman in her position, this case being roughly the equivalent of an airline pilot suing over finding he had a fear of heights, but her former employer, Birmingham City Council, admitted liability and a judge awarded Mrs Watkins an interim payment of £150,000.

'A countryman between two lawyers is like a fish between two cats,' wrote the eighteenth-century American founding father and polymath Benjamin Franklin. How times have changed. The nation's Mrs Watkinses are now richer to the tune of £1 billion a year in the name of human rights. Law is the boom industry of the new millennium, and bright young things are graduating in their thousands to defend our right not to sneeze. As this book is being written, a proposed Commission for Equality and Human Rights in the UK will have a £50 million-a-year budget to hunt down discrimination in every walk of life.

And so today we have a whole new group of carers and outreach workers to protect us from ill health and prejudicial laws, and another group to protect the prejudicial upholders of the law from being sued by those they're trying to protect. We might feel rather proud to be fought over like this, but, alas, while they may defend the right of Muslim children to wear a veil in school, at the same time politicians are banning fox hunting and smoking in public places and pushing through draconian legislation that allows for that pernicious antithesis of human rights – house arrest without trial. Far from bestowing upon us a new freedom, we are being forced into a tyrannical political straitjacket that has been created not by a man with a moustache but an army of men with clipped beards and women with mockney accents. Let's call them the meddling classes.

They inhabit such essential jobs as 'school travel-plan adviser' in Birmingham, a £35,000-a-year 'people team-manager' in Lambeth, or 'five-a-day coordinators' in just about any borough you care to mention – but we'll take Brent, where £28,903 was added to the annual wage bill for someone to persuade people to eat more fruit and vegetables to 'improve health and well-being' and 'reduce inequalities'. Newcastle has sought out a 'partnership coordinator' (£33,642–£35,934, reporting to the manager for programme development and coordination) to ensure that 'local people get the local service they want in the way they want, and to make Newcastle a better place'.

With all these jobs making cities better places and reducing inequalities, it's somewhat bewildering that we're not all living in paradise. There are, after all, thousands of jobs such as these created every year. Between 1998 and 2005, there was a 680,000 increase in the number of public sector jobs – 524,000 of which were in the fields of health, education and social work. And because there are so many new political bodies and pressure groups, and because, by definition, they all want something to do, the tentacles of government are stretching even further into the nooks and crannies of our personal lives. *Strictly No!* is not a tirade against politicians and civil servants – they are essential to a democracy and to the smooth running of our communities – but against the strictures of facile philosophical dogma.

In the same way the old Eastern-bloc countries shared grey, concrete tower blocks, iconic portraits of their leaders and the smell of cheap petroleum, so the West shares public buildings of glass and steel, speed bumps, piazzas, murals, heritage sites and a self-importance among its leaders. Self-righteousness hangs over our society like a mantle.

'Your friends at Jack Daniel's remind you to drink responsibly,' is the cautionary note at the bottom of the liquor company's advertisements. Well, thanks for the advice, friends, but now you have my money, I think I'll be the one who decides how I'll drink it. We live in an age of these soppy exhortations, along with a numbing obsession with jargon and euphemism. Listen to then Cabinet Secretary Sir Andrew Turnbull in front of the Public Administration Committee in 2002 as he ran through the paper on his plans for the next three years. There is 'customer-focused service delivery', 'consequence management' and 'single integrated structure units'. 'Interchange and succession planning' is there, along with 'knowledge management' and that old favourite 'best practice', which turns up many times in Mayor Ken Livingstone's manifesto for London. Who, pray, would opt for worst practice?

This oddly selfish rhetoric, devised in polytechnics and campus universities during the '60s and '70s, is like political correctness itself: while it purports to be inclusive, so it is actually designed to raise the self-importance of its protagonists and exclude those of us outside their exclusive group. The class warriors of the '60s and '70s have become the politicians of today, and their functionaries have unprecedented power locally, nationally and internationally.

There is a separate parliament for Scotland and Wales – the latter, incidentally, employs 3,000 staff – but still a Scotland Office and Wales Office based in London. The European Commission employs 16,000 people to come up with its burdensome edicts, while in the European Parliament staff numbering upwards of 3,600 uphold human rights we thought were ours anyway. In England, there have been desperate – so far unsuccessful – moves for new elected regional authorities to slot in between central and local government. But who needs democracy? Great and important work is being carried out by unelected regional development agencies: 'We also promote the strengths of the region and help people to regenerate their communities' is one of the lines from the pompous manifesto of the South West of England Regional Development Agency. 'All our work is guided by the Regional Economic Strategy.' (Well, of course.)

But while the politically correct like to spend millions of pounds talking about 'regeneration', or tackling 'child' poverty, as their saccharin rhetoric has it, they are not keen on being poor, let alone associating with the poor, themselves. They don't, as a rule, for example, inhabit the housing estates they have created. So Donald Dewar, the first First Minister of the Scottish Parliament, died with a couple of million quid going spare; David Blunkett, the former leader of the socialist republic of Sheffield, disgraced himself not with a down-at-heel local lass from his constituency but Kimberly Quinn, the posh Yank publisher of *The Spectator*; Tony Blair chooses to send his children not to the local Westminster comprehensive but to the snooty London Oratory School six miles away in wealthy Fulham; meanwhile, his wife, Cherie, who makes hundreds of thousands of pounds fighting for poor people's human rights, sees no contradiction in using her position to pick up a reported 30 grand for a lecture in Washington DC. Back in Scotland, the First Minister, Jack McConnell, spent Hogmanay seeing in 2005 not with the locals but with millionaire broadcaster Kirsty Wark at her villa in Majorca. Which brings us full circle:

she is the same Kirsty Wark who was on the panel to choose the architect for the Scottish Parliament building that was budgeted at £40 million and cost, er, oops, £400 million. She'd been invited onto the panel by her friend Donald Dewar, a neighbour in the rather affluent West End of Glasgow. Of the 97 high-value donors to the Labour Party in 1998–99, more than 30 received some kind of government job.

This is what the meddling classes don't want us to know about. Like the tyrants of the past, the nanny state employs huge armies of spin doctors in an effort to ensure that its message is the only message. It is no coincidence that the Government is Britain's biggest advertiser.

Prime Minister Tony Blair's Cabinet Office is double the size of his predecessor's, and in one year alone he recruited 50 staff. In 2002, the Government employed 81 ministerial advisers, costing £4.4 million a year; the government's staff of spin doctors and advisers increased to 64 and, with salaries of up to £90,000 a year, cost more than £5 million. In the year 2000–01, the Downing Street press office headed by Alastair Campbell, who was responsible, too, for overseeing Downing Street advisers, cost just under £1 million. It's a trend that has continued unabated to the point where even the lowliest pressure group has to have an information officer.

This book is here to debunk some of the Orwellian rhetoric these ideological factories churn out – while it's still allowed.

1 Strictly no history

So how did the nanny state come into being? We don't, after all, have a start-point here. A year zero with a baby child in swaddling clothes, a Karl Marx with a headstone in Highgate Cemetery, a Labour Party that traces going mainstream back to the year 1900.

We know that the nanny state is upon us and that it is built upon what we know as political correctness. Yet we cannot vote for a Politically Correct Party. There are no politically correct societies. No Friends of the Politically Correct. There isn't a Campaign for Political Correctness rallying supporters at fundraisers, leafleting our homes, lobbying the Government. Nor is there a group of intellectuals fussing over its meaning, latter-day existentialists scratching their berets and arguing the case for the *Critique of Dialectical Reason*. We don't have a founding father, a Lenin, who has galvanised these words into a political movement – although it would be delightful to see billboards of outreach workers at play, riding their bicycles alongside bendy buses, or setting forth to non-smoking riverside cafés, captured on a grainy video installation by Tracey Emin.

We have these two words – political correctness – now so ubiquitous that even the abbreviation PC has entered the language to indicate a set of values that we all understand perfectly: the moral backdrop to the nanny state.

So how did it start?

For me, it was when I moved into a South London housing

Welcome to a world gone mad . . . Because the thieves of a stolen scooter in Bath weren't wearing helmets, police refused to give chase in case the perpetrators injured themselves and sued

cooperative in 1980. A group of young people had been eyeing this decaying post-war block of council flats for years. At some point in the '70s, they lobbied the owners, at the time the Greater London Council, and asked them what they were going to do with it.

'Don't know,' was the bureaucrats' response.

That was enough for direct action from our young pioneers. In they went, every weekend, replacing rotten woodwork, tidying the yard and painting the windows in order to turn 75 flats into places in which people could live again. Middle-class young professionals, working-class families, black, white and Asian knuckled down in harmony, united by the prospect of a decent, cheap home and, ultimately – like similar projects no doubt in the Bronx and the poor districts of Barcelona and Berlin – nirvana. The young idealists were finally living alongside their working-class brethren, and the Marxist rhetoric that was flowing through the higher educational system at the time became a blissful reality.

But then came the meetings. Oh dear! No sooner had we got to 'Apologies for Absence' than the first objections started to arise.

'I don't know who wrote these minutes, but can I just suggest that "the chairman" should be called "chair"?'

'Each tenant is responsible for *his* interior maintenance.'

'Point of order, chair, I think an amendment should be tabled. We should make clear that applications from prospective tenants are welcome regardless of race, ability or gender.'

'Before this meeting goes any further, I propose a motion that it should be non-smoking . . .'

And so on. The meetings became dominated by drab, dreary professionals from various NGOs and local government offices who fretted and fussed over the minutes and desperately tried to get one up on their fellow tenants with ever more arcane bits of legislation and knowledge that would prove, once and for all, that strengthening the roof was a substantive motion and would

Fylde Borough Council in Blackpool banned the flying of stunt kites on the beach in 2006 after a woman walking her dog became entangled in the string and endured the horror of being dragged to the ground. 'We felt that this is

therefore need a special general meeting. Gradually but inexorably, the painters, mechanics and builders among the tenants – those people who had proved so vital to renovating the block – drifted away.

When a plumber, coming to one of the last meetings before he too threw in the towel, submitted the suggestion that the principal reason our drains kept blocking was a build-up of brown rice, there were one or two titters but a far larger number of knotted brows. The game was up.

Gradually, the middle-class members moved to more substantial houses, and the working classes showed their devotion to the cooperative movement by exercising their right to buy. Then they moved out to the white semi-detached suburbs that girdle London, and all the idealism was traded in for a crippling mortgage and the deeds for a house they could call their own. Perhaps this is the way of all idealistic projects, from the kibbutz to the collective farm, but here it all started when one woman stuck her hand up and said, 'A point of order, chair.'

These weren't bad people. In fact, you could call them rather virtuous, with their commitment to the cause. They weren't crooks, swindlers, wide boys (sorry, chair, wide people), thugs or burglars. Though not very attractive, maybe: the Jeremies and Nigels in their *ouvrier* donkey jackets and Dr. Martens shoes, and the Sarahs and Fionas in drawstring trousers and clipped grey hair oozed middle-class earnestness but had the sex appeal of a hedgehog.

And they were as bossy as your big brother. With their points of order and tabling of amendments, they succeeded in alienating just about everyone for whom this sweet little housing cooperative was designed to benefit: the old, the poor, anyone who didn't have English as their first language, anyone who didn't agree with their politics and even each other as they developed their ideological spats.

an appropriate measure to ensure the health and safety of everybody on the beaches,' said Susan Fazackerley, local Cabinet member for health and safety

These were the tyro-politicians who are in power today. They had brought with them the teachings of E.P. Thompson, Richard Hoggart, Eric Hobsbawm, and they were high on '60s idealism. We'll see them later, building the nanny state, filtering into established institutions and creating new ones, gradually, inexorably, moving the political agenda in the same way as they did in the housing cooperative.

It was an agenda built on what we now know as *political correctness*: two words that have become almost a joke. They come up weekly, daily, hourly in our conversations – 'It's political correctness gone mad!' we exclaim when the council replaces the word 'Christmas' with 'winter' in an attempt to be non-discriminatory. The epithet, which should make us feel warm and righteous – implying inclusiveness, equality, consideration for others – is now used almost exclusively with disdain. This particularly irked one Dave Tuggle, who, on 14 November 2000, wrote to the Random House reader service The Mavens' Word of the Day and asked why this should be:

> It seems that its usage is largely sarcastic and pejorative. Was this the purpose for its coinage, or did it begin with usage more compatible with its concept (that is, being polite and sensitive in the use of language that refers to others, particularly minorities)?

Of course, the expression 'political correctness' was used long before it slid into our consciousness as a concept. On Dave's behalf, Mavens traced it back to 1793, to US Supreme Court Justice James Wilson, who used the term to say a certain toast was not 'politically correct' – but that wasn't going to get a cycle lane built in preparation for the invention of the penny-farthing. H.V. Morton apparently wrote in 1936, in response to the question

A pensioner in Cardiff was thrown off a bus for carrying a tin of paint on. New health-and-safety rules governing public transport list paint as a 'hazardous article'. A spokesman for Cardiff Bus apologised but added, 'The safety of our

as to why St Paul addressed his converts as Galatians: 'Is there any other word that could have described so mixed a crowd? . . . "Galatians", a term that was politically correct, embraced everyone under Roman rule.' Closer, but the Roman Empire was about as PC as Playboy TV.

We need to get to the late 1960s and early '70s before politically correct was being used by liberals and radicals, as is written in Mavens, in the sense of 'conforming to a body of liberal or radical opinion characterised by the advocacy of approved causes or views, and often by the rejection of language, behaviour, etc., considered discriminatory or offensive'. In 1975, the president of the National Organisation for Women was quoted as saying that her organisation was moving in the 'intellectually and politically correct direction' on the lesbian issue.

There's your answer, Dave. This quote has as much meaning as, say, 'washing machine, indeed, banana, car park'. And on that basis alone, you can see why people might be tempted to use the term sarcastically. But you needn't worry: although the words politically correct are often seen as pejorative, if you're of that persuasion you are part of the most potent political force on the planet.

The *Collins English Dictionary* also limits itself to the language element of political correctness, its entry reading, 'adj. demonstrating progressive ideals, esp. by avoiding vocabulary that is considered offensive, discriminatory or judgmental, esp. concerning race and gender. Abbreviation: PC. political correctness NOUN'.

But something very big has been going on here that isn't reflected in this rather bland dictionary entry, lexical mineral water compared to the 100 per cent-proof vodka of, say, Marxism or Muslim fundamentalism. What is wrong, after all, with being polite to our fellow human beings? What is wrong with demonstrating progressive ideals?

The trouble with language is that it belongs to all of us. And as soon as people want to change it, they are saying they know something more than we do. To take this further, they are saying they are better than the rest of us. The woman in the housing cooperative who proposed using the word 'chair' instead of 'chairman', for example, is saying a) I know something about language that you don't; b) by using chairman instead of chair, you are being insensitive to women and their feelings; c) you are more stupid than I am for not having the wit or sensitivity to realise the offence it might cause, even if the word chair does, for you, conjure up a Parker Knoll recliner rather than a rather strict woman in a gilet wearing no make-up; d) I shall be in charge of your lexicon; e) if you don't accept the fact that I'm in charge, you shall be ostracised. This demonstration of politeness becomes, in effect, a group of people led by chair saying we have the right to control what you think. Twenty-five years on, this battle for our hearts and minds is still being fought.

In 2005, the TUC decided that its members – and isn't this an indication that they have secured excellent wages, superb working conditions and unprecedented opportunity? – needed guidance in how to speak without offending their fellow workers. It issued a document with the egregious title 'Diversity in Diction, Equality in Action', which says in its foreword, 'If we are truly to demonstrate respect, understanding and fairness, tackle discrimination and exclusion, we need to ensure that the language we use is consistent with those intentions.'

This extraordinarily dull piece of work, with no subject in its title, drones on for fifty-two pages (the last two of which list another twelve organisations, such as Equality South West, who presumably also have similar documents telling the preternaturally stupid how to talk to each other without one of them marching off in tears).

One assumes, at least, it is for the preternaturally stupid.

'Communication takes many forms,' the TUC document announces in its introduction. Well, we'll be blowed! Tell us more. 'The words we use should give a clear message to everyone we deal with that we value diversity and respect individual differences.' What, *all* of them?

But it's even more complicated than this. 'Communication is not just about words, however, and we should also ensure that our tone of voice, our demeanour and our body language conveys the same message of inclusiveness.'

Now the mind just boggles. The document doesn't, alas, go on to explain how we might alter our body language to convey a message of inclusiveness (genuflecting before all who aren't immediate family, perhaps?); instead, it continues with more self-evident piffle in a new section that starts, 'All communication has an impact on the recipient and may be remembered for a very long time.' Or forgotten instantly.

So we don't get a list of instructions that might say, 'Don't slouch in front of somebody, don't scowl, take your hands out of your pockets, don't talk down your nose at people, don't pick your nose, don't scratch your bottom.' At least not if the person you're talking to is a paraplegic.

The document on first reading essentially seems to be all about what used to be known as manners, taught in every school and by most families, and one of the most envied and prominent features of our society. But it's not. In between every one of these poorly written and ill-conceived lines is the assumption not that we're bad mannered but that when we come into contact with minority groups we turn into boorish, racist oafs. (It assumes, too, that its potentially racist readers are all white, presumably.) The implication that oozes off these pages is that we are rather like unbaptised Christians and it is only through the interference of the Trades Union Congress (and the likes of Equality South West,

compensation after claiming his health was ruined by sawdust in the school workshop

of course) in their role as a secular church, if you'll forgive the oxymoron, that we can become pure and our prejudice can be exorcised.

Good manners, in fact, aren't good enough for the TUC. Being pleasant to each other is actively discouraged, lest it should give offence. Once we've got the hang of using police officer for policeman, actor for actress (and did you know, by the way, that the terms negro, nigger, coon, wog and paki should not be used in 'normal' circumstances? – although quite what the abnormal ones are that make such terms acceptable aren't spelt out), you also have to deal with 'devaluing terminology'. And that means good manners and friendliness as we know them certainly have no place in an inclusive society.

'The terms "love", "dear" and "pet" may be considered offensive by some people,' for a start. Now, let's stop and consider this for a moment, shall we? Imagine a girl, just back from getting a pint of milk from the local shop, head down, tears in her eyes, shuffling into the corner of the room, unable to look the rest of the family in the eye.

'What is it, what is it?' they ask, in their normal inclusive way.

'You wouldn't believe it. The lady said, "That will be 50 pence, dear."' And now, of course, the tears are flooding out. The family is outraged. There is only one course of action left.

'They said *dear*!' says Father, spittle peppering the air. 'I'm not having this. We're going down to Equality South West right away!'

Indeed Hull City Council, which presumably – as the TUC has secured decent working conditions for all its members – has cleaned all the streets, provided top-notch education for its young people and dignified sheltered accommodation for all its elderly residents, took 'Diversity in Diction, Equality in Action' very seriously.

George Knights, a convict serving nine life sentences after a gun rampage, was suing the Prison Service (on legal aid) for £50,000 because he felt his human rights were

A guide to 'professionally appropriate language' based on the TUC document was sent out on behalf of the equalities unit manager, Julie Thomson, and concluded that the words 'girls, elderly, pet and love' were unacceptable. Women should only be referred to as women, according to its advice, while traditional greetings such as 'duck, flower, dear or sweetheart' were obviously deeply offensive.

But when the TUC's publication had been circulated among real people – i.e. everyone who worked for Hull City Council; incidentally, the sort of people who might be TUC members – it was shown up to be utterly useless. The council's employees, as you might expect, took umbrage at being patronised like this. The acting head of equalities – does he come below or above the corporate equalities manager? – had to send out a new letter to everyone who received the council's guide. 'Clearly it caused offence to many people and, for that, I can only apologise,' he wrote.

Behind this document is a belief that we are morons who don't have the perspicacity of senior decision makers at Hull City Council or the Trades Union Congress. Once you believe it to be the case that without their guidance we would remain unreconstructed racist, sexist pigs, then logic dictates that we need more agencies to put us right, to cajole us into using terms that they deem to be appropriate in order to safeguard the future of civilisation. And you don't have to look far to find them.

Enter the Runnymede Trust (at the 'forefront of the fight against social injustice and racial discrimination for the last 36 years'). This organisation, with a mission to 'promote a successful multi-ethnic Britain', goes even further than Hull City Council and the TUC. It flaps away like a worried hen – or should I say cock, or bird of unspecified gender that has difficulty in flight? – over the fact that using any language in any context could be discriminatory.

being breached by not having a cell with an en suite lavatory and because having a single mattress was 'torture, a cruel and unusual punishment'

In his preface to *The Future of Multi-Ethnic Britain*, a report from The Commission of Multi-Ethnic Britain – set up by by the Trust – Professor Bhikhu Parekh states that the commission's members did not like the term 'ethnic group' because it 'traps the group concerned into its ethnicity, and suppresses both its multiple identity and its freedom of self-determination'. If we can read anything at all into this indecipherable jargon, we surmise that Professor Parekh in writing a report on the future of multi-ethnic Britain without having the words 'ethnic group' at his disposal has hit a bit of a problem, and indeed he has.

'Inventing a wholly new vocabulary does not help,' grumbles the professor, 'for such a language would be too abstract, artificial and unrelated to the idioms of everyday life to be intelligible, let alone provide a meaningful dialogue.' 'Integration' is even more misleading, he argues, because it implies 'a one-way process in which "minorities" are to be absorbed into the non-existent homogenous cultural structure of the "majority"'.

All this was highlighted by the journalist Tom Utley in the *Daily Telegraph*. 'Oh what joy if the commission had indeed invented words of its own,' he wrote. 'An "ethnic group" might have become, say, a "crimblepotch". For "integration", the commission might have written "snugglebop" and "majorities" and "minorities" might have been called "clumpkins" and "twiddlekins".' He wonders what Jonathan Swift ('himself an Irishman, and therefore a member of a crimblepotch') would have made of it. He goes on to quote Professor Parekh:

> The movement towards a multi-ethnic, multicultural Britain has been decisive. However, it has not been the result of a concerted decision. Nor is it yet an accomplished fact. It has evolved as an unplanned, incremental process – a matter of multicultural drift, not of conscious policy.

A course on how to change a light bulb was organised for the many workers who might be asked to do the task by Doncaster Council, although a spokesman stressed

Again, let's ignore the appalling writing style. What the professor is lamenting is that, in their own way, people have by themselves become less racist, more integrated. His anger seems to be that they have managed to do this without an important organisation – the Runnymede Trust, say – headed by an important figure – Professor Parekh, say – ordering them to do it. We might also assume that if this is the case, one might question the need for a Runnymede Trust at all. And that certainly wouldn't do.

Once you've agreed that the lesbian issue is moving in the 'intellectually and politically correct direction' in a meeting, regardless of the fact that the phrase is meaningless, you have to do something about it and form organisations and pressure groups to lobby its case. If you've decided that the word chairman is a chauvinistic anachronism, then you are duty-bound to force the world to drop the word forthwith.

What is inherent in this desire to interfere with the language is the notion of a victim. (In this sense, Professor Parekh is right: as soon as you say 'ethnic group', you are establishing victim culture, although this rather overlooks the fact that the *raison d'être* of the Runnymede Trust is coming to the rescue of such victims.) The interference in our language is laying down the foundation for the nanny state because it assumes that so much of society is made up of unfortunates who need to be looked after and protected.

The trouble is, not everyone wants to be saved. One assumes that most people in wheelchairs might prefer it if those who fuss over whether they should be called disabled or not spent a bit more effort trying to get some lifts built in stations. A single mother might put up with being called 'dear' in the post office if Hull City Council managed to get her off their waiting list for a house. There are millions of women for whom the term 'Ms' is an aberration.

Before the Runnymede Trust, Hull City Council and the TUC compose their next tract telling us how not to offend others,

that the two-and-a-half hour course covered a 'whole host of light fittings'

they would do well to peruse *The Pitfalls of Political Correctness: Euphemisms Excoriated* by the late Dr Kenneth Jernigan, ex-president of America's National Federation of the Blind. He wrote of how, at the time of the First World War, shell shock – a simple term, two one-syllable words, clear and descriptive – was the term used to describe the mental illness that resulted from the trauma of battle. A generation later, after the Second World War had come and gone, came the term combat fatigue, which meant the same thing but the two syllables had grown to four. Today the two words have doubled, the original pair of syllables is now eight and we have Post Traumatic Stress Disorder, plus an abbreviation: PTSD.

'It still means the same thing, and it still hurts as much or as little, but it is more in tune with current effete sensibilities,' he wrote. 'It is also a perfect example of the pretentious euphemisms that characterise almost everything we do and say . . . At their worst, they obscure clear thinking and damage the very people and causes they claim to benefit.'

In his case, this is the blind.

He cited a memorandum from the United States Department of Education to the Office for Civil Rights (OCR) senior staff (not averse to a few of their own euphemisms, one shouldn't wonder) with the subject: 'Language Reference to Persons with a Disability'. In it, the OCR noted, 'In all our written and oral communications, care should be given to avoid expressions that many persons find offensive.' So 'a student with dyslexia' should be used instead of 'a dyslexic student' and, naturally, 'people who are blind' or 'persons with visual impairment' instead of 'blind people'.

'In addition,' it read, 'please avoid using phrases such as "the deaf", "the mentally retarded" or "the blind".'

This enraged Dr Jernigan. In 1993, in a passionate plea not to be patronised, the National Federation of the Blind passed Resolution 93-01 at its national convention in Dallas. It reads:

Doncaster also called for rival butchers hawking for trade to cut the noise down at its thrice-weekly market in 2006

. . . the word blind accurately and clearly describes the condition of being unable to see, as well as the condition of having such limited eyesight that alternative techniques are required to do efficiently the ordinary tasks of daily living that are performed visually by those having good eyesight . . .

There is increasing pressure in certain circles to use a variety of euphemisms . . . such as hard of seeing, visually challenged, sightless, visually impaired, people with blindness, people who are blind . . .

[This] euphemism does the exact opposite of what it purports to do since it is overly defensive, implies shame instead of true equality, and portrays the blind as touchy and belligerent.

. . . just as an intelligent person . . . does not insist upon being called a person who is intelligent, and a group of bankers have no concern that they be referred to as persons who are in the banking business, so it is with the blind – the only difference being that some people (blind and sighted alike) continue to cling to the outmoded notion that blindness (along with everything associated with it) connotes inferiority and lack of status.

Stockport College in Greater Manchester certainly didn't feel it necessary to heed Professor Jernigan's entreaty. In an action only a step away from Hitler destroying books that didn't suit his regime, it banned more than 40 'offensive' words and phrases under equal opportunities rules, which staff and students had to follow. 'The blind – not the, visually impaired better,' was right up there on its hit list. Sorry, Dr Jernigan.

'Lady' and 'gentleman' were out because of 'class implications', and 'slaving over a hot stove' was obviously just so outré as to be offensive beyond the pale because, according to the college, 'It minimises the horror and oppression of the slave trade' (of course, 'beyond the pale' could be banned, too, the pale being an area held by a foreign country beyond which civilisation ended – the English Pale around Dublin in the early sixteenth century, say).

Indeed while the college damns perfectly good and inoffensive words – including 'history', which, it states, 'some find sexist' – its own grasp of English is somewhat lacking. The title is one of those that, like the TUC's 'Diversity in Diction, Equality in Action', takes no subject or object. Theirs is called 'Equal Opportunities – Policy into Practice' and goes rather further than the others by including 'mad', 'manic' and 'crazy' on its blacklist – these risk upsetting mentally ill people, obviously.

Oh, and blacklist – well, what do you think?

'We vigorously pursue an equal opportunities policy and we try to be as politically correct as possible, without being tedious,' Richard Tuson, a spokesman for the college, told the press. 'We defend the right to discourage language which might offend someone.'

And the right to be illiterate. The title of the document, of course, is meaningless, just a bit of waffle someone made up because it sounds good, but to ban the word history is shocking beyond belief. If just one of the self-righteous morons who put together this list spoke even elementary French, he or she would know that the etymology of the word 'history' does not denote 'his story'. Did it not even cross their minds that it might be related to *histoire*? Did it not occur to them that the French word for 'his' is *son* or *sa* depending on the gender and first letter of the object? So, 'his story' would be 'son histoire'. Has Greek really (history's root is the Greek word *historia*, meaning knowing or enquiring) gone so far into obscurity?

Obviously, the answer is yes. For Stockport College, political correctness is more important than intellectual or educational rigour.

Police chiefs in Gloucestershire were stopped from issuing pensioners with napkins that gave details of a crime reduction campaign because Tewkesbury Borough Council

So it is across the Pennines in Darlington, whose borough council has come up with an 'Access Strategy (2003–08)'. 'In Darlington, our aspiration is to create a fully inclusive education system,' it pants. 'This commitment to inclusion is based on the belief that education can lay the foundation for achievement and citizenship throughout the rest of peoples [*sic*] lives.'

The aims of the Access Strategy are to:

- raise achievement for all children and young people in Darlington;
- include children and young people in their local schools and communities;
- ensure equality of access to information.

This piffle goes on for pages, as if the idea of schools before this great document was to reduce achievement for children, exclude them from local education and ensure inequality of access to information. Unfortunately, so dense are its authors that they don't realise that 'people' needs an apostrophe when it takes a possessive, or when they write of a 'childrens' services plan', children, being plural, takes the apostrophe before the 's'. Unless, of course, in Darlington they have a plan for their childrens.

A flick through this ridiculous document reveals it is loaded with the words that have become the lingua franca of the nanny state: strategy, equality, inclusion, best value, performance plan, and so on. When it comes to 'Access to the Curriculum', it seems to face similar problems to the Runnymede Trust and its crimblepotches.

'Inclusion is most readily dealt with as a process rather than a fixed state and so it is probably impossible to define what is meant by an inclusive curriculum,' it explains. 'Nevertheless, some aspects of the process by which the curriculum becomes more inclusive can be set out. This would help identify some barriers to

in Gloucestershire had 'health-and-safety concerns'. They needed to carry out a risk assessment to ensure that the elderly wouldn't choke on them

learning and assist in planning to remove them.' You might think the fact that those responsible for education in the borough of Darlington don't know the basics of where to put an apostrophe would be the bigger barrier to learning.

Rather than a bunch of bureaucrats setting out 'the process by which the curriculum could be more inclusive', members of the 'excluded' might appreciate those in charge of their children's education teaching them maths and English – although from their Access Strategy document, there is no evidence that they might have the ability to give them any grounding in even the most basic elements of the latter.

Our educators, though, tire rather of the core subjects. Well, there's no jargon to be used, for a start; nowhere for them to out-perform each other in breaking down barriers and moving forward in the politically correct direction.

The dubious moral world of sex education, however, is perfect for such self-important meddling with the language. Can there be anything so ghastly as a teacher of 14 to 16 year olds telling them that the words 'boyfriend' and 'girlfriend' must be banned from the classroom because they are not inclusive enough? *Sense*, an interactive CD on sex and relationships published by the National Children's Bureau, a charity supported by the taxpayer and Lottery cash, says the word 'partner' must be used instead because it doesn't discriminate against homosexual relationships. What do we make of the fact that it says, 'The terms foreplay and sex imply that everyone has sex in the same way. Instead, use the terms vaginal, oral and anal sex'?

At the age of 14 is no area of life too intimate, too precious to come under the watchful eye of a bunch of nannies who feel they are somehow qualified to tell our teenagers not to use the simple, explicit epithets of boyfriend and girlfriend? How is it that in public life there are now whole organisations, such as the National

Parents who had clubbed together to buy a communal paddling pool with water 12 inches deep were told by Warwick District Council that they should desist from using

Children's Bureau, who have decided that while using the word girlfriend or boyfriend is somehow sinful, it is quite the proper thing to tell children, who might not even be out of puberty, about oral and anal sex? The National Children's Bureau, in case you are wondering, 'undertakes research, evaluation and development projects to provide the evidence base it needs to influence policy and develop best practice'. So now you know.

The rather innocent desire to use language that is inoffensive has mutated into a mumbo-jumbo that has become the bedrock of modern political thinking. It really doesn't matter what is said, so long as it's 'inclusive'. A million megabytes are circulating around cyberspace, taking best practice, strategies, inclusiveness, awareness, diversity, community, outsourcing and delivery to 'stakeholders' and anyone else who'll listen. Forests are being felled in order to publish documents such as 'Diversity in Diction, Equality in Action'. Or how about 'Planning for Housing Provision' from the Office of the Deputy Prime Minister? In this incisive piece of work, it says that there is to be:

> A new policy approach to making the planning system more responsive to the housing market within the overall objective of planning which contributes to sustainable development . . . to ensure that plans and plan policies will deliver land, in the right places, to meet the need for housing going forward.

These words are meaningless. Again, they might as well be writing 'house, inclusive, the, but racist not, and inclusive the conference I agree disenfranchised pillar box star signs'.

Well, if you are a member of the TUC, Hull City Council or the Runnymede Trust, these reports take you a step closer to bringing equality to the world, and when we've all been instructed to speak according to their edicts – let's call it politically correctly – so there

it on a communal green because they weren't insured. The council was unhappy because there was no lifeguard or first-aider present

will be equal opportunities for all, all races shall live harmoniously, and men and women shall exist on equal terms. Moving in the 'intellectually and politically correct direction' has wormed its way into the core of every aspect of public life. This is the argot of the nanny state and, far from being inclusive, if you are not prepared to use it, you certainly should be prepared to be excluded.

We understand political correctness to be a language thing, but it is far, far more than that. Those words are the wrapping paper on a huge parcel of political ideas that were fermenting in academia more than 40 years ago, when a workshop was still where you had your car fixed and delivery was the means by which milk was brought to your door every day.

A mortuary technician who developed a morbid fear of death was awarded £15,000 compensation for being wrongfully dismissed from her job at University Hospital Aintree in Liverpool

2 Strictly no capitalist pigs

Nanny starts recruiting its founding fathers – and mothers – regardless of sexual orientation, race or gender

We think of political correctness as a language thing, as a university thing, as an American thing, but it's the Germans we have to thank for influencing the young darlings who decided that, for the good of us all, our language was going to have to change. Because no one is nailing their colours to the politically correct cause, we rather need to fumble through the swirling mists of late twentieth-century academia and its handling of the two principal intellectual themes of the era – Marxism and Freudianism – to find out the origins of exactly who was planning to impose on us the likes of 'best practice' and 'the visually impaired'.

In the first part of the century, Marx and Freud were still somewhat sidelined in the West, an interesting little diversion while proper academics studied Greek, Latin, literature, logic and the pure sciences. After the Second World War, though, chaps discussing Achilles and the burden of heroism were afforded all the respect Arachne gave to Minerva. Winston Churchill might have led the UK to victory, but the electorate had spoken: now there was a class war on and a bullish Harrovian with a cigar didn't figure. We know this history at least: the Second World War had brought with it a need to educate the working classes, to employ women in traditionally male jobs, to introduce a new bureaucratic infrastructure and to rebuild all the nations involved in this global

---

St James' Catholic Primary School in Millom, Cumbria, barred parents from entering its grounds to drop off children after the father of a pupil was hit by a classroom door and won £22,000 compensation

trauma. The working classes had seen a bit of social mobility and they rather liked it.

And if half of Europe's cities had to be rebuilt anyway, why not condemn the disgraceful slums of the pre-war years to history? Why not construct new towns with decent housing linked by decent roads and dual carriageways? Why not erect new campus universities, centres of excellence that would give our young people the chance to shine and lead us into a new era of scientific and social sophistication? Why not have arts centres and a free health service for all; grammar schools where all children would be admitted on academic ability regardless of their class?

Why not?

In came Labour, bristling with optimism and socialist principles, ready to take us into the future. And we still rightly admire those aims. The only problem was that while the USSR might have picked up a couple of new states and returned to letting Stalin get on with sending the populace to Siberia, Western Europe needed to borrow money from that economic powerhouse the USA to stick into its social projects: nationalisation could go so far, but the White House wasn't going to hand over the Yankee dollar if the new socialist government turfed businesses such as Marconi, Unilever and ICI over to the working classes.

Nonetheless, by the mid-'60s in the UK we had those grammar schools and new hospitals and shiny campus universities. We had the M1. We had the Post Office Tower and the Hilton Hotel towering over Hyde Park, and Concorde was preparing to fly to the US faster than the speed of sound. We were soon to see the reflection of St Thomas's Hospital glinting in the Thames from where it stood opposite the Houses of Parliament, while downstream at London Bridge, Guy's Hospital Tower reached for the clouds – both beacons of a National Health Service offering the latest medical advances to the deprived boroughs of Lambeth and Southwark.

Thanks to an EU 'Working at Height' directive, St Benet's church in Beccles, Norfolk, had to fork out £1,300 so scaffolding with a platform could be erected in order to

In between them, the South Bank arts complex with the National Theatre – oh, how grand, let's italicise it: the *National* Theatre – offering up the great plays for the masses dwarfed the dark terraces behind it. Not only that, this was swinging London. We had The Beatles and the Rolling Stones; Lindsay Anderson was sticking the boot into the public school system, while Twiggy was pulling her boots up to her miniskirted knees. This was the future.

The only trouble was we still had poor people. Millions of coal miners and steel workers, car workers and bus drivers who weren't habitués of the South Bank and whose chances of flying on Concorde were about as good as persuading Harold Pinter to stop wearing a Breton cap and vote Conservative. After building idealistic housing estates with walkways, underground tunnels and brightly coloured playgrounds, this came as rather a shock to the thinking classes, and it bothered them immensely. It irked them that while they wrestled with Sartre's *Critique of Dialectical Reason* in splendid new academic powerhouses, down the road was *Cathy Come Home* country, where the poor were too deprived even to live in a tower block.

At the same time, it wasn't cool to be rich. Or, rather, it wasn't cool to be posh. Posh was tea at the Waldorf, short hair and working in a bank, and who wanted that when you could have as much cannabis as you could inhale and, if you were lucky, free and guilt-free sex to a soundtrack of The Doors and Cream?

So, although the poor themselves were anti-drugs, anti-long hair and anti-free love, and pro solid, hard work and bettering yourself, it was the poor with whom you would align yourself. Here was the birth of the mockney accent. Middle-class kids from the country were coming to the universities and, for the first time, saw a world beyond the pony club – and, *my*, wasn't it exciting. Whether you were a country child who was enjoying the rough and tumble of the inner city for the first time, or a working-class

change five light bulbs. Under new regulations, a risk assessment had to be taken, which ruled out using a ladder

grammar school alumnus who had deserted boots and braces for sandals and loon pants, you were punctuating your diction with 'know what I mean' and 'leave it out', and you definitely felt the poor were entitled to have some of what you were having, whether they wanted it or not. Given that you were a student of a political bent, where would you find intellectual succour to support your worthy and, let's face it, understandable instincts? John Stuart Mill was sort of all right, believing in the welfare and happiness of others, but you were going to go straight for the jugular, tackle the problem head on, let it be known that it was about time the working class had some and had it now. And anyway, like David Hume and John Locke and Thomas Paine, Mill's sort were studied by – spit – posh people in old fuddy-duddy universities. It was time for the means to take over the production. It was time for Marx.

There was the slight problem that there were reports of millions being imprisoned, tortured and murdered in Russia and China at the behest of ruthless dictators, but, seeing as the only people who were actually allowed to visit these countries were *Morning Star*-reading communists who thought it was all marvellous anyway, no one really *knew* that was the case.

And who was telling us that socialism was bad? Capitalists. Squares, in other words. And who could trust *them*? No, the only problem with Marx was that it was rather old-fashioned. OK, there was some cool iconography – Che Guevara, Mao and the Long March, the hammer and sickle – but it didn't really chime with the age of letting it all hang out. Freud did, though.

Although our new breed of proto-intellectuals was terribly worried about the poor, this was the 'me' generation. And no one is more *me* than Freud. Here you could talk about dreams and aspirations: stick him alongside Larkin for your modern literature course – why 'They fuck you up, your mum and dad' – in the same way as you could stick Marx onto your economics degree. It was no longer enough for any academic subject to be studied in isolation. Somewhere along the line, you were going to stitch in one or both of the big Germans. Sociology and psychology became the hip degrees for the latter part of the twentieth century, but whatever you were studying, it was informed by the fact that there was a class war going on.

There's been a long history of philanthropic posh people finding their consciences bitten by the poor. Virginia Woolf would make trips to South London to teach evening classes to 'anaemic shop girls'. In his book *The Likes of Us*, tracing the history of the white working class in South London, Michael Collins relates how Jessica Mitford devoted herself to the class war. Like the 'snob Bolshevik', she had married well and within her class – to the renegade public-school socialist Esmond Romilly, her second cousin and a nephew of Churchill's. They moved to Rotherhithe to a house overlooking the river, with seven rooms over four storeys, costing £2 a month including use of a grand piano. The locals were 'a shorter and paler race of people than the inhabitants of London's West End. In appearance, dress and speech, they form so radical a contrast as to give the impression of a different ethnic group.' The new neighbours gave bottle parties, which brought journalists, writers and nightclub singers across the water. They ate fish and chips, and attended meetings of the Bermondsey Labour Party because Romilly believed the Communist Party membership consisted of too many young upper-class intellectuals like himself. The trouble was the working classes didn't necessarily want to be patronised by a toff who held bottle parties or a woman with mental problems.

Likewise, the poor hadn't wanted to be saved by a proselytiser with a beard in the form of William Booth and his Salvation Army half a century earlier – at least he was of the working class, and there was something genuinely egalitarian in not only bringing the

policies put children's lives at risk

word of God to the poor but telling them that in God's eyes they were equal to the self-righteous Victorian rich. Booth probably had a point when he prescribed temperance in the light of so many working-class men spending their hard-earned wages on drinking themselves to oblivion, but he soon found out that those he was bossing around not surprisingly took umbrage at being told what not to do.

Slowly his mission began to grow, but the work was hard and Booth would 'stumble home night after night haggard with fatigue, often his clothes were torn and bloody bandages swathed his head where a stone had struck', wrote his wife. (Evening meetings were held in an old warehouse where urchins threw stones and fireworks through the window.)

Michael Collins quotes George Orwell, who said that communism was 'never found in its pure form in a genuine proletarian'. He also wrote that the genuine working man 'is seldom or never a Socialist in the complete, logically consistent sense . . . I have yet to meet a working miner, steel-worker, cotton-weaver, docker, navvy or whatnot who was "ideologically" sound.'

Collins notes, too, that the Oxford-educated Alexander Paterson, a teacher who moved to Bermondsey, described in his book of 1911, *Across the Bridges*, how the working man of Southwark rarely stopped to listen to socialist orators on street corners: 'He slides off home, with little thought of revolution in his heart.'

Our free-loving radicals of the '60s and '70s might have lost the ludicrous posh argot of Orwell and his 'navvy or whatnot', but they were to discover the same thing: that the masses didn't want to be saved, even if you did punctuate your sentences with 'know what I mean'. It didn't stop them trying, though, and hasn't stopped them since.

They, too, like Virginia, moved into solid working-class areas, affected cockney accents, joined the Socialist Workers Party and,

Road accidents plummeted in the London borough of Barnet after the council removed speed bumps between the years 2004 and 2005; this was believed to be

if they weren't organising a demo themselves, pitched up at the nearest picket line with a few placards. Indeed, much of student life was spent aping the trade-union movement. The NUS rather sweetly organised sit-ins and strikes, as if one person – with the exception possibly of the bursar and dean of college – in the world could give two hoots whether a Fred Kite wannabe from Kingston upon Thames got his degree in sociology and cultural studies or not.

When the politically minded graduated and started work in the booming public sector, they set up their own unions with shop stewards and conveners ready to drop pencils the moment a comrade was charged with breaking his flexitime agreement. It was hardly the American Federation of Labor's 'a fair day's pay for a fair day's work', but it got the revolutionary juices flowing out on a picket line and, they believed, took them a step closer to socialist nirvana.

But it didn't make them working class. The principal activity of our idealistic, young radicals was setting up events and organisations that suited them in the *name* of equality: *Time Out* listings magazine, a wholesome cooperative that had its darling agitprop section and employed an army of committed young hacks who weren't afraid to swear in their copy; community theatres hosted such delights as *John D. Muggins is Dead* about the Vietnam War. Of course, there were cafés attached, as if there was nothing the local unemployed craved more than somewhere you could drop in and get a decent bit of carrot cake. Law centres were set up on every high street so workers could have representation without having to muck around with capitalist pig lawyers. Adventure playgrounds proliferated across our cities so the 'kids' could get some release and, it was hoped, stop smashing windows and daubing graffiti on the walls for a moment. Our poor neighbourhoods, though, were allowed the dubious pleasure of receiving official street artists to spray

---

because cars didn't accelerate between them and sightlines had been improved

anti-capitalist iconography on the end of terraces. Urban farms, too, sprang up to introduce poor people to the wonders of the cow. And oh, how grateful they must have been to be benefiting from the great works of the community artist to record the goings-on in their neighbourhood.

All this was marvellously idealistic and had the right sentiments behind it. But, surprise, surprise, those it benefited most were young student graduates of a left-wing bent. Youth workers, playwrights, alternative comedians, lawyers, journalists, artists were all being offered grants in the name of improving the lot of the poor. Down the road from my housing cooperative, the Deptford Albany community centre – which morphed into a 'community' theatre – was at the vanguard of this new movement. 'The basic aim in the concept of the work here, that of offering a total environment in which the Deptford residents can realise and develop their potential abilities and interests, and in which they can seek advice and support when and if they feel it to be necessary,' is the long-winded summing up of its work in its report of 1969.

Crucial to the 'support' of the residents of Deptford in the early '70s was the Brighton Combination, a touring fringe theatre company that brought the *NAB Show* to the Albany Hall. The show was based on Aristophanes' play *The Wasps*, then improvised (well, of course it was) by playwright Steve Gooch using research with unemployed people on the dole in Brighton. Albert Hunt, a theatre lecturer, described it as being 'above the heads of the average bourgeois audience' when he saw the show later at the Royal Court Theatre. They didn't clap, then.

This association with the Combination was formed after 'groundwork laid by social and community workers', according to a history of the Albany by John Turner. How the non-bourgeois residents must have cheered when the Combination came to be

A police helicopter was scrambled in order to prosecute a woman from South Tyneside who had held an apple while driving. She was fined £60 plus £100 costs after magistrates found she was not in control of the car

based at the Albany. And you can imagine their joy when John Upton, one of the country's leading muralists, was also brought up from Brighton. On the 'austere and intimidating' front of the Albany, Turner writes, Upton presented an 'X-ray' of what you'd see inside. He painted 'a comic; the social worker at her desk; the photographer at his developing tray; the actors as a prancing comedia troupe'. Even better, our man Upton came from Lewisham, so the Albany could boast of his credentials as an inner-city kid. Turner goes on to explain, 'Upton was part of a generation of British artists who were reacting against the museum and gallery hegemony of art. They believed their art could and should be seen by everybody as part of their daily experience.'

The presumption that everyone in the neighbourhood would be grateful for these broad brush stokes across their buildings lies at the heart of the nanny state that has grown incrementally more powerful since those heady days. Implicit in the idea is that the meddling classes have the ability – and the right – to impose their superior values on the less well off. My memory of the Albany was of students from Goldsmiths College, young professionals from my housing co-op and anyone of a right-on persuasion whooping it up to concerts by local boys Dire Straits – well, local in that they'd moved down from Newcastle to study and work (guitarist Dave Knopfler was a social worker) – enjoying alternative comedy and possibly an alternative play in a cabaret setting. The white Deptford working class were fleeing the area in droves, and the black population seemed not to be particularly interested in our 'Rock Against Racism' gigs and amazingly managed to create their own entertainment in their own clubs without artists painting the insides of buildings on the outside to make them less intimidating.

Although the Albany was, according to Turner, the UK's first and foremost community theatre, this kind of stuff was being

Police rushed fifteen officers, three squad cars and a police van to the scene of a handbag snatch to take a suspect off for questioning in Kensington, West London

replicated across the country, across the Western world. What was to become what we now call political correctness was taking hold and spreading its tentacles among the working classes, but its protagonists – the social workers and actors at the Albany, for example – were quite definitely middle class.

Interestingly, in his account of the Albany, Turner mentions, *en passant*, the question posed by American activist Saul Alinsky: 'What is a people's program?' (All right, all right, I'll tell you: it's 'whatever program the people themselves decide'. The sort of insight you'd need to be, like Saul, a criminologist from Chicago to come up with.) Alinsky, who in the '30s organised the Back of the Yards neighbourhood in Chicago and founded the Industrial Areas Foundation, was considered the 'grandfather of community organising'. He wrote two books outlining his strategies: *Reveille for Radicals* (1946) and *Rules for Radicals* (1971).

'Our rebels have contemptuously rejected the values and the way of life of the middle class,' he wrote in *Rules for Radicals*. 'They have stigmatised it as materialistic, decadent, bourgeois, degenerate, imperialistic, war-mongering, brutalised and corrupt. They are right; but we must begin from where we are if we are to build power for change, and the power and the people are in the middle class majority.'

Someone he considered one of his better students was a young Hillary Rodham, and he asked her to join him in promoting revolutionary leftist causes. Hillary, as we now know, had bigger opportunities to chase, but you can see how a well-kempt young woman like her must have been glad to learn that being a radical didn't necessarily mean dropping acid and taking her clothes off.

What Alinsky describes is essentially a schism within the middle classes. There were the materialist, war-mongering, brutalised and corrupt, who – this was the time of the Vietnam War, remember – were drafting young American men and building huge corporations

Thames Valley Police has given its 120 traffic officers 'aide-memoire cards', which carry a chart awarding different points for catching different offenders. Officers get ten points for stopping a drink-driver – the same number awarded for arresting a rapist

at the expense of the poor, and who toiled relentlessly to fund the American dream. Then there were Alinsky's aficionados, the Hillary Rodhams, who were going to knock the whole damned bourgeois structure down and build it up again, who were going to build Utopia, and it was they who were on the ascendant.

Paradoxically, the young middle-class students really never had it so good. For the first time, large numbers of them had the income to own their own cars (even if they were beaten-up Volkswagens) and they could go surfing in California, kayak down the Columbia Gorge, hang out with the beatniks in Greenwich Village or Carnaby Street and, if they so fancied, fly across the Atlantic to see how each other lived. They could get high on marijuana, discuss Ginsberg and Kerouac in New England cafés and drive to Woodstock to lodge their protest at the way the capitalist pigs were exploiting the poor. They could open theatres like the Deptford Albany, they could sell millions of records internationally and they could call for a brand new world in which everyone would be free to tune in, turn on and drop out.

Perhaps it was because this freedom became so available to so many that the injustices of the rest of the world were put into such sharp relief: the Vietnam War, of course; the terrible Latin American dictatorships of the '70s; a racism that did indeed exist across the West; the fact that there was a proliferation of nuclear weapons that could, within a day, blow the world apart; an underclass for whom Macmillan's 'You've never had it so good' had a hollow ring to it.

Something had to be done, and we weren't talking a couple of Tolpuddle Martyrs, or Ban the Bomb marches, or the Paris riots; we were talking about the civil-rights movement, the emancipation of women, the right to work, the overthrowing of dictatorships across the world (other than those which were communist), freedom for the destitute in much of Africa and the liberation of

- five points for pulling over someone not wearing a seatbelt or using a mobile phone at the wheel. Dealing with an illegal immigrant, a shoplifter or a person breaching bail conditions merits only two points. They aim to get 200 points a month

the disenfranchised of the pernicious Apartheid regime in South Africa. We were talking about peace and love and understanding.

Marx was a good start, given that he was, after all, laying the intellectual foundation for the working classes to rise up and seize power for themselves. But the young radicals needed some way of dragging it out of nineteenth-century Europe, and found the answer in some more Germans – Max Horkenheimer, Theodor Adorno, Herbert Marcuse and a cluster of other Jewish intellectuals.

These men are crucial to why we are giving children head massages in Wales and banning hanging baskets in Somerset. They are the link between the radicalism of the '60s and '70s and the politicians who lead us today. These are the people who were going to make Marx sexy again, despite the bar-less, restaurant-less, car-less, joyless half-light dictatorship of the Soviet Union and the worker-ant communism of China. These were the people who were going to tell us why the working classes described in Orwell weren't rising up under the red flag. They went under the banner of the 'Frankfurt School'.

The Frankfurt School has its origins in Germany in 1923. That year, Felix Weil, the Marxist son of a millionaire trader (naturally), sponsored the 'First Marxist Work Week', a think tank that brought together Hungarian philosopher Georg Lukacs and key German thinkers to discuss the problem of division among Marxists. In the same year, he endowed an institute in association with Frankfurt University. It was originally to be known as the Institute for Marxism, but they obviously didn't have that much confidence in the masses. Worried that being openly Marxist wouldn't play with the workers, they instead named their exciting new venture the Institute for Social Research.

Things really heated up for the institute when, in 1930, it appointed Max Horkheimer, the son of a factory owner (rather than worker, note) as its director. It was he who introduced the

An ambulance carrying an emergency patient with chronic back pain was pulled

thinking of Freud – a heresy that led to Moscow refusing to have any links with it – in making the connection between Marxist economic theory and culture.

The Frankfurt School and its luminaries – Adorno, Horkheimer, Marcuse, Walter Benjamin, Erich Fromm – became the superstars of the academic community. When the Nazis came to power in 1933, this intellectual equivalent of The Beatles, being Jewish as well as Marxist, fled to New York City and re-established the institute with the help of Columbia University. They turned their study towards American, as well as German, society, and Marcuse (whom we can thank, incidentally, for the phrase 'make love, not war') became a key figure in the Office of Strategic Services (the predecessor to the CIA), while Horkheimer and Adorno chose the Hollywood sunshine as the base from where they could pontificate.

These dazzling intellectuals took Marxism into the modern world by introducing psychoanalysis, dialectical philosophy and avant-garde art into their orbit, coming up with 'Critical Theory', which, along with the concept of 'Cultural Superstructure', would open up every bourgeois capitalist cultural institution to criticism. Even if you didn't agree with them, it was potent philosophical stuff.

'Radical feminism, the women's studies departments, the gay studies departments, the black studies departments – all these things are branches of Critical Theory,' said William S. Lind, director of the Center for Cultural Conservatism at the Free Congress Foundation, an American right-wing think tank that deals with culture as well as economics, in a speech entitled 'The Origins of Political Correctness'.

For both the classical Marxist and cultural Marxist have a method of analysis that gives them the answer they want. For

over by police in Hartlepool for having a faulty brake light

the classical Marxist, it's Marxist economics, for the cultural Marxist, it's deconstruction. Deconstruction essentially takes any text, removes all meaning from it and reinserts any meaning desired. So we find, for example, that all of Shakespeare is about the suppression of women, or the Bible is really about race and gender.

Here is the intellectual root of our meddling classes, the DNA of the nanny state. Meet Eric Fromm, who wrote that masculinity and femininity were not reflections of 'essential' sexual differences, they were derived instead from differences in life functions, which were, in part, socially determined. Sexual differences, in other words, are a construct: bourgeois, naturally.

Marcuse argued that mass media and culture, advertising, industrial management and contemporary modes of thought all reproduce the existing system and attempt to eliminate negativity, critique and opposition. The result was a 'one-dimensional' universe of thought and behaviour in which the very aptitude and ability for critical thinking and oppositional behaviour was withering away. Or Theodore Adorno anyone? He argued that capitalism fed people with the products of a 'culture industry' – the opposite of 'true' art: false needs that keep them passively satisfied and politically apathetic.

The Frankfurt School nurtured and expanded the notion of the victim into whole new areas. The working classes now are failing to work towards socialist nirvana because, effectively, *EastEnders* is numbing their brains. Women are repressed because of their socially defined roles. Wars are fought to protect capitalist imperialists. Listen to the critics of the BBC today and the same crackle of discontent informs intellectual discussion from the ICA to the Department of Media, Culture and Sport.

Another ambulance driver on an emergency call was fined £30 and given three penalty points on his licence after Thames Valley Police caught him exceeding a

As a founding student of the country's first degree course in media studies at the Polytechnic of Central London, I remember this enthusiasm well. Fuelled by subsidised beer and table football in the Student Union bar to a soundtrack of The Clash and the Sex Pistols, we wouldn't rest until the walls of the fuddy-duddy repressive capitalism (in effect, our mums and dads) came crashing down and we could build a new utopia based on . . . based on what?

Well, based on the Frankfurt School. There were to be no more prissy girls in skirts, frightening divisions between the theatre and the football terraces, pansies in the closet, rich people having posh parties from which we were excluded while we students shared bus stops with the working classes. We celebrated our new internationalism, crowed over our liberalism and acceptance of black culture (a couple of rich Africans who'd been to English public schools) and praised a new culture of street artists, punks and socialist sloganeering that fitted seamlessly into our academic pursuits.

Unfortunately, the masses yet again followed form and took no interest in this whatsoever. Red Robbo took his British Leyland staff on strike for the maximum pay for the minimum hours, not on a long march to cultural emancipation. Arthur Scargill led the miners to the streets and the picket lines, but the only time they mingled with the audience at the Deptford Albany was with collection boxes to fund the strikes that would contribute to their inevitable downfall. So, the students decided to declare UDI and build a socialist utopia without them and, in a little aside from the class war, turned their attentions on each other. We had Militant, the Socialist Workers Party, the Communist Party and the Workers Revolutionary Party.

And so it was to be across Europe. Even in America, where making such overt displays of political leftism was somewhat

30 mph speed limit by 6 mph while delivering organs as quickly as he could to Oxford from Gatwick

akin to drinking cranberry juice in a shebeen, this play-politics was still taken extremely seriously, with every university boasting instead a black society, Hispanic society, women's society, and so on.

'The totalitarian nature of Political Correctness is revealed nowhere more clearly than on college campuses,' writes Lind in his lecture, 'many of which at this point are small, ivy-covered North Koreas, where the student or faculty member who dares to cross any of the lines set up by the gender feminist or the homosexual-rights activists, or the local black or Hispanic group, or any of the other sainted "victims" groups that PC revolves around, quickly find themselves in judicial trouble. Within the small legal system of the college, they face formal charges – some star-chamber proceeding – and punishment.'

These students are now at the core of modern political thought. While capitalism suits them too well ever to advocate the hoisting of the red flag again, that socialist background – the notion of the victim – informs the political establishment in the way it used to be informed by tea parties in university quads. Gordon Brown, when he was rector of Edinburgh University, edited *The Red Paper on Scotland*, published by Edinburgh University Press. Some 30 years later, in 2005, it was reprinted (exciting features included 'Power to the People!: Scotland's Public Services' by Dave Watson), with a nod to its past, noting that Mr Brown's paper exuded 'a confidence in the inevitability of socialism that is today almost shocking given the retreat that socialism has experienced'.

Jack Straw, Britain's former Home and Foreign Secretary, was president of the Student Union in Leeds. Peter Hain, the Northern Ireland Secretary, was a founder of the Anti-Nazi League. Geoff Hoon, a Blair favourite who led the Labour Party for the 2005 election, left Lancaster University and returned to his native Newcastle to run a radical bookshop, Days of Hope (apparently

Avon and Somerset police cars caught by camera during the first nine months of 2003: 419; number of officers prosecuted: 1

given the charming spoonerised nickname 'Haze of Dope' because of the hippies who congregated there).

In 2006, a BBC Four documentary, *Lefties*, showed just how dominant these students have become: the right might have won the economic argument, but these people hold the cards in every other area of our political and cultural life, from education and movies – when was the last time you saw a right-wing film? – to social services and pop music.

They are not though, in general, members of the working classes they sought to emancipate those three and four decades ago. Their culture is of intellectual pursuits, which they inherited from their posh forebears. While they desperately tried to persuade the poor to come to acting workshops and yoga classes, the problem was that the working classes, deemed to be the principal victims of this cultural oppression, weren't having any of it. As we moved into the '70s, much to the chagrin of this new class of publicly employed worker whose sole purpose was to educate and enlighten the poor with street theatre, it became apparent that they couldn't care less about seeing *The Last Benefit* at the Deptford Albany.

The truth was, the poor didn't want to be middle class, they wanted to be rich.

A driver in Kent was ticked off by police after they spotted snow apparently 'billowing' off his roof

3 Strictly no white men

Nanny says we're all homophobic, racist and sexist

Well, now we're richer than ever before and our young radicals are running the world. Hillary Rodham's boyfriend, Bill Clinton, became her husband and the most important man in the world, and that handsome young student Tony Blair from the band Ugly Rumours is running the UK. Outside lavatories have been flushed into the ether of history and replaced by central heating, washing machines, video players and mobile phones. Employment opportunities have never been more exciting or widespread. There is a minimum wage and motor cars are no more the domain of the rich than Old Trafford is every week crammed with so many thousand men in cloth caps. A raft of legislation brought in by our young idealists means that no one can be discriminated against on the grounds of race or sex; local authorities spend £10 billion a year on social services as outreach workers stride out across council estates nationwide lest somebody doesn't know how to claim their unemployment benefit.

But things still aren't right. No, no, no, not right at all.

Despite the tireless work of Addaction, ATD Fourth World, Barnardo's, British Association for Adoption and Fostering, BVSC, Caritas, Centrepoint, Child Poverty Action Group, Childline, Children's Links, Church Action on Poverty, Citizens Advice, Contact a Family, Coram Family, Council for Disabled Children, Daycare Trust, Disability Alliance, Family Rights Group, Family Service Units, Family Welfare Association, Fathers Direct, Frank

---

A speed camera on the A27 trapped 12,500 drivers and raked in £750,000 in just two months during roadworks when the speed limit was reduced from 70 mph to 40 mph . . .

Buttle Trust, Maternity Alliance, National Children's Bureau, National Civil Rights Movement, National Youth Agency, NCH, New Policy Institute, National Family and Parenting Institute, NSPCC, One Parent Families, Oxfam, Parentline Plus, Poverty Alliance, Rainer, Refugee Council, Save the Children, Scope, Shelter, TELCO, The Children's Society, UK Coalition Against Poverty, YWCA England and Wales, and a few thousand other charities, we still have some people who are poorer than others.

Our grown-up radicals claim to be terribly disappointed by this disturbing inequality, and if they believe in their own rhetoric, so they should be. Hillary Rodham, after all, became the wife of an American president and is now herself a senator, where she has a direct influence on the richest and most powerful country on earth. Tony Blair is running the fourth-largest economy in the world and has a direct line to the world's most powerful man, President George Bush. For the past 30 years, their influence has been at the heart of every area of political and corporate life, and unprecedented amounts of money have been channelled into helping the disadvantaged. If anyone can help, surely it should be them.

Their political idealism has fermented into this brew we now know as political correctness. As its potency has increased inexorably, and those ideals transferred from halls of residence to the corridors of power, so you would have thought that the disadvantaged would have decreased in number. But no. Although the Student Union activists of the '60s and '70s now have the wherewithal to build radical theatres wherever they damn well like and send outreach workers into the darkest corners of our inner cities, we have victims in unprecedented numbers.

Why should this be? Could it be that the proponents of political correctness have failed? Or that despite being the dominant – if tacit – political force in the Western world, they have singularly

while the Treasury earned an estimated £642,000 from speed cameras which caught 10,700 drivers exceeding a 40 mph speed limit during roadworks on the M25

failed to bring about the changes they claim are necessary for a fair, equal and just society?

No, of course not, that would be impossible.

So perhaps it is *our* fault. Far from failing, despite the obvious theoretical righteousness of Eric Fromm and Herbert Marcuse and their manifest moral higher ground – equal rights for all, language to be non-offensive, poverty to be eradicated along with racism and homophobia – an amorphous rest of us are unreconstituted stick-in-the-muds who simply aren't getting the message. What we need, therefore, are more charities, more NGOs and more human rights groups. And therefore they need to spend more public money on more right-thinking people in more jobs until we change our simplistic, selfish ways.

The nanny state needs to be expanded, in other words. The work of the meddling classes needs to be redoubled and endless laws must be enacted to force us into behaving as they say we should. Certainly the British Government seems to think so – in 2004 alone, 240,000 new state jobs were created. To justify these jobs, there need to be victims and oppressors. For there to be a 'smoking cessation officer', there need to be smokers. The existence of the Runnymede Trust demands that there be racists. For there to be poor people who need our help, there need to be capitalist exploiters. For women to suffer sexual harassment, there need to be sexists. Most of us would think ourselves as none of these things; indeed, we surely buy into a world where they are quite rightly frowned upon. Isn't this a measure of the success of the modern Western world and a pluralistic society? Shouldn't our political leaders be thanking us for our tolerance and leaving us alone to continue living in such an urbane, civilised manner?

Not a bit of it.

Our culpability is raised time and time again as a barrier against their unstinting work towards a fairer society. Let us take, for

Council staff in Birmingham painted yellow lines around cars parked on a street,

example, the immigrant community of Tower Hamlets, where we came into this book, one of the poorest boroughs in the United Kingdom despite the fact it abuts the City of London, workplace of the richest people in the world, and boasts within its borders opulent riverside apartments overlooking Tower Bridge. Much is made of the fact that some of the poorest people in the country are living a stone's throw away from where many of the richest work. The simple fact of their juxtaposition tells us we are sinful in allowing such differences in wealth between the haves and have-nots.

The children's agency UNICEF, for example, in a report in 2000 bemoaned the fact that one British child in five lived in poverty, a figure worse than Turkey, say, or former Eastern-bloc nations such as Poland and Hungary. 'The persistence of child poverty in rich countries . . . confronts the industrialised world with a test both of its ideals and of its capacity to resolve many of its most intractable social problems,' the report concluded. In response to these findings, Steve Webb, a Liberal Democrat spokesman, called for tax increases on the better off to help defeat poverty (taxes attract Liberal Democrats like gold chains attract Puff Daddy). And while it's all very dramatic, why should Steve Webb *believe* this report, compiled by some very rich people working for the mightiest NGO in the world – 'advance humanity' and 'unite for children' are UNICEF's nonsensical slogans – searching for and finding victims? Any sensible person would surely question how UNICEF could possibly claim that children in the UK should suffer greater poverty than those in Poland, Turkey or Hungary, when this is patently not the case.

The reason is, of course, that UNICEF's measure defines poor families as living on incomes less than half the national average. And the reason for measuring it that way is political expediency. The fact is that the income of an average British family was and

then traffic wardens slapped £60 fines on their windscreens

still is beyond the wildest dreams of most families living in Turkey, Poland or Hungary. This is why the poor of Tower Hamlets aren't upping sticks and moving to Gdansk, while the workers of Poland are coming to London in their droves. Indeed, while UNICEF tugs at our heartstrings by talking specifically of 'child' poverty – there is a notion here of rich parents gliding around our cities in BMWs while their children are left in a dingy cellar to play with a burst balloon and a doll with a missing limb – it misses the most obvious point that poor people live in boroughs such as Tower Hamlets *because* of the City of London. The immigrant population hasn't moved to the borough because of its website translated into four languages and its massive social-services department; they have come to Tower Hamlets because they want to be rich. And who can blame them?

Huge political capital is made out of the relative poverty that exists in Tower Hamlets. Moreover, it scores double on the victimometer because some 50 per cent of its population is not only poor but first- and second-generation immigrant. There's an underlying implication that racism is holding its citizens back. But is it? If you are a young Bengali, say, you could make for Calcutta or Dhaka and try and make your fortune in one of the state capitals with presumably no danger of racist abuse. Or, if you have the contacts and the money to get yourself a flight, you could take a chance and join your mates in the East End of London. The fact that you are unskilled, have a poor grasp of English and no capital might hold you and your children back; indeed, you could say that the poverty will hold you back, just as the indigenous poor population of any city in any country in the world doesn't have the opportunities afforded to the rich. Likewise, the child of a poor farm worker in Shropshire, by dint of the fact that he doesn't have ready access to books and his mum and dad don't have the resources and quite possibly the desire to drive him to

A retired teacher, Betty Wilbraham, 82, was requested to take off her hat in a pub, the Hereward in Ely, because, since it was difficult to see faces under

every sports club within a 30-mile radius of their house, may also be held back.

But you could surely argue that far from the rich exploiting the poor, the new poor are exploiting the opportunities and charity offered by their rich city neighbours. Poor Mexicans, for example, aren't clambering into makeshift boats to cross the Caribbean to the people's paradise of Cuba; instead, they pour their life savings into traversing the Rio Grande. No, it is the Cubans who are risking their lives trying to make it to the vibrant, edgy, risky, capitalist melting pot of the United States.

Is it really true that Tower Hamlets residents suffer from racism? Well, statistics show that in Britain, Asian children do rather better in school than their white counterparts. By this argument, there is positive discrimination that works in other parts of the country but a weird Tower Hamlets warp that works against the Asian community. If you look at the yobs who hang around Shadwell DLR station, admittedly, you get the feeling there's a reason that they're not part of that positive statistic. Because race is much more complicated than Asian children doing better or worse in schools. In this case, it's also about Bangra beats and driving a Nissan with skirts and illuminated wheels. This is as much part of the identity of the youth as the traditional dress worn by their fathers, or the skull cap worn by the Jewish community who lived there two generations ago and managed, without the help of any politically correct groups whatsoever, to, ooh, run a multimillion-pound entertainment group, say, as did Lew Grade, who came to London to escape the anti-Jewish pogroms still rampaging through Tsarist Russia – now that *was* racism.

And Asians in much of the country are doing the same thing as Sir Lew. There's an Asian rich list and Asian business awards. Tariq Ali and Hanif Kureishi are two of the country's most prominent intellectuals. But modern-day political correctness has deemed

hats on CCTV cameras, wearing it posed a security risk

that Britain, far from being a rather tolerant country that for centuries has offered opportunity for immigrants, is a nation of bigots who will at minimum discriminate against anyone because of the colour of their skin and in the worst instances set upon them in a vicious attack in the same way despicable yobs laid into the black youth Stephen Lawrence in Eltham in 1993 in a case that became a cause célèbre.

Our intellectual mores have spawned inter alia the Commission for Racial Equality, 'Kick It Out' (against racism in football), the Campaign Against Racism and Fascism (CARF), the National Civil Rights Movement, the National Assembly Against Racism, the Student Assembly Against Racism, Black Information Link, Black Racial Attacks Independent Network (BRAIN), Nazism Exposed and, of course, the Runnymede Trust. And worthy as these causes are, in order to justify their existence they all have a vested interest in there being visible racism in our society. Charity, after all, is a £65 billion-a-year industry and chief executives of these organisations enjoy six-figure salaries. It is, and has been since the '70s, fashionable to be anti-racist, and quite rightly so. The notion that people should be discriminated against because of the colour of their skin, their sex or their accent is obviously abhorrent, but all the evidence seems to point to the fact that there are very few people who hold racist views.

What we have to ask ourselves is: without these organisations, without the constant hectoring and pointing the finger at a theoretical mass, would our society be any more racist than otherwise? I remember well in 1978 young, white middle-class students and members of left-wing groups, Socialist Workers Party banners aloft, lobbing bricks at young, white working-class National Front members as they exercised their right to march down the New Cross Road, in one of the most racially mixed areas of London. I was there, doing my bit. How those

A 'Women Unlimited' exhibition, part of a drive to get more women into work, proposed that women should look for employment in the vacancies columns of their

young working-class 'have-nots' – angry, disgruntled, out of work – would have loved to have broken through the police lines there to 'protect' them and given us posh, young stone-throwing 'haves' a good kicking.

Two things were interesting here. First, the black community didn't feel it necessary to come out in force and attempt to stop the march – presumably they would have been happy to ignore it and just let this sad little group stomp and snarl and boot-march through empty streets. Second, the fact that a generation before, the National Front marchers at whom the anti-Nazi protestors were now lobbing stones would have been the very South London poor whom the young communists wanted to emancipate.

The truth is that much of the racism and sexism and poverty in Britain is so much more complicated than the sloganeering self-righteousness of the meddling classes would have us believe. This doesn't make those National Front marchers right – on the contrary, their views deserve the opprobrium they receive – but the one thing they share with some of their Muslim counterparts is at root a visceral hatred of the Jews. Look at the way a West Indian talks to a Chinese server in a takeaway, or the reaction of the community if an Islamic girl should have a white boyfriend. These are difficult, complex issues that simply aren't covered by the facile rhetoric of 'inclusiveness' and aren't necessarily best served by a load of well-meaning graduates doing very nicely on government grants. And there are a lot of them.

The Commission for Racial Equality (CRE), in its search for a 'chair', described in its advertisement how the successful applicant must make sure that the Race Relations Amendment Act 2000 is implemented effectively. The Act requires more than '40,000 public sector bodies to promote race equality as they carry out their functions'. One can't help thinking that many in our black communities would rather their rubbish was collected on time

newspapers and Job Centres; it also pointed out that some vacancies are 'still filled by word of mouth'

than have council workers spending endless hours in anti-racism meetings with the CRE.

Trevor Phillips, the man who in 2003 became that chair, saw the organisation swing into action with a report revealing that while 10,000 Afro-Caribbean men are in jails in Britain – a significantly higher proportion than for other ethnic groups – the number of black men at university is about half that. Mr Phillips described the figures as 'devastating' and demonstrated the need to eliminate discrimination in society, although he didn't say how.

But is this figure entirely down to discrimination? In fact, although the black community hasn't exactly had an easy ride over the past 30 years, it isn't doing too badly in the UK. A study published by the Joseph Rowntree Foundation in 2005 found that black Britons are more socially mobile and less likely to be working class than the white population. In contrast to the '70s, when nearly 80 per cent of British people of Caribbean descent were in the lowest socio-economic groups, the figure was now just over 22 per cent. The proportion of whites stuck in these groups was 25 per cent. The report found that more than 45 per cent of British blacks were in managerial or professional jobs. 'Caribbeans have a 22 per cent greater chance of ending up in the professional classes than otherwise comparable white non-migrants,' it stated.

'This sort of research is to be welcomed and reflects the progress of black women,' said Diane Abbott, MP for Hackney North and Stoke Newington and the first black woman elected to parliament, 'but it masks continuing underachievement and higher rates of unemployment among black men in their teens and 20s.'

She rightly points out the complexity of the issue but, nonetheless, if we follow the report's logic, this must mean that Trevor Phillips's racism works in strange and mysterious ways. If it is discrimination at work holding back young black men and forcing them into prison, there must also be some kind of positive

An Irish woman won £3,000 compensation after a colleague wrote a list of fineable sins on a whiteboard at a fire service control room in Berkshire as part of Comic Relief Day in

discrimination taking place elsewhere that allows the majority of the black population to achieve more social mobility than its white equivalents. Similarly, in education, where Asian and many black African children out-perform their white counterparts, there must be a racial discrimination going on that works against some immigrants and not others.

Or maybe it's just the fact that if you uproot yourself and your family from friends and neighbours to move to a new country, initially you will be forced into the lower-paid jobs, but the gumption and initiative you needed to tear yourself away from friends and family in the first place will rub off on the next generation.

Who knows?

Obviously, despite this positive news from the Rowntree Trust and elsewhere, racism still exists and is clearly horrible. It is one of the most blatant manifestations of bigotry, in that it makes no attempt whatsoever to judge a person by who they are; it reduces whole nations to being nobodies because of the colour of their skin. But that is different to bigotry itself. A bigot, for example, could easily be black and dislike posh people, or southern people. He or she is not necessarily a racist. A bigot could also be xenophobic, but although a xenophobe is by definition bigoted, it is different to being a racist. A white racist will quite happily share a beer with a white South African or a Pole, which would be anathema to the xenophobe. A xenophobe likewise could be black and hate the idea of white people and Asians living in Africa, as did Idi Amin (who was probably all three) in Uganda in the '60s, with the effect that the UK instantly benefited from the business acumen of so many refugees who arrived at its shores during that time, despite the fact that our young intellectuals were denouncing Great Britain as being run by racist bigots.

It is incredibly easy – and fashionable – to tar an anonymous

2003. Her sins were 'being Irish' and 'not wearing a tie', and were punishable with a small fine for the charity. She was awarded the money for 'injury to feelings'

population with a racist brush. Especially if those making the accusations depend on it to make a living. The Scottish Executive in 2002 published a survey that suggested that one in four Scots was racist. Quite what this meant in a country that is 98 per cent white wasn't really clear, but it did decide that £1 million should be spent tackling the 'problem'. Presumably this meant employing lots of Trevor Phillipses to furrow their brows and moan about our racist environment.

What this survey didn't seem to pay any attention to was discrimination against the English. None of those millions spent on tackling the 'problem' prevented the Scottish Executive's Minister for Environment and Rural Development, Ross Finnie, calling the director general of the CBI, Digby Jones, 'an English prat' at around the same time as the report was published. What, one wonders, would have been the reaction had he called a non-white businessman a 'Bangladeshi prat' or a 'Nigerian prat'. Ross Finnie, in fact, is the same race as the English businessman he was upbraiding. It wasn't a racial slur, but it was bigotry. And bad manners.

The truth is, fashion plays a large part in whom we defend and why. The politically correct have gone, for example, from defending the white poor to Jews to blacks to Muslims on little more than a whim. Oh, how much more fun it became in the '70s to hold Anti-Nazi League rallies, flex your political muscles against a group of dejected saddos who had left their traditional homes as local industry crumpled and align yourself with some reggae artists who had found a whole new market at Rock Against Racism gigs, than bother with the boring old white working class. Of course, a real black gathering, like an appearance by Yellowman, say, or Buju '*Boom Bye Bye Shoot the Battyman Dead*' Banton, or any number of blues parties being held around London would have been far too violent and risky for a young middle-class white man or woman to contemplate.

The Red Lion pub on Whitehall, yards away from Downing Street, had its application for a licence to open until 1 a.m. as part of the Government's legislation allowing

Nonetheless, there were no outreach workers going into the homes of working-class whites to maybe talk to them about their pain and the problems they encountered dealing with the changes going on around them. I remember seeing an old lady hanging out of the window of her first-floor flat, traffic roaring past the building, looking in despair as reggae music blared out from the window next to her. Were the likes of her being racist in their lack of understanding of the new and mysterious community that had moved in alongside her?

But Afro-Caribbean people are now out of fashion, too. The days of Rock Against Racism gigs and murals daubed with the colours of Ethiopia have gone the way of Austin Allegros, and light and bitter. Following the 9/11 bombings in New York and the 7/7 Tube bombings in London, the politically correct are unstintingly bringing to our attention the peace-loving majority of Muslims, who might now be the focus of attacks, and wagging their fingers at us should we encourage this racist uprising. We haven't even done anything yet and we're being upbraided for the possibility that we might.

The reality is that despite the outrage at the bombing of innocent, defenceless people going about their business, there have been almost no repercussions. It is a tribute, surely, to a secure, tolerant society. But this hasn't stopped the nanny state bossing us all about and telling us off for our potential racism.

In the run-up to Christmas in 2005, two in three bosses banned 'offensive' tinsel to avoid upsetting non-Christians, according to a survey conducted by the employment law firm Peninsula. Of course, this was a nice bit of propaganda for the agency, but it got the publicity on the back of councils such as that of Waveney, Suffolk, which planned to scrap grants for Christmas lights because Christmas does not fit in with its 'core values of equality and diversity', and Lambeth, which insisted on renaming

extended opening hours turned down on the grounds of 'public nuisance' and 'public safety'

its decorations 'winter' lights. Whether you're a Christian or not, the one thing Christianity respects are core values of equality and diversity – a simple fact lost on the priggish leaders of Waveney Council. Most Muslims would surely assume that in a country where the national religion is Christianity that Christmas might just be celebrated in some way.

'I don't think any Muslim community would object to Christmas decorations,' said Sir Iqbal Sacranie, the newly knighted secretary general of the Muslim Council of Britain, of the Peninsula report. 'Maybe the companies are using it as an excuse to save money.' If only such common sense prevailed among the white community that decides to ban the word 'Christmas' from, well, Christmas cards and call Christmas lights 'festive lights'.

Meanwhile, the word inclusiveness has permeated every school in the country, with the perverse result that while inclusive councils ban Christmas, so our schoolchildren are taught to celebrate Eid and other religious festivals that for the majority have no immediate bearing on their background.

One primary school in St Albans decided to take its six- and seven-year-old pupils on a trip to the Regent's Park Mosque, where the poor little mites were upbraided by an Imam for not paying attention while he droned on for 40 minutes in praise of the Muslim faith. Why were they taken to a mosque when they hadn't yet visited a church, let alone the city cathedral down the road from their school? Why, indeed, did they have to go at great expense to that mosque rather than the one in the city? And what were they taught in the name of inclusiveness? Here is a place where men worship separately as part of a religion that at its most extreme forces women to hide their faces in public, enforces arranged marriages, punishes homosexuality, sticks fatwas on those who criticise it and blows up innocent citizens in the name of Allah. And these are children who still believe in Father Christmas.

The Prime Minister's wife, Cherie Blair, presented the Labour Party with a bill for £7,700 for the services of her personal hairstylist during the 2005 general election campaign

So much part of public life has political correctness become, and so obsessed have we become with it, that basic moral values and principles seem to have been left behind. A Pandora's box of rights has been opened up that has led to a sclerosis of morality. We have got to the stage where, in one case, travellers illegally camped next to a wildlife reserve and a site that had been given special scientific interest status in 2004 demanded £62,000 from residents to move on. The group of three traveller families had bought the four-acre site in Yatton, North Somerset, for £27,000 and, despite being denied planning permission for their six caravans, ripped up hedgerows and put down areas of concrete hard-standing. Then they moved in portable lavatories and industrial generators.

One has sympathy for the travellers, of course. There is less and less common land available to them, and their community has become ever larger. One has sympathy for the council, too. The travellers' group lodged an appeal against North Somerset Council's decision to reject their retrospective planning application – a method used by increasing numbers of travellers to stay on land – and so they stayed and the argument rumbled on. But the fact remains that in an era that worships the cult of the victim, residents couldn't rely on the rule of law to protect their interests. Their 'rights', you could say. Indeed, in 2005, the Government announced that £8 million would be put towards new and refurbished residential sites for travellers. Just up the road from Yatton, £1.5 million of it was going to be spent on a scheme at South Liberty Lane in Bristol.

There was no sign of that in Yatton, of course. Despite the fact that the travellers' action was illegal, immoral and obviously distressing to residents, it was always unlikely that the local police would be down in a hurry. Our public figures – policemen, teachers, politicians, lawyers – seem so concerned with prostrating

An 82-year-old Labour Party member Walter Wolfgang was ejected by bouncers from the party conference in 2005 after shouting 'Nonsense' as former Foreign Secretary Jack Straw defended the decision to invade Iraq

themselves before the altar of equality that what they're meant to be doing gets left behind.

In 2005, the chief of the Metropolitan Police, Sir Ian Blair, was so irked by a major issue that he felt compelled to speak out against it. Was it the fact that street crime had increased dramatically? Or that only one in 100 crimes go to trial? Or the fact that more motorists than burglars are jailed? No, of course not. What troubled Sir Ian was the 'racist' reporting of murder. After the front-page coverage of the horrific, cold-blooded murder of Tom ap Rhys Pryce, as he walked home from Kensal Rise Tube Station after an evening with friends, in which his last words were 'You've got everything', Sir Ian criticised the racist press for not affording similar coverage to the murder of blacks. Not only was this crassly insensitive, it was patent nonsense. The murder of the black youth Damilola Taylor in Peckham (which the police, incidentally, made a pig's ear of investigating, with two trials of two different groups of youths failing to secure guilty convictions at an estimated cost of £20 million), Stephen Lawrence in Eltham, Victoria Climbié in North London and Charlene Ellis and Letisha Shakespeare gunned down in Birmingham all made front-page news.

And even if he did have a point, why did he choose to make it so publicly? Either he is completely blind to the sensibilities of the nation or he felt a need to ingratiate himself with his paymasters at the Home Office. He was, in effect, displaying his politically correct credentials.

Everyone recognises the police have had their issues with racism; but when the term 'institutionally racist' was coined, it did the most terrible damage to the police, and especially to the black community living in high-crime areas, where the young black men who strutted round the locale, forcing their law-abiding neighbours to live in fear, were largely allowed to roam unfettered because the police were scared of picking them up and being labelled racist.

Labour MP Jean Corston, Chairman of the Labour Party in 2001, said MPs should get free counselling because of Parliament's long hours. 'I do think there is an argument

Who suffered? Well, the mainly black law-abiding citizens who lived nearby. The police's fear of racism, and fear of being labelled racist by their political masters (all right, and mistresses) in the Home Office, led to the immigrant population receiving inferior policing compared to white areas. How racist is that?

Now the police, guided by a PC government, are obsessed with 'hate' crime. All 45 forces in Britain have been issued with a document entitled 'Hate Crime: Delivering a Quality Service' – note the word 'delivery' again – which insists that all hate crimes be rigorously followed up, whether or not they have any merit. Lord knows how any decent copper is going to have time to plough through its 114 pages – but, needless to say, there is all the usual jargon of best practice and the like.

We all agree that the police force hasn't been the most liberal of institutions. But rather than quietly trying to clean up its act with a supportive government, it is on the back foot, constantly trying to justify itself. Staffordshire force, for example, felt the need not to brag about its record on fighting crime, or how much more peaceful the streets of the county had become, but the fact that it had per capita more gays in its workforce than is the case across the nation. The force's 'delighted' chief constable, John Gifford, granted an interview to *Guardian Society*, the house journal of the politically correct.

'How would you describe your leadership and management style?' asked Mary O'Hara, in what is probably the least-challenging interview in the history of journalism.

'My style is to enable people and so get the best from them.'

None of us approves of hate crime, but crime is crime. Why should it be that the police force is so concerned with being nanny's favourite rather than telling us that it is getting stuck in and trying to make some impact on the antisocial criminal behaviour that is endemic in the UK?

for counselling provision which is in no way stigmatised and which obviously would have to be entirely confidential,' she said

As one Staffordshire resident, Mrs M. Reader, pointed out in a letter to the local *Cannock Mercury*:

> I am sure that the good people of Staffordshire are delighted that Staffordshire Police has been named as Britain's most gay-friendly employer. Thanks to their positive targeting in recruiting drives, one in 10 of the county's 2,309 officers are either lesbian or homosexual.
>
> However, a Staffordshire Police spokesman states that these officers are entitled to attend up to three Gay Pride rallies a year in paid time. With 230 officers being eligible, this could result in nearly 700 days of patrol time lost while being financed out of public funds.
>
> I would suggest that this a gross misuse of police resources and public money at a time when the sight of a patrolling police officer is a rare event.

Meanwhile, Avon and Somerset Constabulary was accused in 2005 of discarding almost 200 job applications because the candidates were white males. Some 800 hopefuls applied for 180 jobs, but 186 applications sent by white men were rejected at the first stage. The force admitted that they were ruled out because its workforce was 'over-represented by white men'. Could it not be that, for whatever reason, more white men than other groups tend to apply to join the police force? Even Batook Pandya, director of the Bristol-based Support Against Racist Incidents, said, 'We need a police force that reflects the community we live in, which means having officers from all sections of society, but this is not the way to get it.'

But there are many of Batook Pandya's contemporaries who believe it is. The mayor of London, Ken Livingstone, repeatedly calls for his staff to reflect the society in which we live. How is this meant to work? In London as a whole, ethnic minorities form 29

Kent drama group The Coxheath Players, planning a pantomime of Snow White and the Seven Dwarfs, were shocked to find when they received a script that all references to the word 'dwarf' had been removed and the characters instead referred to as 'gnomes'

per cent of the population; the figure in some boroughs is 50 per cent. Does this mean that the workforce of every organisation has to reflect this mix? And if so, does this mean that employers in Scotland, with its 98 per cent white population, would be obliged to make sure that 98 per cent of its employees are also white?

In 2005, the former Trade Secretary Patricia Hewitt admitted breaking the Sex Discrimination Act after overruling advisers and appointing a woman to an influential post at the South West Regional Development Agency. Merchant banker Malcolm Hanney used the Freedom of Information Act to obtain notes taken during his interview and found he had been described as by far the strongest candidate. But Ms Hewitt decided instead to appoint the third choice, Christine Channon, who was approached by a headhunter when she was the leader of Devon County Council.

Her action is in keeping with the attitude of the Labour Party to which she belongs, which advocates and enforces women-only candidate shortlists with the stated aim of ultimately 50 per cent of its MPs being women – the logic being that it reflects the population they 'serve'. These worthy democrats have conveniently forgotten that in a democracy ultimately it is the public who put people into office, and even if 50 per cent of candidates fielded were women, that's no guarantee the same percentage would be elected. What to do then? Lob out the surplus men or women, however the bias might fall? While a public culling of these rather pampered individuals might result in a certain *Schadenfreude* among the general public, it is hardly the way to conduct the democratic process.

And how could this ever be reflected in the real world? While the general population comprises 50 per cent women, the general population doesn't have the same aspirations. Many women quite understandably decide that once they've had children, they would rather stay at home and raise them. This means that you can do a

or 'guardians of the forest'. The name of Bashful had been changed to Basher to avoid offending shy people

number of things. You can insist that 50 per cent of all employees must be women, as Labour wants to do with its MPs, but to reach this nirvana logic dictates that the number of women who choose to stay at home to raise their children will have to be matched with unemployed men, or the quota will never work. Or you force all women to work. Or you could go the other way and say that there have to be an equal number pro rata of men and women in the workforce, which would mean a permanent majority of men. Which would be absurd.

Or we could muddle along the way we are with the democratic ebb and flow of a flexible workforce meeting the demands of a flexible employment market and ignore the silly theories of the nanny state.

In fact, while women are among the victims who are trotted out as needing special and deserving attention in our society, this too is more of a myth than one imagines. Career women in middle and top management jobs, for example, earn nearly as much as their male counterparts. A survey in 2003 by the Chartered Management Institute and analyst Remuneration Economics found the average female department head earned 1 per cent less than her male equivalent – £53,257 a year compared to £53,732. The researchers found that traditional prejudices were disappearing and women were breaking through the 'old boy network'. Indeed, many were the biggest wage earners in their family. They found, too, that almost 30 per cent of women were managers, up 9.5 per cent from 1994, while on average women received pay rises of 5.9 per cent compared to 5 per cent for men.

Meanwhile, British Government figures show that there are now more female millionaires aged between 18 and 44 than there are men. In an episode of the BBC series *The Money Programme* entitled 'Filthy Rich and Female', the businesswoman Nicola Horlick estimated that within 20 years 60 per cent of the United Kingdom's wealth would be controlled by women.

Liz Beattie told her colleagues at the Professional Association of Teachers conference that the word 'failure' should be banned and replaced with the term 'deferred

But this is of no use to the politically correct. If racism has little part in national life, and black people are actually doing better than their white counterparts, where is the need for all those important groups campaigning on their behalf? What can the Commission for Racial Equality do other than dig up cases of racism and defend them – fine – and then hold them up as an argument for the fact that racism is endemic in our society – not fine. Similarly, what will happen to women's rights groups if it really is true that women are doing better in the workplace than men? Will a new glass ceiling come into being and women's groups be replaced by men's organisations? Will coffee mornings be replaced by park football afternoons, and ladies who lunch by men who lager?

This need for victims is no better illustrated than by Teignbridge District Council in Devon, which spent £3,000 on research to ensure equal access to services for minorities. After three years of effort, no gays could be found. David Corney, a councillor, said that it was 'incredible' that consultants had been unable to find any in the area, which had many organisations for minorities. He was concerned that the research hadn't been done properly. Lynn McElheron, Teignbridge 'community initiatives' manager, said that they were concerned that no minority groups had been contacted but to continue looking for them would have been too expensive.

What is so extraordinary is the disappointment of the councillor and community initiatives manager, who are desperate, absolutely desperate, to find minority groups to be discriminated against. What would be wrong, pray, rather than hunting down the only gay in the village, with scouring a few village fetes and looking out for old ladies living on nothing more than a diet of plum jam?

The reason Teignbridge council wanted to track down these minorities was obviously not just to satisfy themselves that they existed but also to discover that they were being discriminated against, too. They needed actively to seek out homophobes and

success'. 'Failure is very hard to cope with,' she said. 'Education is too important for that; we need to keep people striving on'

racists who were denying these victims 'equal access' to services.

In his pamphlet on political correctness, 'The Retreat of Reason', Anthony Browne argues that the perceived glass ceiling for women's employment is due almost entirely to their bringing up children. They will take lower-paid jobs in order not to have to succumb to the pressure of the late and unpredictable hours that modern professional life imposes. Indeed, my wife, with a degree in history from Oxford, works part time as a classroom assistant at the local primary school so she can be at home to look after our two daughters. What would happen if, under a quota system, I were to lose my job because I was a man? Would she then be forced to work against her wishes?

Even more pernicious is the fact that when seeking out predjudice is the *raison d'être* of your working life, you can paradoxically perpetuate that predjudice by giving it credence. So, points out Mr Browne, teaching underperforming black boys in school to see themselves as victims of white racist teachers is not to help them but to discourage them and their families from looking at the cultural attitudes to education that might be the root of the problem.

In a heartfelt piece for the *Sunday Times*, the writer Nirpal Singh Dhaliwal told of his school – an all-boys comprehensive in Ealing, where the pupils were overwhelmingly black and Asian – and how they were let down by the idealistic teachers who had 'read Marx and Malcolm X and done an elective in post-colonial theory at polytechnic'. 'We ate those suckers alive,' he wrote:

> Desperate to empathise with our persecution, they were knocked dead by our indifference and rampant misbehaviour. At the first sniff of guilt-ridden middle-class weakness, the feral instincts of teenage boys were unleashed and the class descended into anarchy. They thought we'd been crazed by

Smokers who work for Tower Hamlets Council have to work 30 minutes a day more than their non-smoking colleagues

oppression, so didn't want to come down too hard on us. They wanted to understand instead. When it did get too much for them and they threatened to march one of us to the headmaster's office, our immediate protest would be: 'You're a racist!'

They'd cower behind their desks, mortified that we'd recognised some deeply suppressed prejudice within them, while we got back to hurling insults, beating the crap out of each other and rolling joints to smoke at lunchtime.

It was only, writes Dhaliwal, a group of stalwart traditionalist teachers who prevented them from leaving the school illiterate. One teacher, a Mr Garrett, who had high expectations of how they should behave and apply themselves, flew into thunderous and terrifying rages whenever the boys failed to meet them. For some children, he was the most solid male presence in their lives.

I have a friend who teaches, and he says it's normal for teachers not to reprimand badly behaved black kids because 'they suffer enough oppression as it is'. The soft bigotry of wet liberals is as insidious as the racism of white supremacists. Lowering the bar for children because you consider them oppressed has the same effect as expecting little of them because you think them inferior.

Indeed, a school in South London has opened, offering young, black male students the chance to receive the sort of education that the state is not providing. Rather than being mollycoddled by frightened teachers terrified of being accused of racism, they are taught discipline, hard work and good manners. It is a condition that parents are involved in the school, and any transgression of the rules leads to expulsion. Eastside Young Leaders Academy in

At a course for new managers at the Home Office, equal opportunities guardians asked staff to consider 'beardism' and to note their reactions to facial hair

Plaistow, East London, is run by Ray Lewis, who used to be the governor of a young offenders' association. He doesn't want to hear about his charges becoming DJs or footballers; he expects them to go to university and enter top professions. Three days a week and on Saturday mornings they are taught maths and English, given order in their life and taught social skills – how to speak to people at dinner, how to talk to women, tidiness. They are taught discipline, on the basis that they can only build self-control and self-confidence if they respect adult authority. They aren't allowed to say 'yeah' or 'right'.

'After a few months,' Mr Lewis told the writer Melanie Phillips in a piece for the *Daily Mail*, 'all of them are expected to be able to speak to an adult with humility, honesty and courtesy.'

'At school, they'll give you 50 per cent for work that you should only get 1 per cent for,' one boy told her. 'Here they are straight up and tell you if you have to do something again.'

'I don't believe in attention deficit disorder,' Mr Lewis continued. 'If these boys can concentrate on PlayStations for hours, they can listen to me for half an hour. Our boys have got too much self-esteem. We need to take this out of them, and then we build them up. We love them and we believe in them, which is why I won't listen to this rubbish.'

How many children have suffered, how many of those black people in prison Trevor Phillips is 'devastated' by are there because school teachers have been scared to do what Ray Lewis is doing for fear of being jumped on by the Commission for Racial Equality?

We all know about racism and sexism and homophobia. The reality is that black people want proper policing as much as whites. The immigrant population of Tower Hamlets want a proper, strict education for their children, not some right-on organisation simpering on about how Christmas may or may not be appropriate in a multi-faith borough.

Fiji villagers, whose ancestors killed and ate a British missionary, said they were sorry in a ceremony of reconciliation 136 years after his death in 1867

One of the great advantages of being a Western woman at the start of the twenty-first century is that there is a flexible marketplace for jobs and that they are neither forced to stay at home – as they surely would be in many Muslim countries – nor to undertake high-powered jobs against their wishes. It isn't surprising that country people object to traveller camps setting up at the bottom of their gardens with 24-hour generators on the go, the whole atmosphere of their village changed. This isn't racism as the politically correct insist on defining it, just an understandable desire to have some peace and quiet in their lives. When top orthopaedic surgeon David Nunn stopped an operation at Guy's and St Thomas's Hospital because the nurses could not speak English, was he being racist? Did he deserve the threat of disciplinary action from his bosses?

It is astonishing how in this age of equality it has taken the setting up of a school such as the Eastside Young Leaders Academy to give black youth a fair start in life. Everybody recognises the need for special interest groups. But our democracy is under serious threat if its processes are undermined by a set of values that demand there be victims and oppressors. Of course prejudice is wrong and pernicious, but the politically correct thinking that coalesced in the '60s and '70s has the same uniformity of thought that presided over the revolutions in Russia and China. There is an absolutism that is dangerous and unhealthy. Even more worryingly, it is being fed and nurtured by the universities to such an extent that independent thought itself is under threat. We should remember H.L. Mencken's words: 'The urge to save humanity is almost always a false front for the urge to rule it.'

Highland Council has banned its employees from taking cigarette breaks in office hours because 'they will be doing themselves harm in company time'. So now it is a criminal offence to harm yourself

4 Strictly no maths

While we're jolly pleased to live in an age of mobile phones, iPods and unprecedented medical benefits, the science that has given us these huge advantages isn't sexy science. It isn't what gets our politicians' juices flowing, and it isn't what makes the headlines.

Nor is it what is encouraged by the nanny state. What nanny wants is science driven by sentiment. Headlines are made by such vital contributions to the pursuit of greater human understanding of the world as, 'Taller children will grow smarter, claims IQ test study', 'Swimming with dolphins can significantly alleviate depression', 'The more TV, the fatter your child could be', or conversely, 'Couch potatoes sprout bigger brains'. How about 'Smearing skin with broccoli can help reduce the risk of cancer'? Or 'Pomegranate juice can help your heart'?

These are the caring, sharing, touchy-feely studies that chime with the nanny state, pumped out in ever greater number with finger-wagging warnings about dangerous pursuits such as watching television.

So, a survey of this ilk published in 2004 by the market research company TNS – an organisation that includes Gallup as a subsidiary and takes on research for the European Commission – that reported that six in ten children aged under ten admitted to feeling 'stressed out' is emblematic of nanny's intellectual pursuits. Like so many studies, it provides a nice little conversation piece over a cup of coffee when the children have gone to school – or

---

Measures outlined by the Government in 2006 proposed rewarding youngsters with 'good behaviour cards', enabling them to spend up to £25 a month on

even, perhaps, a bit of dinner-party chatter on Saturday night when parents can talk about how little Henry gets down in the mouth sometimes, before going on to talk about the difficulty of getting him to eat pear purée, or how soon the children might be old enough to enjoy a gîte in France.

We rarely stop to ask why TNS OK (Online Kids, if you please) should have wanted to ask children about their mental well-being. This basic question certainly doesn't figure in press reports; even the company doesn't make clear what prompted it to carry out research into this pressing area.

TNS certainly asks lots of people lots of things, though. So many things, in fact, that the European Commission has chosen the company to run its Standard Eurobarometer, with its subsidiary Gallup Europe measuring public opinion on social, economic and political issues across 33 countries. And the European Commission isn't known for its reluctance to part with its money for a social survey or two. Thanks to TNS's unstinting work, we shall no doubt learn lots of things about ourselves and our European compatriots.

The meddling classes, not least our political masters in such institutions as the European Commission, are forever instituting tick-box consumer surveys on what we eat, what we watch on television, how often we drive, where we live, what our jobs are, what gender we are, what race we are, and so on. These questions are to our bureaucracies what iron ore is to the steel industry. Information such as what makes our children stressed is churned out by the yard. But no one seems to question either why these surveys are instituted in the first place, or the methodology behind them.

What, pray, did TNS ask the children who turn out to have so much on their minds? Was it a direct question? 'Hey, kids, do you feel stressed?' Tick either box 'Yes', 'No' or 'Don't know'. Or

sport and leisure facilities to deter them from misbehaving

perhaps the four to six year olds surveyed were given the statement 'I feel stressed and it's doing my head in' and asked to please mark from number one to ten, where one is 'strongly agree' and ten is 'strongly disagree'. Or maybe, recognising that reading isn't a four to six year old's strong point, TNS OK simply wrote, 'Parents/carers: my kids are, like, really hassled a) never; b) sometimes; c) often; d) always. Please don't include trips to McDonald's, Legoland or play zones.' One is not impugning TNS's competence or its ability to run serious research projects, but it is an example of how much we take for granted when we read daily about these surveys and research results.

Research of this kind is a symptom of our age. There is no limit, it seems, to the subjects that come under academic scrutiny. We can learn from research papers from other organisations over the past couple of years that, variously, jogging on your own is bad for you, children are advised to keep mobiles away from their heads and laps, women's 'lifestyle' raises cancer risks, Mozart makes maths easier, children are too clean for their own good, illness could all be in the mind, eye cancer is caused by mobiles, the unborn child can detect language, there are benefits to drinking beer, harsh words can deform children's brains for life, even that the bizarre visual effects of migraines may have inspired Picasso's paintings.

This new type of science also stems from the big Germans – and the rapid growth in sociology in those heady campus university days of the '60s and '70s. Sociology can serve you up some good old Marxist statistics on the plight of the poor and any other victim you choose to scrutinise, while psychology satisfies the Freudian urge to glorify the self. If the TNS survey could be taken up by another NGO and the conclusion reached that *poor* children are more likely to be depressed, then the Marx and Freud buttons would have been pressed simultaneously.

'Wearing of this garment does not enable you to fly' on a child's Superman outfit, 'Do not turn upside down' on the bottom of a tiramisu and 'This product moves when

If we really believe these results, the logical conclusion we should draw from them is to get the kids on Prozac forthwith.

As the doctor Theodore Dalrymple wrote in *The Times*, 'Children learn psychobabble early these days. It is part of growing up, like smoking dope and stretching condoms on bananas. After all, children must be taught a lack of resilience as soon as possible, or else what would become of the army of social workers, counsellors, psychologists and therapists upon whom the future growth of employment in this country so strongly depends? They are the Jesuits *de nos jours*. Give us a child for the first seven years and he is ours for ever.'

While this sort of research isn't going to send us to concentration camps, it has slowly and insidiously given succour to a range of values and beliefs that, 50 years ago, we'd have thought nonsensical.

Sheila Lee, the head teacher of Treverbyn Community Primary school near St Austell, Cornwall, didn't go quite as far as putting her pupils on drugs, but she was one step ahead of that TNS report. She decided that stress was a real problem for her wee charges and instituted a regime where, before morning class began, children gave one another shoulder, neck and head massages to rid themselves of the tensions that we all know beset primary school children.

A visit by a therapist so impressed Mrs Lee that she commandeered £300 from school funds to run a six-week trial project for five year olds (after seeking parents' permission, it should be mentioned). Then she secured a grant of £2,000 from a government fund to help 'disadvantaged' children to extend the programme to pupils between three and eight, and massage expert Lin Hudson was brought in once a week to teach the children the skills needed.

Mrs Lee also introduced t'ai chi for nine to eleven year olds to help them relax before national tests – probably just as well, because the

used' on a children's scooter are just some of the daft labels spotted by readers of *Which?* magazine in 2005

school's results were below the national average in English and maths in 2002. And Mrs Lee had rough-and-tumble in the playground to contend with. 'This was deliberate tripping and pushing, and then the children were laughing at the pain they had caused,' she said. 'Within two to three weeks, the complaints started to drop back. It did not solve the problem – we still have incidents – but they are at a much lower level than they were previously.'

The only trouble is, of course, that although 'stress' is a word we love to bandy around, it doesn't buff up well under academic scrutiny, as Sean Perrin, a clinical psychologist at the Institute of Psychiatry, pointed out in *The Times*: 'The word stress is completely meaningless because it does not distinguish between ordinary, everyday stressful events and those that have a lasting effect on our self-esteem.'

When we read the TNS study, it is impossible to differentiate between children who are worried about getting their homework done on time and those who are undisciplined, live on a diet of junk food and have no routine in their lives. But in either case, children are learning early these days that there is much that isn't their fault.

How curious that we are undertaking these nebulous enquiries in an age in which, thanks to science, we are blessed with immunisation against most of the traditional killer diseases that used to wipe out children by the score; quick and reliable personal transport; technology to heat our homes to the temperature we want when we want; rapid, safe transportation to every corner of the earth; birth control that gives us the ultimate choice over when we reproduce and the size of family we want. How curious that we, who can 'stand on the shoulders of giants', to borrow from Newton, and benefit from 2,500 years of wisdom, should now pour our scientific efforts into discovering that six out of ten children under the age of six are 'stressed out'.

De Montfort University in Leicester was caught in 2004 lowering a pass mark to 26 per cent to prevent widespread failure of trainee pharmacists. Marks for five

The benefits we enjoy today are largely the result of empirical enquiry and, for that, we can give thanks to the likes of Isaac Newton, Robert Hooke and Edmond Halley through to Humphry Davy, Michael Faraday and Alexander Fleming. What is striking about their extraordinary achievements is that they undertook their research largely unfettered by political control or expediency.

In 1662, the Royal Society was formed. Admittedly, it was essentially a gentlemen's club, but while it received no money from the state, men such as Newton and Christopher Wren could carry out their work independently of the sovereign, or any vested interest group that was in a position of power at the time. Not only that, it was a focal point, where great scientists from around the world could send their work and continue the debate.

Today it seems the academic rigour that those great men strove for has given way to science that seems to reinforce the prejudices of the political establishment. We imbibe scientific information without questioning its provenance or thoroughness.

In his book *Bad Medicine*, Christopher Wanjek, a journalist and senior writer for NASA, questioned scientific findings that we've somehow translated into certitudes. He reports, for example, how the myth of brain cancer from mobile phones is steeped in our irrational fear of radiation. For radiation to cause cancer, he notes, it must break chemical bonds in the body, and only certain types of radiation – ionising radiation – can do this. While ultraviolet radiation, X-rays and gamma rays could cause illness over time, visible light and radio waves are always safe. Radiation travels as photons. A high-energy X-ray photon acts like a golf ball and smashes a window. Radio photons from mobiles are millions of times less energetic, like puffballs, he writes. You can throw as many puffballs as you want, but you will never break the window. This is the essence of quantum mechanics. And it debunks the paper, gleefully reported by a hungry press, that mobiles might somehow

modules were increased by 3, 6, 9, 12 and 14 per cent, depending on how badly students performed

cause eye cancer. If your ear feels warm after a conversation on a mobile phone, it is because you are holding a machine with a battery pack against your head.

Similarly, there has been mass hysteria, particularly among the educated middle class, over MMR (measles, mumps, rubella) injections being related to autism. Despite the fact that studies in the US and the UK have shown there to be no association between the two, the myth has spread to the extent that there is a real risk of measles, mumps and rubella spreading again. The reality is far more likely to be that autism appears at the same time in life that a child gets the MMR jab. Even if the scaremongers are *right*, statistics would also tell you that the risk of death or serious, life-damaging illness from the side effects of measles are greater than the risk of autism through the MMR jab.

Indeed, one of the reasons our life expectancy has so increased – again thanks to our forebears, who practised real science – is because of mass immunisation. According to Immunisation Action Coalition, measles accounts for 30,000 to 35,000 deaths a year in Afghanistan. So why is it that we are so keen to challenge proper science, yet imbibe this new science until we're fit to choke? Maybe it's down to mass education itself.

The British Government is determined to put 50 per cent of children in England and Wales through further education. In 1970–71, the UK had 414,000 graduates. By 2000–01, the number had more than doubled to 1.113 million, a figure that soars to 2.1 million when you include postgraduates and part-time students. Never have so many people been so educated, yet we seem to be willing ourselves to believe in hypotheses that have little basis in fact. At the same time, perfectly respectable polytechnics and colleges are now universities, the definition of which, in the UK, is that they undertake research.

When the universities are offering degrees in everything from

Even though he didn't light up at work, a sales executive was sacked from his job at the Boxes and Packaging manufacturing company in Swindon for smoking at home

golf to PlayStation, it's hardly surprising that their postgraduate departments should come up with research along the lines of a 'formula for tying your laces' and 'women spend on average 117 hours a year ironing compared with 68 hours for men'.

When entrance to university is based on exams that everyone can pass, and when students are introduced to a world of semi-literate jargon in pursuit of nonsense degrees, it is unsurprising, too, that such piffle should pass for knowledge.

History should tell us that with a relatively small number of people in further education, advances in science have led us to pave the way for mapping our genetic make-up and the nature of the world in which we live. The scientific endeavour that contributed so much to the development of the human race was based on making the complicated simple; the science of the meddling classes is to make the simple complicated.

It's great fun to snigger at Buckingham Chilterns University College's BA (Hons) in sports management and golf studies – with the added opportunity of gaining an NVQ in greenkeeping – or Plymouth University's degree in surfing, or even a four-year degree in folk music offered up by Newcastle upon Tyne University, but in all these universities there need to be research departments, and all these research departments have to come up with studies. The more studies published, the more recognition, and therefore funding, for the university. It is a vicious circle that is easily exploited.

We can make up a theory here and now that if we were to send out a press release under the auspices of any university, it would easily make the pages of the national press. In fact, let's do one. We'll say that fizzy drinks could cause stomach cancer. Nice scare story, isn't it? We can ask stomach cancer victims about the number of fizzy drinks they've consumed. They will probably be relatively old, have probably drunk a lot of fizzy drinks and will probably be

A patient will be refused treatment from a nurse or care worker at home if they smoke under a directive from the Ashfield and Mansfield Primary Care Trust in Nottinghamshire

rather grateful for something to which they might attribute their disease. Then we'll get a control group, hopefully of the same age, feeling perfectly healthy, who will naturally play down the fact that they've guzzled a couple of thousand lemonades over the past ten years. The headline is ready-made there at the top of our press release: 'Fizzy drinks could cause stomach cancer'. No need for definitive figures to back up our findings; all we're saying is 'could'. Add in the words 'up to' and we can make even greater claims: for example, 'Adults who drank at least one fizzy drink a day were up to five times as likely to suffer stomach cancer as those who didn't.' This statement, of course, is meaningless unless you know how many of them are likely to contract stomach cancer in the first place, and about the other possible cancer-causing victuals they might be taking on board throughout their lives. Then, of course, we are adding in the 'up to', which means, well, 'we don't know' – 1.13278 times as likely would still fit the criterion but would be statistically as insignificant. But by now we have proudly presented the press reports of our findings to our professors and will soon be on to the next project: setting out to prove that five year olds who play tiddlywinks are up to three times as likely to go on to further education as those who don't.

This sort of science is a product of our age, stimulated by the work of the great Germans, who introduced sociology and psychology into institutions whose funding depends on seeking out new lines of enquiry. It's interesting, too, that our academia produce so many papers – on passive smoking, road accidents, global warming – that chime in with the thinking of the meddling classes.

In May 2004, for example, it was reported that a waiter, barman or nightclub worker dies every week in Britain because of the effects of breathing in second-hand smoke. The basis of this astonishing claim was a study by Professor Konrad Jamrozik

In 2003, a judge stripped a schoolboy of over £4,000 compensation which he was awarded when he sued Isle of Wight Council after he fell off a swing during his primary school's sports day. Mr Justice Gross warned that if he had allowed the

of Imperial College London. His report said that passive smoking was responsible for an 'estimated' (note), but very specific, 49 deaths a year in the hospitality industry. A further 700 people were killed by environmental smoke in the workplace, while another 4,000 deaths could be attributed to passive smoking in the home.

There is an extraordinary precision to these figures, yet how could this possibly be? First, there is no disease called passive smoking, so these 49 unfortunates presumably died of various smoking-related diseases, such as lung cancer, emphysema, etc. On what basis were these diseases selected and isolated from the non-smoking-related diseases hospitality workers might also have died of?

Second, for these statistics to carry any weight those 49 people must have been non-smokers, or their deaths would presumably be attributable to their own habit rather than the passive inhalation of other people's smoke. How was it established that these workers didn't themselves smoke, or hadn't until recently smoked?

Third, the hospitality industry is a wide and varied one. A barman working in a smoky local will breathe in far more smoke than a waiter in a Conran restaurant, where a few punters might spark up after a long meal, or maybe have enjoyed a post-prandial cigar with the great man himself. How were these differences taken into account in the assertion that these deaths take place across the hospitality industry?

Fourth and similarly, the length of time people work in the industry must surely make a difference to their intake of passive smoke. How were the figures adjusted for the fact that many hospitality workers only stay in the industry for a short time, while they're studying, for example? Were these groups split from veterans who had worked for decades in clubs and bars and,

payout to stand, it would jeopardise similar events. 'The probability is that sports days and other pleasurable sporting events will simply not take place,' he told the High Court in London. 'Such events could easily become uninsurable'

therefore, have breathed in far more smoke (although miraculously survived)?

And so, fifth, was age factored into the equation? For the figure to be significant, those 49 deaths obviously had to be premature. How was that established? Was there a cut-off age? And, finally, how were these hospitality workers isolated, and where did the control group work? There must, presumably, have been a group of people who don't work in hospitality with which to compare them. And they, too, must have been non-smokers. How was this established?

When the study is widened to assert that 700 people are killed by environmental smoke in the workplace, how do we know that their fellow workers – presumably all not working in the hospitality industry, this being a separate category – who survived weren't in the control group with whom non-smoking workers in the hospitality industry were compared? Or the 4,000 people whom the report claims died from passive smoking at home? Were they asked about the amount of smoke in their environment before they died? Given that until the 1980s people were free to smoke just about everywhere in Britain, and just about everyone passive smoked to a degree, how were these people isolated so it could be established that they were victims of passive smoke in their homes, rather than their workplace?

In 2002, Greece was top of the league of smoking nations, with an average of 8.6 cigarettes smoked per person per day. Third in line was Japan, with a figure of 6.8. Yet if you're Japanese, your life expectancy, at 81.6 years, is beaten only by those lucky people of the duty-free haven of Andorra. Similarly, life expectancies in Greece (equal with Germany on 78.3 years) and Spain (79.3, in joint sixth place with Canada), another country with a large percentage of smokers, are very high – people there live longer

If a study published in the *British Medical Journal* is to be believed, passive smokers have an increased risk of coronary heart disease of 'up to' 50 and 60 per cent on average than those in the UK, say, or low-smoking countries such as Singapore and Australia. What must be a very high rate of passive smoking can't be killing the populations of these countries. A recent feature on people who worked under Churchill in his bunker – surely about the densest passive-smoking environment imaginable – revealed a group of sprightly octogenarians and nonagenarians of both sexes.

And we know, too, that Professor Jamrozik is an ardent anti-smoker. 'It is extremely hard to fathom why a nation that has led the way in documenting the harm done by smoking has been so slow to act on the evidence and adopt a comprehensive programme of tobacco control,' he said in a release earlier in 2004. It was entitled, 'The British Government is not doing enough to stop people smoking, claim doctors from the UK, leading to the death of one Briton every five minutes from tobacco-related diseases'.

And this is how much of contemporary science and its funding works. In 2001, an Imperial College release announcing the appointment of Professor Jamrozik (an 'outspoken' authority on public health from Australia) bragged that 'to date he has succeeded in attracting more than AUS \$6 million (GBP 2.3 million) in competitive grants and has published over [should be more than] 100 papers in scientific literature'. This keen oarsman and cyclist says himself, 'It is increasingly apparent that we have to go beyond the individual patient, beyond the individual doctor and beyond the individual practice and primary-care team to think about delivery of the best possible health care to whole communities.'

'Delivery' of the best possible health care to whole communities is typical of the parlance of the nanny state. What the professor seems to be saying is that your doctor having a quiet word about your chest is not good enough. We need to be nannied by non-elected experts.

Being exposed to cigarette smoke at work more than doubles the risk of asthma, according to reports from the European Congress on Lung Disease and Respiratory Medicine

Professor Jamrozik is obviously at the top of his tree and highly respected by his peers, and he carries out worthwhile and important research, but when these papers are reported, we are given no idea of how these dramatic statistics are arrived at.

As a layman reading Professor Jamrozik's paper, I found it impossible in his methodology to find the answers to the questions listed earlier, so I wrote to him and countless organisations publishing similar papers asking how their results were calculated. No one has given me the answers. Professor John Britton, chair of the Tobacco Advisory Group of the Royal College of Physicians – which presented Professor Jamrozik's figures at a conference called Environmental Tobacco Smoke and the Hospitality Industry – simply referred me to the Department of Health website. 'Our own government, the US Surgeon General and many other well-informed and independent organisations around the world agree that passive smoking is harmful,' he wrote. 'Therefore I don't think there is any reason to argue about that.'

Well, of course not, we're only vilifying a quarter of the population. Yet if we don't know where these figures come from, it is arguable that some of this research amounts to little more than poking your head round a pub door and saying, 'Ugh, isn't it foul? It must be killing people.'

And while we might be giving up the fags, by God we're putting on weight. We don't, of course, need any science to tell us that an ever-increasing proportion of the population, particularly in the UK and the USA, is, to use an old-fashioned word, fat. But here multifarious politically correct organisations are flexing their publicly-funded muscles, clamouring to tell us how many people are overweight and why, where they are from, whether they are male or female, what the cost of treating fat-related diseases is to the health services and how many fat people there will be in the future, plus the fact that there is a preponderance for working-

Coffee drinkers who have more than three cups a day are 'up to' 64 per cent 'more likely' to suffer a cardiac arrest said a study published in the *Journal of the American Medical Association*

class people to become obese. (Never mind the fact that a lack of competitive sport and an extraordinary lack of discipline among our youth has been largely fostered by the nanny state.)

The nation's weight problem is costing the Government £7 billion a year and the NHS £3.5 billion. On statistical trends, nanny says, half of all British young people will be overweight by 2020. (Simon Jenkins pointed out in *The Times* that, on similar 'trends', half will also be media studies graduates, cocaine addicts and in prison.)

The underlying fact is modern government, and the agencies of the politically correct, are using this evidence firstly as a basis for exerting ever-stricter controls on those who elected them, and secondly to create a society based on *their* values. There is plenty of scientific research proving that obesity is a health hazard among the beer-swilling, junk-food-eating working classes, but it doesn't seem to be a problem if it's brought on by guzzling down litres of cabernet shiraz and overdoing it on the polenta. Indeed, olive oil, that favourite of the meddling classes just oozes with goodness, while proletarian vegetable oil will lead to a premature death.

Science is being used to justify the meddling classes' ever more profound intrusion into our personal lives, while simultaneously it is being exposed to less questioning than at any time in our history.

So when law-abiding citizens get twitchy at the fact that 1.4 million motorists in 2002, who one presumes in most cases had committed no other crime that year, were convicted of motoring offences, the Government acts by commissioning independent research from University College London that claims that cameras were reducing casualty rates in road accidents by 40 per cent and saving 100 lives a year. 'These figures prove that cameras save lives,' said Alistair Darling, Transport Secretary at the time.

Oh do they?

The University of Bristol found that female fertility is reduced by passive smoking, with the odds of a woman taking more than 12 months to conceive increasing by an extraordinarily precise 14 per cent

Note here the use of again – as for passive smoking – notional deaths. The research is based on the fact that, for example, I could have died on the Clapham Road on my way home from work were it not for the placing of a (neatly hidden) speed camera. The fact is that the Department of Transport's own statistics have shown that at some camera sites casualty rates have gone up. And anyway, speed is responsible for only 18 per cent of road deaths (a Department of Transport study based on analysis of 36,000 crashes found 'loss of control of vehicle' was the key element at 43 per cent): translated, you have more chance of being murdered than a speeding vehicle being responsible for your death.

Doctor Oliver Johnson in a letter to *The Times* responded to a claim that at eight trial locations where cameras were installed the number of people killed and seriously injured fell by 47 per cent. It is entirely possible, he said, that this was due to figures being skewed by positioning cameras where accidents have occurred before. Consider a corner, he wrote, where a fatal accident occurs every five years. If one of these occurs in 2000, a camera is installed and none happens in 2001, this counts towards a fall. Of course, the chances are that the same effect would be observed without the camera. This, he said, might explain why overall road deaths remain 'high' – so no libertarian speed freak, then – despite the local falls reported.

In fact, Alistair Darling's pompous declaration that 'speed cameras save lives' was proved to be nonsense just a week later when the Government published figures showing that in 2003 the number of road deaths exceeded 3,500 for the first time since 1997. In the decade before speed cameras were introduced, from 1984 to 1993, road deaths fell by 32 per cent. In the decade since, deaths had dropped by only 3.8 per cent. Astonishingly, in one in seven sites casualties increased. Whatever is contributing to road safety, in other words, it doesn't seem to be speed cameras. The science of their efficacy is fundamentally bogus.

Using real figures in the real world, speed cameras might have no effect on reducing road deaths, but that doesn't stop the proliferation of speed-camera partnerships between police, councils and road-safety groups, which are allowed to keep some of the revenue. The more drivers they prosecute, the more money they earn, so more cameras can be erected, and the bigger and more important their organisation can become. On the basis of the flimsiest of statistics, so the self-righteous are inflating their power (and their incomes) and the nanny state becomes ever-more powerful.

Just as in the sixteenth century your career as a bishop wouldn't have got far by claiming the earth revolved around the sun, now you're not going to get a job in a research department with the hypothesis that really passive smoking makes sod-all difference to anyone's health. Similarly, pitching up at a town hall with the view that buses are noisy, smelly, inefficient polluters that travel around virtually empty for much of the day while fuel-efficient private vehicles take people exactly where they want to go is unlikely to precipitate your swift rise in the ranks of the Department of Transport. And try getting someone to employ you on the basis of your theory that global warming is a phenomenon largely perpetuated by those whose careers depend on the public worrying about global warming. If you aspire to being a successful scientist in the nanny state, then your calling will be made far easier if you can prove what nanny wants to hear. Furthermore, if you can be scarily, hysterically predictive, then hopefully there is more chance of your research getting noticed. And, when it comes to global warming, it don't get much scarier.

The Government's chief scientist, Sir David King, warned in 2006 that even the most optimistic projections 'suggested' that

Smokers are 'twice as likely to lose their sight in later life' if an analysis of age-related macular degeneration (AMD) is to be believed

carbon-dioxide levels would reach double their pre-industrial levels, increasing temperatures by three degrees Celsius or more. Without action to mitigate the effects of this global warming, 400 million people would be at risk from starvation because between 200 million and 400 million tons of cereal production would be lost, he told the *Today* programme on Radio 4.

In 2003, the UK had a particularly warm summer. Global warming was to blame. In 2004, it chucked it down throughout August and was for the most part pretty damn cool. Amazingly, global warming was at the root of this inclemency, too. (Although the UK, with its temperate climate, is the last place on earth you'd choose to seek out meteorological trends.) Hurricane Frances, Hurricane Ivan – yep, global warming, although as far as we know, hurricanes have been a feature of the Caribbean for as long as we can remember. British Prime Minister Tony Blair has gone as far as saying global warming is the biggest problem facing the world. You would have thought that any scientist, any person who has been trained in rigorous, logical analysis, might have been taking a long, hard look at the effect changes to the movement and activity of the sun might have on our climate. But no. This extraordinary phenomenon that is undoing the entire balance of the planet seems to be down to a load of factories opening up in China and posh mums insisting on driving their children to school in rather large SUVs.

A little bit of history: the UK has had, in the course of a few millennia (and that is a fraction of a millimetre in a kilometre of evolution) climates that have ranged from the tropical to the Arctic, which might suggest that the population – whom our politicians are proposing to bully out of their cars – have about the same effect on the world's temperature as a hairdryer in a cathedral. We are currently living in an ice age that began 40 million years ago with the growth of an ice sheet in Antarctica but intensified during

Passive smokers appear to have an increased risk of developing diabetes, suggested

the Pleistocene age (starting around 3 million years ago) with the spread of ice sheets in the northern hemisphere. Since then, the world has seen cycles of glaciation, with ice sheets advancing and retreating on 40,000- and 100,000-year timescales. The last glacial period ended about 10,000 years ago.

Patently, none of this had anything to do with our new-found desire to centrally heat our houses or drive ourselves to work rather than ride a bicycle. Not that we shouldn't be aware of what we're doing to the planet. Common sense tells us that it's good to recycle, to cut down on energy where we can, not to send sulphuric smoke up into the atmosphere, to minimise landfill sites. But that is totally something other than claiming that due to the efforts of man, the earth, if we don't mend our ways, will become an uninhabitable cauldron/covered by sea/subject to a new ice age, or whatever doom-laden prediction you might care to believe.

Somehow though, we are now at the stage where the politically correct feel it is their right to protect the earth by installing monstrous – indeed weather-changing, if not climate-changing – wind turbines, by creating massively polluting traffic jams as they try and boss us out of our cars, and by chastising parents for packing their children's lunches in aluminium foil under the auspices of 'good citizenship'.

Scientists tell us that there has been a steady increase in the world's temperatures (despite massive reductions in pollution by factories in the West, or huge increases in insulation in our houses, or massive reductions in vehicle emissions), but even this simple fact is up for question. Readings that produce this perfectly plausible evidence are taken from stations on land, which covers only 30 per cent of the world's surface. Knock out Antarctica, the Sahara, millions of acres of mountain and the beloved rainforest – still wild and, to all intents and purposes, uninhabited – and man only occupies around 15 per cent of the world's surface.

research by American scientists published in the *British Medical Journal* in 2006

Of that 15 per cent, cities account for about 1 per cent. Fly over even the most crowded of nations, such as the UK, and check out the amount of wilderness. Unsurprising, then, that satellites that have circled the globe throughout 25 years of intense industrial activity and increasing use of motor cars have shown the earth's temperature to have barely changed at all.

This is a complicated subject, but what arrogance to presume the influence of man on this vast and volatile planet, rotating at the equator at 1,000 mph, travelling around the sun at 66,600 mph, a molten upper mantle only miles below us, bubbling away at up to 800 degrees Celsius, heated by the sun (which itself can be likened to the continuous explosion of millions of hydrogen bombs) for millions of years from between 91.4 and 94.5 million miles away, yet still we have humid rainforests and the continent of Antarctica with ice sheets 7,000 feet thick. The power of the natural world is awesome.

Even if you do accept these land-recorded readings, does this slight warming of the twentieth century, which, when you get to the bottom of it, seems to be about one degree Celsius, represent a trend?

Nigel Calder, author of *The Manic Sun: Weather Theories Confounded*, points out that the 1730s were nearly as hot as the 1990s, this warming occurring before the Industrial Revolution when the ecology of the world was largely left to its own devices. There followed a period known as the 'Little Ice Age', with 1816 remembered as a year without a summer after a huge eruption in the East Indies darkened the world's skies. The 1920s and '30s saw another spell of continuous warming, followed by a decline, with the climate growing chilly once more in the '50s. The winter of 1962–63 was the worst since 1740.

In truth, Calder writes, the sun is the master of climate. Two hundred years ago, the astronomer William Herschel noticed that the price of wheat was higher when there was a scarcity of dark sunspots on the sun's face. Scientists who have monitored the parallel histories of the sun and the climate know sunspots indicate intense magnetic activity on the sun's surface, and in the depths of the Little Ice Age, around 1700, the sun was in depressed mood.

Calder may or may not be right, but isn't it amazing that this rather non-sexy science is ignored? It's ignored because it doesn't mean rushing off in gas-guzzling aeroplanes to Kyoto to stay in energy-sapping air-conditioned hotels, to write thousands of words on millions of pieces of paper for endless reports that can be disseminated among thousands of functionaries who will declare that millions of pounds of our money should be spent developing an industry that will pour thousands of tons of concrete into the earth's bed to support huge and hideous wind turbines. It's ignored because the hobby horses of the nanny state have permeated the mainstream. So, in a speech to environmentalists, the ever-credulous Tony Blair says that climate change is the gravest threat facing the planet. In other words, he believes the evidence to be incontrovertible. 'By the middle of this century, temperatures could have risen enough to trigger irreversible melting on the Greenland ice cap – eventually increasing sea levels by around seven metres.'

Yeah, right.

Very pompous and very grave. But the key word here is 'could'. The Prime Minister could have worked himself up into more of a lather a few weeks later when it was reported that carbon-dioxide levels in the atmosphere are rising more quickly than at any time since records began. 'Global warming clock begins to tick faster', panted the *Daily Telegraph* in 2004, as the late Dr Charles Keeling, who in 1958 began the longest-running carbon-dioxide measurements at the Mauna Loa Observatory in Hawaii, said the unprecedented rise was 'a cause for concern'.

intelligence when it published a report from a study by the University of Michigan

Well, maybe. But what does it mean? Scientists have determined that before the industrial era, concentration of carbon dioxide in the atmosphere stood at around 280 parts per million (ppm). Average concentrations in 2003, the Mauna Loa records show, were 375.64 ppm. What 'concerned' Dr Keeling was that concentrations of gas rose by 2.08 ppm in 2002 and 2.54 ppm in 2003, the first time successive years have seen an increase of more than 2 ppm. Previous peaks such as the largest rise of 2.87 ppm in 1998 coincided with the weather phenomenon El Niño. And according to the US agency that runs the observatory, the rise for 2004 was likely to be just under 2 ppm. Sir David King is predicting it will go up to 500 ppm, thus promoting the disastrous climate change.

The huffing and puffing this research produced was hardly surprising. But it points to a number of things. One, of course, is that this increase is unlikely to be man-made; scientists can only assume it to be natural phenomena. Another is that El Niños cause a lot more damage to the world than a load of Americans driving about in unsightly four-wheel drives.

Curiously, this rise in 2003 was not predicted by climate models, so Tony Blair's doom-laden assessment, based on current climate models, is presumably debunked. The fact that these figures are worse than predicted shows how dubious are the words 'up to' and 'could'. These grand theories keep pressure groups, scientists and bureaucrats employed but do little else. Dr Spencer Fitz-Gibbon, Green Party spokesman on climate change, said that it is 'too early to draw conclusions' from this report. Really? This is uncharacteristic of those who make political capital of the most dubious of scientific theses. Oh no, false alarm . . . 'There's been an observable pattern in recent years not merely of the increased frequency and severity of extreme weather events and the breaking of long-standing records,' he said, 'but also reports from eminent

Men who smoke at a young age are more likely to have overweight sons, says research from northern Sweden and the UK

scientists saying global warming is worse than we thought.' And that isn't drawing conclusions, Dr Fitz-Gibbon?

But the facts of the matter are of little importance to the politically correct. We are now informed not by rigorous theoretical knowledge constantly tested and updated by the cream of academia, but by a slavish allegiance to the mores of a ruling elite: the people who run the town halls and NGOs, national government and its departments. No one, it seems, is prepared, or has the desire, to work outside these remarkably simplistic hypotheses.

We quite rightly believe this hegemony of thought to be repugnant when we look back at the pseudoscience undertaken to give credence to the racism of Nazi Germany and the pogroms of Stalin's USSR; but in the twenty-first century, we seem to accept it as happily as the majority accepted those horrendous regimes. OK, we're not sending smokers to Siberia (yet), or drivers to Auschwitz, but the academic processes and the kowtowing to the powerful groups sponsoring this scientific research lend themselves to the tyrannies of the past rather than the free thinking that has led to real scientific breakthrough.

The values of the meddling classes have created a hysteria that is feeding the most controlling, interfering instincts of our politicians. Meanwhile, the population of the West lives in a state of high anxiety, fed by reports that tell us of the shocking asthma toll on British children, that aerosols may make women and children sick, and drinking coffee during pregnancy increases risks of miscarriage. Soon we are to see health warnings on bottles of Newcastle Brown Ale, and there is talk of obesity warnings on chocolate. The extreme claims of current scientific thought are empowering the meanest of bureaucrats to the highest of politicians. There is no area of life too small or too private for them to interfere with.

Smoking shortens women's lives by 'up to' seven years, according to the Continuous Mortality Investigation (CMI)

5 Strictly no fox hunting

Nanny takes away our liberty

A sign on the noticeboard of my daughters' school reads, 'Kids Cook Quick'. Its message, in a ghastly vernacular that is presumably designed to ape the parlance of the illiterate lest they won't otherwise understand it, is telling us parents to smother them in suncream and make sure they wear hats.

Similar notices are abundant across the nation: 'Please Go Slow' scrawled in a child's hand under a drawing of a tortoise is stuck up at the side of a speed-bumped road running through housing estates in Kennington, South London; 'Kill Your Speed' signs in red and white uglify many a street in the borough of Wandsworth. And better not go too fast along the empty roads of the New Forest because 'If you kill a pony, its mummy will be lonely'.

We are a nation awash with these simpering pieces of doggerel. They are pumped out on the basis of the scientific research we read about in the last chapter and, this time, the victimisation goes beyond being black, or poor, or a woman, and is directed at all of us. The nanny state has created an atmosphere of near hysteria that can be quelled only by the intervention of our politically correct crusaders. Without these signs, the roads would be dominated by Mr Toads careering off the pavements, mowing down mothers and children, gleefully parp-parping and leaving the injured in their wake. It's only thanks to the intercession of some government department or another – Education, Health, Environment? – and a strategically placed illiterate sign that our schoolchildren are not

Drinking large amounts of coffee creates smaller babies is the claim made in studies

at best red-raw with sunburn and at worst running the risk of skin cancer.

These statistics, drummed up by the infinite flow of research students, are deployed daily to back up a set of truths that support a set of prejudices that are absolute. They run roughly as follows: cars and roads are very bad; buses and trains are very good; planes are probably very bad, but we love flying around the world so we'll put them in their own 'not great but essential to the economy' category; bicycles are good beyond belief; smoking is very bad indeed; other drug taking is good, especially when it involves counsellors, support workers, etc.; charities: good; big business: bad; Third World countries: good, but can be bad through no fault of their own; USA: bad, and often the reason behind Third World countries not being quite as good as we'd like them to be; Palestine: good; Israel: bad; fox hunting in the traditional manner: bad; raising rare-breed sheep and slaughtering them in the traditional manner: good; countryside: good; Countryside Alliance and people who live in the country: bad; McDonald's: bad; polenta: good. And so on . . .

To think otherwise is anathema. As of 2007, I cannot on the grounds of public health, for example, open up a restaurant in Britain with a sign saying 'Smokers Welcome', despite the fact that smoking is legal, the countries with the highest life expectancies have the highest rates of smoking and there has already been a proliferation of non-smoking restaurants and bars with no legislation in place at all. It's called freedom. There was to be some compromise in the smoking legislation whereby one could still smoke in private members' clubs and bars that didn't sell food, but even that little concession to liberty was a step too far for our PC leaders.

In the weeks leading up to the vote on the ban, anti-smoking pressure groups bombarded us with statistics telling us how

carried out by the London School of Hygiene and Tropical Medicine

such a compromise would adversely affect the poor. A piece of research undertaken by the Croydon Primary Care Trust is typical. It found that 88 per cent of pubs in the wealthiest areas served food compared with 46 per cent in poor areas. The inference is obvious: while the well off would quaff red wine and cassoulet in some non-smoking gastropub with their health intact, the poor would be coughing to their early deaths in a bar where the only nutrient would be a bag of pork scratchings – cue instant heart attack there, too.

This research serves up everything the politically correct stand for. First, it follows an agenda: that smoking is very bad for you and should be banned everywhere. Second, it provides a victim in the poor. Third, it concludes that there should be legislation policed by people who know better – in this case the busybodies at the Croydon Primary Care Trust, who feel that the best way to spend the public's money is on this spiteful piece of research.

Because spiteful it is. The truth is that the poor more than the rich enjoy a cigarette with their pint, which is accepted by this report. By banning smoking, it is they who will be adversely affected to a much greater extent. What will happen as a result of the smoking ban – as has happened in various American states and in Ireland – is that the smaller pubs and bars will simply lose their clientele and the poor will lose their local. The prettier ones that survived have become theme bars, sparsely populated relics of a bygone age, frequented by middle-class non-smokers on a break from a day out rambling, pretending that they are enjoying a traditional, wholesome local pub.

Except that the locals – unless it is pretty enough and in a posh enough location to serve the local wealthy – aren't in it. People such as my wife's Irish uncle, a single man in his 50s who, at six o'clock every evening, would take the paper to the local pub and spend an hour or two unwinding with the crossword, a pint of

Guinness and a pipe. Not any more. He could no more have the Guinness without the pipe than you could eat jam without the toast. This law-abiding citizen had one of his principal pleasures snatched away from him on the say-so of an elite who have decided they have the right to treat him as a child.

The politically correct, from whom this legislation emanates, are telling this poor majority – and anyone else who dares to light up – that if you don't quit your nasty habits, you no longer have the right to meet in public.

This mania for regulation at best and banning things at worst is rapidly becoming their trademark. Along with smoking, fox hunting is deemed a crime. You are no longer allowed into central London without paying a tariff to its egocentric mayor. In Scotland, disciplining your child with a smack can have you hauled up in front of the courts. These controls satisfy a lust not only for power but also a desire to control the way we think; indeed, a moral code is being imposed upon us, and its list of interdictions and the extent to which it is forced is rising inexorably.

Up until February 2006, as their forebears had done for centuries before fox hunting with dogs was made illegal, English country folk would pitch up to the local pub on their favourite horses and, in a wonderful spectacle of colour and sound, gallop off in the bracing country air in pursuit of a fox or two. It was a link to the past that employed thousands of people, was a focal point for communities across the countryside and a living element of our traditional culture. Not so great for the fox, perhaps, but brer fox was never going to benefit from this piece of legislation anyway: the moral argument was not that killing foxes was bad; more that it was a moral crime that a load of toffs were enjoying themselves by pursuing these rather handsome animals.

Since the legislation has come into place, the net effect is that yet more law-abiding citizens have had a vital part of their culture

overweight said a study by American doctors in the journal *Circulation*

taken away from them and foxes have died in rather greater numbers, as farmers who used to let hunters gallop across their land in what was quite often a futile pursuit of their foe now keep the number of these predatory animals down with high-powered rifles. If they get a clean hit, the fox might die in less pain. But if the first bullet, say, hits the leg, then you could argue that to kill a fox in the way it would be killed in the wild – generally a weaker animal being quickly torn apart by a pack of other creatures – is far more humane. To think such a thing in the nanny state, though, makes you a cruel, somehow retrograde philistine.

Indeed, when thousands of members of the Countryside Alliance, an organisation formed as a direct result of plans for this legislation, marched on London, they were mocked by the oh-so-superior metropolitan elite. 'At 9 a.m., an hour before the start, the queue at the Piccadilly branch of Starbucks was longer than the one for joining the demo,' wrote Emma Brockes in *The Guardian*:

> Protestors had come to march against 'smug Londoners' meddling in their lives, but first they stopped to fortify themselves against the autumn chill with that symbol of metropolitan pretension – the café latte.
>
> It was clear from the outset that, in central London yesterday, the Liberty and Livelihood march would be a mixture of charm, idiocy and flat contradiction.

Well! Would you credit it? A load of country bumpkins drinking café latte! How dare they? Of course, a café latte in Starbucks is about as much a symbol of urban sophistication as a Bacardi and Coke in T.G.I. Friday's – and probably about the only refreshment available in Piccadilly at nine on a Sunday morning. But, well, all the same, shouldn't they have been drinking a mug of tea poured from a tartan-wrapped Thermos?

Dr Ciaran Simms and Professor Desmond O'Neill wrote in the *British Medical Journal* that four-wheel-drive vehicles should come with a health warning because the shape

And, anyway, in London we're allowed to kill our foxes.

The urban fox population – 15,000 of them within the M25 – generally make a pest of themselves by rummaging through litter bins and compost heaps, chewing through security-alarm wires and aiming to eat as many songbirds as they can catch. Pest-control expert Bruce Lindsay-Smith, armed with a high-powered rifle, can kill 30 animals in a week. In one night, he took out eight foxes that had caused £24,000 of damage to the Hampstead home of a rock star. He shot 23 animals after they'd dug up £30,000 worth of greens on a golf course. One wonders what the legality of urban fox hunting would be, with rifle-carrying hunters with a pack of mongrels burning across the city on off-road bicycles.

Mr Lindsay-Smith carries out his work, week in, week out, quite legally on behalf of those who are prepared to pay him. Crude sentimentality has it that as soon as you mount a horse to do the same thing on a far lesser scale in Gloucestershire, you will have the full force of the law upon you.

There is, of course, a legitimate ethical case against fox hunting – that we humans shouldn't be allowed to pursue a wild animal for *pleasure* – but if you are going to adopt that moral argument, then you have to ban fishing and hunting with raptors or guns. Indeed, game fishing involves using bait to lure the fish to a hook, then a barb ripping through the upper part of its mouth. The whole idea is to play with the animal until it is so exhausted it can fight no more: the greater the fight, the greater the sport. The real fun is spending hours 'playing' a marlin as it leaps from the water, shaking its huge body like a tragic waterborne puppy with an old slipper in its mouth, trying to escape the barb that's ripped through its flesh and attached it to the fisherman's line. It makes hunting with hounds seem positively humane.

Indeed, if we are going to superimpose human values and emotions onto an animal, wouldn't you rather take your chances

of the front of the cars increases the risk of injury to the head and upper body for pedestrians

as a fox than be a bear, chained and muzzled for a miserable lifetime in India, forced to dance for the entertainment of humans, or trapped in a cage barely bigger than your handsome torso in China, so that you can be drained of your bile? Or maybe a female sow, locked into a pen so small you can't turn round and used as a breeding machine before you're turned into bacon? Or a bird trapped in a cage in Malta, your cries attracting fellow members of your species who fly down and are caught, then sold in the caged-bird market? Or one of the nineteen hens per square metre kept on a farm that the red tractor symbol deems an acceptable minimum in the United Kingdom? Or even a domestic dog tethered to a drainpipe outside a supermarket, wondering if it has been abandoned for ever? Surely the years of effort spent by the anti-fox hunters would have been so much better spent trying to eliminate this terrible quotidian cruelty to animals. But the facts don't come into it. Fox hunters, like smokers, have simply fallen foul of the ruling elite by happening to live in an age where it has been decided they don't fit into a politically correct view of the way the world should be.

But by far and away the biggest group to be on the receiving end of nanny's opprobrium is motorists. Obviously they can't be banned in the way minorities such as smokers and fox hunters can, but they are mercilessly picked upon, taxed and bullied on the grounds that, far from contributing to a booming economy and offering mobility, liberty and happiness to millions of people, the motor car is taking the planet to an inevitable end.

But this simply isn't true. Our cities are cleaner now than they have been for hundreds of years. A 1996 Ford Fiesta emitted 20 times less pollution than the first model that was launched 20 years earlier – a 2006 model less still – but anti-car snobbery is all the vogue among the meddling classes, and so drivers must pay, and pay heavily, for not sharing the views of their political masters.

Jogging on your own could be bad for your health say a team of Harvard University psychologists, who compared the benefits of solo jogging with those of exercising in a group. In a series of experiments, they monitored groups of rats given exercise wheels

Ken Livingstone hates drivers so much he introduced a congestion charge to use central London roads even though before he introduced the charge, car use in the centre of the city hadn't increased for 20 years. The reason was simple: the marketplace meant that a finite number of roads and parking places – charged to suit the market – automatically restricted the number of cars coming in and out of town. But that wasn't enough for Ken.

Like Alistair Darling, a socialist with an apparent antipathy to cars, he didn't like cars in the first place, one suspects, because they connote wealth and capitalism and the exploitation of the working class. The fact that nasty old capitalism has meant most poor people can now afford a car and bypass the disastrous, inefficient public-transport system overseen by Ken and Alistair just adds to their resentment of people going where they want to go when they want to go.

Ken wasn't having any of that, and neither was Alistair. At vast expense, Ken has introduced a congestion charge for using roads motorists have already paid for many times, which will raise millions of pounds every year with the justification that it reduces traffic by dissuading us from driving into town. It ignores the fact that one of the main reasons we have such good highways is that in the early days of motoring, road tax from motorists was ring-fenced to pay for them. The fact that a city even as higgledy-piggledy as London has fine paved streets, which benefit cyclists and other road users, is because of the development of the car. The reason we have pavements, where pedestrians can walk in safety, is the motor car. If Ken's political ancestors had taken his attitude, the mayor would be overseeing a city paved with cobbles and mud. It would be impassable by cyclists, and pedestrians, picking their way through the effluvium, would be splattered by filth thrown up by the passing omnibus as they cowered in a doorway to let it pass.

---

separately and in groups and concluded that those running in a group had generated twice as many new brain cells - 'neurogenesis' - as those who jogged alone. Your solo jogging rat had also undergone less neurogenesis than those that had done no exercise

Now, everything possible must be done to restrict the driver.

With the twin justifications of road safety and a greener environment, traffic lights stay almost permanently on red, forcing cars to queue for hundreds of yards for non-existent pedestrians who have the right to cross the road instantly whenever they choose. Speed bumps, which have the side effect of making the lives of anyone living next to them hell, with white-van men crashing over them in the early hours of the morning, and if you believe the statisticians cause far more deaths by delaying ambulances than save lives, bring traffic on major thoroughfares to a crawl. Roads in London have been closed to traffic by the dozen on the basis that drivers might want to use them.

I asked Transport *for* London – TfL – the body that has spent millions of pounds bringing London to a standstill – why it felt it necessary to turn what were once quite civilised thoroughfares into snarling traffic jams and close others altogether. 'Records show that the total number of pedestrian casualties in London has declined from 11,000 in 1991 to some 9,000 in 1999 – the number of pedestrian fatalities has fallen by almost 40 per cent in the same period,' Peter Heather, then assistant director of street management, told me in a letter. 'This is attributed primarily to the introduction of safer crossings for pedestrians of the London road network,' he went on. 'In the short term, such measures may indeed involve a reduction in capacity and consequent increase in vehicle journey times. Bus priority measures will help protect bus operations from the associated delay.'

What 'a reduction in capacity' means is TfL is creating traffic jams across the city in the hope of forcing people onto buses. Not only that, the only travellers who are net contributors to London's transport infrastructure are, through the congestion charge, to be whipped into paying even more money in an attempt to get traffic

Left-handed women 'could be' more at risk of breast cancer researchers at Utrecht University Medical Centre claimed

flow back to what it was before the politically correct introduced all these traffic schemes in the first place.

Let's leave aside the fact that these 'records' on pedestrian injuries have no source. Let's leave aside, too, that the vastly superior brakes and visibility of modern vehicles might have something to do with this reduction. Let's leave aside the fact that, in typically arrogant fashion, there is no evidence at all that this reduction in pedestrian injuries is primarily due to the improvement of crossings – the figures aren't broken down in this way. And anyway, none of these initiatives existed in 1999. 'This is attributed to' translates to 'made up by someone with a political agenda'. Unless the figures are broken down to cover injuries on crossings, Peter Heather's reading of the figures is pure supposition.

He, however, is positively moderate compared to Darren Johnson, Green Party member of the London Assembly and environment adviser to Ken Livingstone. Mr Johnson's responsibilities are: chair of the Environment Committee; member of the Commission on London Governance; member of the Health and Public Services Committee; member of the Transport Committee; member of the 7 July Review (London Resilience) Committee; member of the London Fire and Emergency Protection Authority. His 'key issues and concerns' are traffic reduction, planning and the protection of open space, the promotion of waste reduction and recycling, and equality and the provision of opportunities for ethnic minorities, gay men and lesbians, and the disabled. His vision was to go much further than Ken's and introduce a 'car-free' zone where buses and taxis would be allowed but no private vehicles in large parts of the capital.

'It's going to be a much safer [that word again] environment for everyone in central London – better for tourists and for the people who work there,' he said. 'If you start to reduce road space, then the traffic will reduce accordingly. The whole point

---

Researchers at the University of Bristol said that children who grow taller grow smarter because there is a link between a child's IQ and the level of growth hormone circulating in their blood

of the congestion charge is not actually to raise extra revenue for the Greater London Assembly, it's to deter people from making unnecessary car journeys.' As if anyone gets in the car for the pleasure of sitting in traffic jams created by him and his band of politically correct colleagues.

He said he would introduce a 20 mph speed limit throughout London – although presumably not for buses – and would introduce fees of up to £3,000 a year on company parking spaces. 'If business is concerned about the cost of that, then it can immediately reduce that cost by cutting the number of spaces and introducing washrooms for cyclists instead,' pronounced this zealous little prig.

If the mayor so much as glanced at the areas so far pedestrianised in London, created in the name of protecting the environment and safety – Leicester Square, Covent Garden Piazza and now effectively part of Soho – he might notice that they've been taken over by fast-food vendors, tacky trinket shops and scores of Coca-Cola-swilling teenagers. Londoners give them as wide a berth as possible. Visitors to these car-free havens can be transported by rickshaws pedalled by Australians on working holidays; proper taxis no longer get near them because the surrounding congestion is so bad. Around the periphery are smelly open-topped tourist buses, which, incidentally, are not charged for the privilege of driving into a city whose infrastructure is paid for by the souls who are to be deprived of using it.

These schemes are, for the politically correct, today's equivalent of the boulevards and arcades of a more urbane past. In smaller towns and cities, pedestrianised zones have all the atmosphere of a railway terminus. Millions of pounds have been spent to provide a night-time hangout for yobs and drunks. The city centres of Oxford and Bath have become mutilated by street furniture, decorative paving and bollards, making them *Camberwick Green* cities, in the

Children are suffering from an epidemic of eczema and asthma because they are being washed too often, said a study from Bristol University

process distinguishable only by the integrity of architects such as Christopher Wren and Nicholas Hawksmoor, whose buildings still stand tall so long after their deaths.

This stands to reason. A hardware shop in the centre of a town where residents are banned from driving is going to do poor business. So it will close. As will the independent toyshop, the interesting stamp dealer's, or quite possibly, God forbid, the bicycle store. What these pedestrian zones favour are Starbucks, McDonald's and some odious gift shops.

Indeed, a group of MPs in early 2006 bemoaned the loss of the corner shop and interesting high streets. Members of the All-Party Group for Small Shops warned that newsagents and their ilk had a 'very, very bleak' future unless action was taken. In 2000, there were 30,000 small shops; now, there are only 20,000. This is indeed a massive reduction.

Needless to say, it is nasty supermarkets that have stolen all this business. Well, maybe they are part of the problem, but it also coincides with the most intense period of prohibition in the history of the motor car. This committee of career politicians with their local government histories demanding 'action' are the same people who have been busy banning cars in high streets across the land. These little Darren Johnsons, by trying to un-invent the motor car and turn our cities into mini Beijings awash with bicycles and buses, militated against motorists parking up for a couple of minutes while they popped into the butcher's for a couple of chops, the newsagent's for a paper or the baker's for a large white bloomer. In their place are the barren town centres these politicians are now moaning about.

In a rather brilliant way, we in the West have built up a series of very little roads that join on to bigger roads that join on to even bigger fast roads that will take you from the door of your house to wherever you want to go. The car will take you to the supermarket

Women spend on average 117 hours ironing compared with 68 hours for men, according to a survey from Audience Selection

and to Grandma's for the day. Then it will take you and Grandma, who can't walk as well as she used to, for a run out to the seaside, or to a remote country inn. It will take all your rubbish to the dump (where it can be recycled). When a mother goes into labour, it gets her to the security of a hospital – it isn't customary for women about to give birth to make their way, TENS machine in one hand and overnight bag in the other, to the bus stop and wait for the next 85.

The justification for this attempted prohibition is that the motor car is taking the earth to its death. Traffic is increasing at such a rate that our roads will come to a standstill unless 'something is done'. Cars are throwing carbon dioxide into the atmosphere in such volume that the planet is on the verge of coming to an end. But although the number 85 is aesthetically pleasing and provides a useful service for those who can't, or don't want to drive, it is not a green alternative to the car.

The UK's National Environment Technology Centre (Netcen) has shown that one diesel-engine bus emits as much pollution as 128 modern cars, while Japanese scientists have identified one of the most carcinogenic chemicals known to science (3-nitrobenzanthrone) in the exhaust fumes of diesel-engine buses when their engines are under load – as they are when pulling away from bus stops. Other estimates see an average bus contributing 34 times as much pollution as a car. Meanwhile, according to Dr Jeff Llewellyn of the Government's Buildings Research Establishment, the air in the average UK home is ten times more polluted than city smog. But these statistics are of no apparent concern to politicians since there would be difficulties in introducing a tax on air in homes and polluting buses are in vogue at the moment.

Buses also have to run a regular service, so regardless of whether passengers are on board or not, they trundle up and down their route. Every bus that runs into the centre of town full has to run

Scientists from Leicester University, in a report published in the *British Medical Journal*, claimed that swimming with dolphins relieved depression. They took patients with mild to moderate depression to Honduras and compared those who swam with

back out again empty to collect the next passengers. It needs to run at night, it needs to run early in the morning however many people want to use it. The car, pumping out 34 times less pollution, is used only for the exact journey the individual wants to take.

These are the facts Dan and Ken don't want you to consider, because then there would be no justification in taking millions of pounds in congestion-charge payments. There would be no justification in creating little empires headed by little bureaucrats whose sole justification is to earn the maximum profits possible from the nation's motorists. There would indeed be no justification for setting up thousands of cameras to track cars as they move across London.

Nationwide, thanks to the proliferation of speed cameras across the road system, income from speeding fines rose by 500 per cent in England and Wales, from £19 million in 2002 to a far more substantial £114 million in 2004. Let us humanise these fines and, for once, think of the otherwise law-abiding citizen who comes home to find in an envelope on his doormat details of a crime he probably didn't even know he committed, a photograph of his car number plate shining out at him; he's three points closer to losing his licence and all the freedoms a car gives him, £100 worse off and with no mitigating circumstances – such as he was the only car on the road in beautiful weather and was going 5 mph over the speed limit.

So, when he was Secretary of State for Transport, Alistair was looking on enviously, his civil servants hungrily drawing up their own plans to charge motorists by the mile to use the country's highways. Fed by the dubious science that says cars are ruining the environment and their use must be curtailed, transport ministers are licking their lips at the prospect of whipping the car driver into their own vision of how the world should look.

And we should be very afraid.

dolphins and those who swam alone. The former showed 'significantly' greater improvement

A system called Galileo gives them the possibility of tracking every vehicle in Europe. And how enticing is that for our self-righteous political masters? The European Union is planning to use Galileo to enforce road tolling across the Continent. You won't be able to drive anywhere without a bureaucrat knowing where you are going and at what speed you are travelling. Manufacturers could be forced by law to fit Galileo devices to all cars, and you wouldn't be able to start your vehicle without one.

Police are already putting the finishing touches to a central database in North London that will link 3,000 closed-circuit cameras across the country with automatic number-plate recognition of the type used by the mayor to snoop on us as we travel across the capital of England. The system will be backed by 'intercept units' stationed in every police force, which would halt vehicles police urgently want stopped. Police think that about one in a hundred cars spotted by the cameras each day could come into this category. So one in a hundred of us is of interest to the state enough to warrant our being stopped.

Why should it be that as soon as we get into a vehicle our civil liberties can be taken away like this? Let's take away the metal box and wheels around us and imagine the Government enjoying similar powers. One day you hurry across the road before the pedestrian light is on green – oops, ten days later there's the photo of you crossing the road and a demand for the fine. Jaywalking is an extremely serious offence, you know, causing any number of premature deaths. That collision with the youths hanging around Tesco? The camera shows you weren't looking: three points on your right-to-roam licence. One more misdemeanour and you'll be under three months' house arrest. In Japan, this has become a step nearer to reality. A new law has been passed dictating that from 2007 you won't be able to buy a new mobile phone there without a satellite-navigation system. In other words, its government is

Stepping on cobblestones is good for you and could help you live longer was the conclusion of a study in China by the Oregon Research Institute, which watched the

legislating for the right to know where all its citizens are at any one time.

Even now, the average Briton is filmed 300 times a day. The Government is proposing a new way of assessing our council tax that will enable local authority officials to come into our homes, poke around and look at the view to decide if it is scenic enough to make the house more valuable than we say it is. Refusing to let in one of these spies will mean a proposed fine of £500.

Why should we accept this from our politicians? Why should they travel around the world on expenses in fossil-fuel-guzzling aeroplanes, snarfing gratis champagne while we are castigated for driving to the shop? Why should we be considered guilty until proven innocent by a bureaucrat with a digital camera? While socialism has been largely discredited, these busybodies are claiming powers that were previously familiar to us only in tales from totalitarian states such as the USSR and Cuba.

While burning fossil fuels is bad for society if the proles are doing it, important people such as green-loving politicians are driven round in expensive vehicles. In 2012 in London, there is to be a special lane for Olympic officials to be whizzed from their hotels in the glamorous west side of the city to the not-so-glamorous east, being 'regenerated' by the building of the stadium. The green argument only applies, therefore, to little people. Our politicians, naturally, will be able to glide by the London motorists who are contributing to the economy that is making all this happen. Stuck in an even bigger traffic jam as road space has been reduced to make room for this Olympic lane, they can mull over the fact that it is they who are paying an indefinite surcharge on their council tax for the Games to be held in the first place. And who will receive a proposed £5,000 – yes, £5,000 – fine should they have the temerity to use the lane. And after the Games are over, what will happen to this stretch of Soviet bossiness? Will it

local population walking, standing and sometimes dancing on the stones in the belief it was beneficial to their health

be dismantled, or will it just remain for politicians and the police, who already scream around London looking for hate crimes while we sit and fume in our cars? Well, what do you think?

By then, they will have more grounds for arresting us. The day after the anti-smoking bill was passed in 2006, Parliament decided that the nation would be forced to carry ID cards on the grounds that terrorism is such a threat that the freedom to go where we choose without having to prove our identities to any busybody the state cares to employ should be taken away from us.

We have now got to the stage where the Government is to force us to submit our fingerprints and iris patterns for a state-run archive – perhaps it can run next to the one logging details of 22 million homes? The information will be included on a national identity register, the NIR. But who has the right to call up the information? Given the Government's disastrous record with computers – the £6.2 billion computer project central to the National Health Service reforms had made only 20,000 appointments by 2005 when it was supposed to have made 250,000 six months earlier and was meant to be capable of making 9.5 million first hospital appointments every year – how do we know that our identities won't be called up in the erroneous belief that we are someone else? What if a criminal steals our identity? And why is it that we should suddenly be accountable to those who for so many centuries have been accountable to us?

It is an extraordinary irony that one of the first people who will have a police record for life for a 'thought crime' is Mark Wallace, who campaigned against ID cards outside the Labour Party Conference in 2005. He was detained under the Terrorism Act 2000, which gives police powers to apprehend anyone in a designated area, whether or not they are acting suspiciously. This designated area while the conference was taking place, by the way, was the whole of Brighton. For having the temerity to exercise

Microbiologists from the New York Medical Centre of Queens concluded that doctors' ties are a breeding ground for potentially lethal infections, finding that while 48 per

his right to free speech, Mr Wallace will now be on police records indefinitely, and a video of him collecting signatures for a petition against ID cards will be kept for seven years.

'It was bad enough that I was subjected to this unjustly, but why am I now registered for life as linked to anti-terrorist investigations, despite my innocence?' he said to the *Daily Telegraph*. 'It worries me that this could damage future travel plans or even attract suspicion in future cases, when all I have done is use my freedom of speech.'

While the children in our schools are being treated as adults, with sex education lessons for seven year olds, citizenship classes and visits to mosques to teach them the sort of morality that was previously reserved for honours degrees in religion, their parents are being treated as children.

Indeed, while the police will apprehend the likes of Mr Wallace simply for asking his fellow citizens to sign a petition, they are absolutely terrified of arresting the feral teenagers who roam free around our town centres. This is the domain of the politicians and the armies of social workers and experts who feel their pain. Along with pounds, shillings and pence, and saluting AA men, the idea of a clip round the ear to keep your charges in any sort of line has gone out of the window. In 2002, a French tourist fell foul of nanny for doing exactly that when he was arrested for smacking his child on the bottom in an Indian restaurant in Edinburgh. Most of us would probably be relieved to see a parent discipline an unruly child. 'He had annoyed everybody,' said the father, who wasn't named. 'I was trying to reason with him, but he wouldn't listen, so I slapped him on the bottom once and he allowed himself to fall over.'

Witnesses didn't see it this way. One couple said that the boy was left 'whimpering like an animal' on the ground. But who should we believe? The witnesses, after all, had been drinking

cent of physicians were found to have contaminated ties, just 6 per cent of security staff carried traces of bacteria

before and after a rugby international. The father spent two nights in a police cell following the allegations by witnesses whom he claimed were drunk. Although Edinburgh Sheriff Isobel Poole said she was satisfied the boy was not injured as a result, she found the father guilty of punching and kicking him.

Maybe this was more than a *claque* delivered sharply to the bottom. We don't know. But how many times have we marvelled at how well behaved French children are compared to the spoilt individuals who run around British restaurants.

The Scottish Executive was at the time considering proposals to ban smacking children under three years old, but the move was opposed by the Scottish Parent Teacher Council. Judith Gillespie, the group's development manager, said that the trial of the Frenchman could set a dangerous precedent. 'What's significant is that police, once involved, have no option but to charge the person with smacking,' she said. 'And the same situation would apply with all parents and, therefore, it would open the way to people mischievously charging each other with having smacked children, which I think is quite a risky road to go down.' Well, too right it is, if we don't want to go all the way to becoming a new USSR.

But the notion of arresting people because they might harm themselves or others – the equivalent of putting reins on a toddler – has arrived in the form of the smoke police, who are ready to bang people to rights even though they have committed no crime.

Drinkers in Edinburgh can be comforted by the knowledge that the city council is spending their money on 'undercover agents' who will disguise themselves as drinkers and snoop on bar owners or customers who flout the ban. They will be inside the premises to stop smokers and outside to fine them for putting out cigarettes on the pavement. Just to be particularly spiteful, some local authorities aren't authorising the placing of litter bins

Climate change will make seas 'surge up to 16 feet', says a document entitled 'Avoiding Dangerous Climate Change' based on a conference hosted by the UK

for cigarette ends outside pubs. Every household in the city will receive a leaflet telling them how to inform on 'rogue' pubs.

Our authorities are for the first time in British history acting with the moral imperative of Stalin and Castro, in which the citizen is being encouraged to sneak on his neighbour to try and get him shopped. Posters screaming, 'Racism is a crime. Report it!' are put up in public places, while claimants are asked to pry on neighbours who are cheating the unfair, complicated and virtually unworkable social-security benefits system. Water companies in the Southeast are asking residents to snoop on their neighbours and report back if they spot them giving the rhododendrons a quick spray.

In her book *A Short History of Tractors in Ukrainian*, author Marina Lewycka paints a picture of the horror of the paranoia that infects a society in a totalitarian state, perpetuated by the secret police but, more significantly, by the fact that every friend and neighbour is a potential enemy.

> It soured the relations between friends and colleagues, between teachers and students, between parents and children, husbands and wives. Enemies were everywhere. If you didn't like the way someone sold you a piglet or looked at your girlfriend, or asked for money you owed, or had given you a low mark in your exam, a quick word with the NKVD [Russia's secret police, the People's Commissariat Internal Affairs], a stint in Siberia would leave the coast clear for you. However brilliant, gifted, or patriotic you might be, you were still a threat to somebody. If you were too clever, you were sure to be a potential defector or saboteur; if you were too stupid, you were bound to say the wrong thing sooner or later. No one could escape the paranoia, from the lowliest to the greatest; indeed the most powerful man in the land, Stalin himself, was

Meteorological Office, 'if' temperatures rise by about 1 to 3 degrees Celsius

the most paranoid of all. The paranoia leached out from under
the locked doors of the Kremlin, paralysing all human life.

Now, in the West, in the land of the free, snooping by the state
is already at an advanced stage and is starting to be encouraged
among its citizens. Don't like somebody? Ring this number and
tell the authorities they're a racist. Let them try and prove they're
not. Your boss holding you back at work? Wait till he's having
a cigarette in the back room of a pub and ring the police. You
think that woman over the road fancies your husband? Ring the
authorities and tell them she's smacking her child. These 'crimes'
are so nebulous, they are desperately hard for anyone to defend
themselves against: what, exactly, constitutes being racist?

What an easy collar it is for the police to pick on a tourist giving
his son a smack on the bottom, or a man collecting signatures for a
petition outside a political conference, compared with, say, fighting
their way through the army of social workers and solicitors, and
arresting the relatives of Victoria Climbié, killed tragically after
months of systematic abuse in the home of her aunt and uncle,
where she was ritually tortured.

Meanwhile, in 2006, a judge criticised the Crown Prosecution
Service for pursuing a case against a boy of ten who allegedly
shouted racist insults at another boy in the school playground.
The boy was brought before Judge Jonathan Feinstein at Salford
Youth Court for allegedly calling an 11 year old a 'Paki' and 'bin
Laden'. The judge said that the decision to prosecute appeared
to be 'political correctness gone mad'. In the old days, he said,
the headmaster would have given them 'a good clouting' and
sent them on their way. 'I am not condoning what he supposedly
said, but there must be other ways of dealing with this apart from
criminal prosecution.'

We have entered an age where we are policing those who are

Sea levels would rise to at least 20 feet, drowning the centre of London and displacing
millions in Britain by 2100 according to two international teams reporting in the
journal *Science*

willing to be policed, and where serious crime is being ignored. Our citizens are being prosecuted in ever-increasing numbers for matters that even a decade ago wouldn't have been considered an offence. Snoopers' charters are being introduced by the back door, with our legal processes edging towards those we always assumed were the preserve of the totalitarian states of the last century.

And to back it up, we have the propaganda to match.

Maoris filed a lawsuit for damages against the New Zealand government, saying that successive governments had encouraged them to smoke and profited from the taxes raised on the cigarettes and tobacco they have bought

6 Strictly no bad news

Nanny insists on good propaganda

When the England cricket team won back the Ashes trophy from Australia in 2005, we were treated to the spectacle of our boys parading through central London on an open-topped bus in a blaze of glory worthy of our Second World War heroes. It was over the top, perhaps symptomatic of our childish age, when any achievement has to be lavished with praise (the players went off to the Indian subcontinent and got a good thrashing a couple of months later by Pakistan), but crowds turned out in their thousands from their central London offices in a display of genuine goodwill after our cricketers' efforts.

This is the sort of approbation our politicians dream of but, in a democracy, almost never achieve. Stalin and Mao managed to conjure up phoney adoration on the pain of at worst death and at best a visit from the secret police; the Queen enjoys genuine affection from her subjects; but, with the exception of the Party faithful, our elected politicians are generally greeted by, if they are lucky, a couple of moaners with an axe to grind, a cat, an egg-thrower, some old ladies and two teenagers with a penchant for pulling faces. And so it was almost inevitable that Prime Minister Tony Blair would want to shoehorn himself into the act to share a bit of the cricketers' glory and after the procession invite the team to 10 Downing Street for a bit of a drink and a chat.

The Prime Minister has patently put hours of work into spontaneity, carrying that coffee cup down to the press office,

Scientists from the Institute of Atmospheric and Climate Science in Zurich claimed that global warming would be triggered by a brightening of the sun due to a decrease

and developing the Bill Clinton point, where you pick out somebody in the throng and point to them knowingly, a matey acknowledgement that you have real relationships in this unreal world – the England captain, Michael Vaughan, got the Blair point at the Downing Street shindig.

In our more sophisticated age, with its advanced mass media, we are supposedly more suspicious of government now: should a new Chamberlain stand at the steps of an aeroplane and wave a scrap of paper agreeing to peace in our time, we sophisticates simply won't believe it. Yet that's clearly not the view of the meddling classes. Otherwise why should Britain's Prime Minister have forked out £1,375,894 on his Number 10 press office during 2001–2002? Why is it that Labour's army of spin doctors and special advisers – 64 of them – cost the taxpayer more than £5 million in 2001, with salaries of up to £90,000 a year, or that the Government is Britain's biggest advertiser?

If you live in London, you are simply bombarded with information from Mayor Ken Livingstone. In 2003, he had 27 press officers under his control – 14 in the mayor's press department and 13 in Transport *for* London of which Ken is chairman. The combined cost of the two departments was £1.5 million a year. He spent £18 million on advertising, including £4 million on the congestion charge and £6 million on London's transport services.

Ken dominates London as Lenin dominated the Soviet Union. Since he came to power, his face has loomed out of poster sites across the city; every advertisement for London's infrastructure, and even such items as the Oyster cards we are bribed into using for public transport, carries the slogan 'Mayor of London'. Our civic information could be coming straight out of the Soviet Department for Agitation and Propaganda.

We have leaflets, newspapers and poster campaigns across the

in dust, smog and other pollutants, particularly from the old Soviet Union, between 1960 and 1990

capital telling us how wonderful civic life is under his leadership. 'Poll finds praise for "exciting" London,' crowed one headline from *The Londoner*, an occasional newspaper from our leader, a pompous little *Pravda*-esque publication. 'I notice that in some parts of London the bus stops have indicators, like those in railways stations, stating bus times and when the next bus is expected to arrive,' writes a concerned K.J. Webb on the 'Letters to Ken' page. 'Is it possible to speed up the provision of this facility to all parts of London?' This faux criticism then gives Ken a chance to tell Mr/Mrs/Ms/Miss/Comrade Webb that he/she is 'quite right' and assure him/her that there will indeed be more indicators.

It's not all good news, though; some of us aren't obeying the edicts that are coming out of City Hall. We have, for example, the 'Needless Jam: made by drivers who stop on red routes' posters, which look down from billboards onto miles of stationary vehicles created by Transport *for* London's traffic lights. There is not a car parked in sight. Or how about 'Say Cheese! More cars caught on camera. More £100 fines. GLA, Mayor of London' – the hilarious joke on the back of one of Ken's buses?

These advertisements and publications are issued by councils across the land, millions of pounds spent on persuading us that nanny is working tirelessly and flawlessly on our behalf. As if *The Londoner* isn't enough, in the capital we've also been issued with *LondON* (geddit?) magazine. The front cover of the summer 2002 edition led with the splash, 'Ken: Getting London Moving – 200 extra buses this year and every year', while the back cover read, 'Ken: Making London Safer – 1,000 extra police this year and every year'. Well, good on you, Ken. We should soon see the last of murder on London's streets then.

Except, obviously, adding policemen and buses every year is propagandist nonsense. There are a finite number of buses and policemen that are desirable even for Ken. Unless, of course, he's

A website *It's Not Your Fault*, set up with the help of a £62,000 government grant to help children cope with divorce launched by the charity NCH Action for Children, advised its young visitors, 'You might wish Mum and Dad would get back together.

replacing old, worn-out policemen and old, worn-out buses with new policemen and new buses every year, in which case the cover lines are simply a con. Needless to say, too, that London is more congested than it's ever been. And anyone who lives in the capital knows that street crime there is endemic.

The piffle continues inside. Little cover lines such as 'ON the home front: the Mayor's target is for 50 per cent of new homes to be affordable' are typical of this worthless publication. What does affordable mean? For someone with the means of the mayor of London – salary £133,997 – affordable is probably a house in the capital and a weekend getaway in the country. For one of the 400 staff who were working for him, earning less than the £6.70 an hour he deemed a 'living wage' for Londoners, it might, if they were lucky, be a house in Mitcham.

What the politically correct want, but can't politically say, is to offer 'cheap' housing to those people they deem worthy of it. And cheap, too, is relative. There is plenty of quite reasonably priced housing in Dagenham out on the District Line, but nanny is far too snobbish to want anything to do with areas like that. What Ken really means is that there should be cheap housing in expensive areas. And rather than the market deciding what the price should be, that too should be down to the bureaucrats who work for the Mayor, who will also decide on what should be built, where it should be built and who should have the right to buy it. Will it be the impoverished social worker, or the impoverished shelf-stacker at Tesco? You decide. Or rather, they decide.

Under the headline 'Helping Londoners Get a Home' (helpful picture of Ken enjoying a cup of tea with nurse and another non-uniformed person we take to be her friend, so we know what a home looks like), we are told that the housing problem is particularly acute for those working in the public services. Well, of course. Statistics detailing public-sector wages, which in recent

This probably won't happen . . . Try to be polite to the new friend . . . Your parent's new friend could be fun'

years have outstripped the private sector, are obviously nonsense. What it really means is middle-class teachers don't want to live in slummy areas with lorry drivers and builders.

Among its sixteen pages (seven featuring another picture of Ken lest we forget what our leader looks like), *LondON* helpfully explains how 'going out in London can quickly become a problem if you can't get home easily and safely at night. That's why Mayor Ken Livingstone has made safer night-time travel a priority' and how 'the Mayor's campaign to boost theatre attendance following 11 September was a hit with London audiences'. The price of producing and distributing this glossy nonsense to more than three million homes for the 2001 edition, which, to be fair, included the BVPP (Best Value Performance Plan), was £767,000 of our money.

The 2002 magazine sadly didn't include a BVPP, but instead we were offered the *LondON* annual review, with performance targets for police, the fire services, transport, economic development and the mayor of London (of course). It covered such vital topics as 'Meeting London's challenges', 'Working for a safer London' and 'Improving London's transport system': 'Transport *for* London is working to transform London's transport system into one that is appropriate for a great capital city.' Which means what, exactly?

In a sop to democracy, there was a little survey. Surveys and consultations are a key element of the politically correct propaganda machine. They fuel press releases and the justification for, say, extending the London congestion-charge zone west, even though residents and fellow Londoners patently oppose it. These surveys work rather cunningly by specifically not offering what you would think is the basic question: 'Do you want a charging zone in this area of London? Yes/no.' Instead, 'questions' take the form of 'I would like commercial traffic to move more quickly across central London,' against which you can tick boxes ranging

Professor Sherwood Burge, a consultant in respiratory medicine at Heartlands Hospital in Birmingham, told an inquest that the facility was 'not a terribly safe

from 'agree strongly' to 'disagree strongly'. And who would want commercial traffic to move less quickly across London?

So it is with our little section on, say, 'mayoral priorities': 'A Growing City – do you agree or disagree with the Mayor's case that London should plan positively for a growing population, and meet challenges in public infrastructure like transport and affordable housing through increased investment? [my question mark, the *LondON* editors obviously haven't reached this level of literacy]' Again, we tick the boxes from agree strongly to disagree strongly. By disagreeing strongly, of course, you are saying that London shouldn't be planning positively for a growing population, etc., etc. The mayor can then claim 90 per cent of Londoners support his spending pots of our money to carry out whatever schemes he thinks appropriate for the capital.

This snivelling, underhand form of questioning is replicated across the country. The *Times* columnist Mick Hume in 2003 wrote of a survey sent out by his north-east London council canvassing opinion on possible anti-car measures. In it were yes/no questions, such as 'Are you concerned about the implications on health (such as higher rates of childhood asthma and respiratory disorders) of poor air quality resulting from increasing car use?' We should demand that a 'just go away and leave me alone' box be included in this nonsense, he wrote.

In Scotland, the city of Glasgow is setting out its own plans for a transport 'strategy' and has issued a document, published online, entitled 'Moving Glasgow Forward' that includes a questionnaire. (The nonsense illiterate jargon keeps cropping up, I'm afraid. Who's 'moving Glasgow forward'? And where, pray, are they moving it to?) You pretty much get an idea of Glasgow's agenda with the first question: 'There should be more pedestrian priority areas in the city centre even though this may inconvenience and restrict other traffic' – strongly agree, strongly disagree, etc. Not one of these

place to be' because of the risk of infection

questions even mentions roads, though. There is no statement, for example, that says 'There should be priority signals to speed traffic in and out of the city centre – strongly agree, etc.' Or 'Bus lanes should be removed because they do little to speed up bus journey times and create unnecessary congestion – strongly agree, etc.' Expect in five years' time a group of politicians worrying over how the heart has been torn out of the centre of Glasgow.

These surveys, press releases and advertisements are unrelenting and unrelentingly patronising. A press release from TfL, 'On Your Bikes, Get Set, Go!', promoting Bike Week 2004 and BikeFest in Trafalgar Square – including a nice multiracial twist with Bollywood on Bikes – is simplistic beyond belief. 'Cycling makes sense as part of city life,' said TfL's then managing director of surface transport, Peter Hendy. 'The average four-mile journey in central London takes just 22 minutes by bicycle and cyclists can park for free and don't have to pay the congestion charge.'

Well, just how grand is that?

Nasty things, like smoking, of course, get the opposite treatment. 'Smoking "causes half of all deaths"' was the headline in London's freesheet *Metro* in November 2004. This we all know just can't be true given that only 25 per cent of the population smokes. People die from falling off walls, car crashes, old age, heart attacks, and so on and so forth. It would mean every smoker has to die of a smoking-related disease, prematurely, plus another third of the non-smoking population has to come to some smoking-related fatality. In fact, to compensate for the smokers who die in car crashes, terrible sporting accidents and, God forbid, even the odd non-smoking-related disease, there would have to be even higher numbers of non-smokers somehow falling foul of the weed.

The title of the report on which these figures were based, published by the Health Development Agency, is 'The Smoking

In 2003, a report for the Centre for Policy Studies said that the number of health service managers hired since 1997 had soared by 50 per cent. It reported that

Epidemic in England'. Epidemic? Twenty-five per cent of the population and falling? Er, not an epidemic then. Statistics like these end up clouding the real issues. The propaganda gets so ridiculous that smokers will end up ignoring genuine science into the dangers of the habit.

Under the nanny state, all these bodies are compelled to ratchet up their propaganda to gain the biggest headlines, which in turn justify their existence. What use is the Health Development Agency if we're actually not really in bad shape? A competition is taking place between rival NGOs in which spin is as much a part of a pressure group as doing the job it is supposed to do. In Rwanda, post-genocide, there were 50 charities competing for funds to do their work there and in the refugee camps of what was then called Zaire. If Care International, or Médecins Sans Frontières, or any of the other 48 charities are to exist, they have to sell a version of events that is so extreme that without our money millions will die: through lack of resources, lack of medical aid or whatever the charity concerns itself with.

We live in an age where doing good relies on sophisticated marketing departments selling us a version of the world in which we must have faith. So a charity such as actionaid (note lower case 'A' to attract more attention) is prepared to fork out £50,000 for a communications director for its unstinting work to make poverty history. If Greenpeace and Friends of the Earth are to expand and prosper by persuading us of the importance of their work, they need there to be a constant stream of press stories and television events that support the fact that without them we are heading for ecological disaster. Greenpeace, with its largely symbolic blockading of whaling ships, and Friends of the Earth's high-profile vision of a world destroying itself have largely infiltrated the public's consciousness.

Spin is at the forefront of the work of the nanny state. Given

there were 270,000 bureaucrats running an NHS that had 185,000 beds

that we aren't completely childlike, it needs constantly to justify actions that logic otherwise dictates are highly questionable other than to employ greater numbers of meddling classes. When it comes to global warming, there are very few dissenters – indeed, to question the fact that the world is warming up at an alarming rate is the twenty-first century equivalent of heresy. Ask anyone why global warming should be occurring at such an alarming rate and there will be the pat answer of greenhouse gases. Ask what those are and there is the pat answer of carbon dioxide. Ask them the percentage of carbon dioxide in the atmosphere and they won't know. Ask them how this tiny percentage of the atmosphere (0.03 per cent) should create such an effect and that too will be a mystery. The spin has done enough to win the hearts and minds of the population – although, admittedly, not enough to stop them taking skiing holidays, or buying green beans flown in from Egypt and televisions shipped from China, currently building 500 coal-fuelled power stations to keep up with demand for its products. If global warming really is the biggest threat to mankind, as Friends of the Earth and Greenpeace claim, then surely the airline industry, the car industry and the tourist industry should pack up. Now.

Michael Crichton, creator of *ER* and *Jurassic Park* and the author of *State of Fear*, a novel of how green pressure groups try to manufacture ecological disasters to create the headlines that will ensure funding, has introduced the concept of the PLM – politico-legal-media complex. The PLM, he writes, is dedicated to promoting fear in the population under the guise of promoting safety.

'Western nations are fabulously safe. Yet people do not feel they are, because of the PLM,' he writes. 'And the PLM is powerful and stable because it unites so many institutions in society. Politicians need fears to control the population. Lawyers need dangers to

Between 1997 and 2000, the number of qualified NHS doctors and nurses rose by 15 per cent, while the number of patients treated rose by 2 per cent. The number

litigate, and make money. The media need scare stories to capture the audience. Together, these three estates are so compelling that they can go about their business even if the scare is totally groundless.'

Crichton cites the example of breast implants claimed to cause cancer and autoimmune diseases. 'Despite statistical evidence that this was not true,' he writes, 'we saw high-profile news stories, high-profile law suits and high-profile political hearings. The manufacturer Cow Corning was hounded out of the business after paying $3.2 billion. Four years later definitive epidemiological studies showed beyond a doubt that breast implants did not cause disease. But by then the crisis had served its purpose and the PLM had moved on, a ravenous machine seeking new fears. This is how modern society works – by the constant creation of fear.'

The Independent has been at the forefront of this hysteria with its green stories, but it excelled even itself when in January 2006 it published a piece by James Lovelock, author of the hugely influential *Gaia: A New Look at Life on Earth* in which he conceived the theory that the Earth functions as a single organism. 'My Gaia theory sees the Earth behaving as if it were alive, and clearly anything alive can enjoy good health or suffer disease,' he wrote, continuing:

> Gaia has made me a planetary physician and I take my profession seriously, and now I, too, have to bring bad news.
>
> We have given Gaia a fever and soon her condition will worsen to a state like a coma. We are responsible and will suffer the consequences: as the century progresses, the temperature will rise eight degrees centigrade in temperate regions and five degrees in the tropics.
>
> Much of the tropical land mass will become scrub and

desert, and will no longer serve for regulation. This adds to the 40 per cent of the Earth's surface we have depleted to feed ourselves.

Curiously, aerosol pollution of the northern hemisphere reduces global warming by reflecting sunlight back to space. This 'global dimming' is transient and could disappear in a few days like the smoke that it is, leaving us fully exposed to the heat of the global greenhouse. We are in a fool's climate, accidentally kept cool by smoke, and before this century is over billions of us will die and the few breeding pairs of people that survive will be in the Arctic, where the climate remains tolerable.

Blimey!

A month later, the newspaper told us that 'greenhouse gases are already past a threshold that spells disaster':

A crucial global warming 'tipping point' for the Earth highlighted only last week by the British Government has already been passed, with devastating consequences.

The implication is that some of global warming's worst predicted effects, from destruction of ecosystems to increased hunger and water shortages for billions of people, cannot now be avoided, whatever we do. It gives considerable force to the contention by the green guru, Professor James Lovelock, put forward last month in *The Independent*, that climate change is now past the point of no return.

You would have thought the green lobby would have been delighted at this forceful propaganda on their behalf. But not a bit of it. Since this scare story has now been ratcheted up to such a degree that we are all beyond saving, it slowly occurred to them that there really isn't any point in green politics any more. Let's build fleets

The future of the pipe organ in our churches and cathedrals was under threat from EU Directive 2002 95/EC RoHS (Restriction of Hazardous Substances) and EU Directive 2002 96/EC WEEE (Waste Electrical and Waste Equipment) because they use lead in

of new aircraft, make motor racing a compulsory school sport and party while there's still time.

And that, of course, is anathema. So we need to get back to a nice sensible point where all is not lost and, if we behave ourselves, then we might, after all, save Gaia.

'It is late, very late [to save the planet], but not, as Professor James Lovelock suggests in his book *The Revenge of Gaia*, too late,' ran a leader in the *Independent on Sunday*. 'The solutions are known, the technologies available, and we have perhaps a decade to make the radical change of direction to save the planet. If we act together, swiftly, we can yet preserve a habitable world for our children.'

Considering all the tree-felling, paper making and transportation, printing works, heating and lighting of offices, sending reporters around the world in cars and aircraft and using the many distribution lorries and vans that newspaper publishing entails, readers could start, perhaps, by giving up buying the *Independent on Sunday*.

Spin of this type is integral to the working of the Government and the world's NGOs. Greenpeace and Friends of the Earth – and all the jobs that go with them – can only attract funding while we believe that the planet is on its way to certain doom. Yet the doom cannot be so certain that some men with beards tearing around the world on gas-guzzling aeroplanes and setting off into the oceans in RIBs powered by petrol-guzzling outboards can't save us. So prevalent are these stories, and so unchallenged have they become, we are at the stage where we accept these truths virtually without question.

It is only when things go terribly wrong that we get a glimpse into the propagandist machinations of our governments and the cynicism behind these publicity operations. Most famously, Jo Moore, employed in the government's Department of Transport,

the form of traditional tin/lead alloys, which are needed to form the sound-making organ pipes, meaning they cannot be built or repaired

Local Government and the Regions, issued an email on 11 September 2001 – the day Muslim extremists flew planes into the World Trade Center – saying that it would be a good day to bury bad news. The crass insensitivity of the message is bad enough, but it also illustrates how total is the commitment to spin.

Jo Moore, who eventually and inevitably resigned the following year – as did fellow civil servant Martin Sixsmith, who became caught up in the row – worked in Labour's Millbank press office in the years up to the Government's 1997 victory. She spent two years at the lobby organisation Westminster Strategy, part of the PR group Grayling, before going to the Department of Transport, where she worked two days a week for a rumoured £50,000 a year. She was part of the spin machine that characterises the modern political environment.

In an article for the *Daily Mail* in August 2003, Martin Sixsmith described life as a senior civil servant in charge of official departmental communications where he had daily contact with Alastair Campbell and Peter Mandelson – the masters of New Labour's publicity campaign – and Ms Moore. 'What struck me then was the iron hand with which Downing Street ran the Government's contacts with the outside world,' he wrote. 'No Minister, no department could say anything of importance to the media without Alastair Campbell's knowledge and authorisation.'

The reason is that the modern politician has an absolute terror of a free press. Since the UK is a democracy, the meddling classes grudgingly have to accept another point of view. But they don't like it one little bit. Neil Kinnock, when he was vice-president of the European Commission, accused British newspapers of 'continually pumping out bilge which simply doesn't have a basis' in order to discredit the EU. He was commenting on a story in which our European masters were allegedly thinking about removing national motifs from the European Union passports, and

In 2005, £9 million was spent on art in NHS hospitals

this heinous misrepresentation of the facts was just de trop for our Welsh European.

But why this anger? He's not doing so badly. Hired in 1999 at a salary of £139,000 plus expenses to sort out mismanagement, fraud and incompetence in the handling of the EU's £63 billion budget, he wasn't exactly working in an environment where he could be fired any minute, particularly not as a result of a few press reports questioning its actions. In fact, given that it's a bloated, undemocratic bureaucracy that costs us billions of pounds, the European Union has done pretty well out of the press coverage it receives. Looking at it from another perspective, the Conservative Eurosceptic peer Lord Pearson of Rannoch claimed in 2000 that the BBC's *Today* programme was twice as likely to feature pro-Europeans as Eurosceptics. Between 22 May and 21 July that year, *Today* featured 87 pro-European (defined as those in favour of joining the euro or greater EU integration) and 34 Eurosceptic (defined as against euro entry or further EU integration) speakers. His report for Minotaur Media Tracking said, 'Given the controversial nature of the issues being discussed on Europe, Minotaur finds the breakdown of the number of the speakers over the period as a whole hard to explain or understand.'

Could it be, perhaps, that Neil Kinnock was angry that the press should question the fact that each year, according to the EU auditor, Jules Nuis, in 2003, more than 5 per cent – or some £3.5 billion – of the budget managed to go unaccounted for? Could it be that the free press quoted whistleblower Marta Andreasen, the European Commission's former chief accountant, who tried to expose this incompetence before being suspended and then fired? In fact, what is more remarkable is what an easy ride the press has given Mr Kinnock and his fellow commissioners . . . for not knowing what's happened to what Euro MPs estimated could

Farm workers could be prevented from driving tractors for more than three hours a day because of proposed European Union rules restricting the amount of time employees can be exposed to vibrations from machinery

be £3.5 billion. Let's repeat the figure – £3.5 billion. And again. THREE POINT FIVE BILLION POUNDS.

In a democracy, surely we should be tearing up the building and not stopping until we find out who has spent this unaccounted for money and what they've spent it on.

The European Commission, though, can't accept such a thing. Indeed, it spends even more of our money (that at least this time can be accounted for) on *Press Watch*, which claims to be a 'digest of bias and error'. But as Charles Moore pointed out when he was editor of the *Daily Telegraph*, this institution made of paranoia makes no clear distinction between factual error and the holding of opinions that it does not like, and between comment pieces and news articles.

Our friends the Runnymede Trust appear again here, saying that the 'race card' is part of a hand and that Euroscepticism is another card in the same hand. So to criticise the European Commission for, say, oh, losing £3.5 billion of our money is somehow racist. *Press Watch* condemned, for example, a *Daily Mail* headline from February 2000 that said, 'New charter will give Euro court power over UK laws.' This, apparently, was an example of scaremongering. Yet Charles Moore pointed out the EU's charter of fundamental rights was a text referred to by the court in the UK in arriving at its judgments.

In the main, we don't kick up about this. There are some 1,200 accredited journalists in Brussels who pop along to the commission for their daily briefing at noon. Back it comes pretty much unquestioned and reported as fact.

The journalistic part of Michael Crichton's PLM is relying ever increasingly on press-release journalism. Lord Northcliffe's adage, 'News is what somebody somewhere wants to suppress; all the rest is advertising,' is a relic of an age that disappeared with seamed stockings and a glass of mild. In our sophisticated

---

The part privatisation of the London Underground is costing the taxpayer 20 times more than the state-run system, yet, according to a Transport Select Committee

electronic age, with its supposedly media-savvy population, by his definition pretty much all we're served up is advertising. The BBC's local London news often consists of stories each one of which is based on a press release – little advertisements for a new show that's opening, or credulously taking at face value traffic statistics from the mayor and his officials.

In its news on the introduction of speed cameras, for example, in East London's Limehouse Link Tunnel – a dual carriageway with no pedestrians, no shops and no junctions, which has a 30 mph speed limit – we were offered an interview with a policeman telling us how many lives will be saved, a picture of a smashed car, although not necessarily in the Link Tunnel, the relative of someone who had died in it and the news that such cameras could track cars across London to keep them within the speed limit. What we didn't get was the amount of money this draconian measure might earn, nor were we told how many people had died in the tunnel to make this a priority for the police over trying to bring down street crime in East London, including 'Murder Mile' up the road in Clapton, where lives have certainly been lost.

Our politicians have come to expect this from our news organisations. Indeed, when a free press has the temerity to question their actions, to move off the press release, as it were, they seem rather shocked: like your father telling you not to be so stupid when you suggest he's trying to put the jack of the car in the wrong way, so the truth is only to be what they pump out.

'Since 1997 Britain has been ruled by political correctness for the first time,' says Anthony Browne in 'The Retreat of Reason':

In the topsy-turvy politically correct world, truth comes in two forms: the politically correct and incorrect. The politically correct truth is publicly proclaimed correct by politicians and celebrities and it is wrong, while the factually correct truth is publicly

report published in 2005, it had not improved despite the fact that £1 billion was to be pumped into the system that year

condemned as wrong even when it is right. Factually correct truths suffer the disadvantage that they don't have to be shown to be wrong, merely stated that they are politically incorrect.

Mr Browne cites various examples of headline news that have opposing politically correct and factually correct truths. A rise in anti-semitic attacks, for example, is accepted as being down to white skinheads, while the factually correct truth is that it is Muslim youth carrying out these extra attacks. The explosion in HIV is due to teenagers having unsafe sex rather than African immigration. Africa, meanwhile, is getting poorer because the West is not giving enough aid, while it is bad governance that is actually largely to blame. 'PC has a vice-like grip on public debate and policy making, setting out what can and can't be debated, and what the terms of the debate are: anything or anyone who digresses from the PC script is automatically controversial,' he wrote.

The flip side to this propaganda, of course, is the stuff you *can't* say. On a simple level, it can simply be an awareness of spin that prompted an edict in 2000 from the Treasury Chief Secretary, Andrew Smith, to use the term 'taxes and social security contributions as a proportion of GDP' rather than the straightforward 'tax burden'. Tax burden tells it like it is, surely; but given that it pays for the meddling classes, it is unthinkable that it should be a burden. Similarly, the word 'spending' has been replaced by 'investment', while 'partnership' is used in place of privatisation.

We still live in an age of a free press, however. Malleable though it is, it's not *that* malleable. It is still the only place where – in between lobbying and phone calling and the virtual reprinting of press releases that are at times about as believable as *The Chronicles of Narnia* – our politicians get called to account. Ken Livingstone, the nation's most blatant propagandist, has a loathing for Northcliffe Newspapers that borders on the pathological. Unfortunately, they publish the *Evening*

Vice-admiral Adrian Johns, Second Sea Lord and Commander-in-Chief Naval Home Command, said that he was 'heartened' that a significant number of gay and

Standard, a publication that he feels should be the house journal of the Greater London Authority. Alas, Ken's politics emanate from Lenin and the *Standard*'s from John Maynard Keynes. So when Oliver Finegold, an *Evening Standard* reporter, had the temerity to approach the mayor in 2005 after a reception at City Hall, the home of the London government with spectacular views over the Thames and Tower Bridge, London's man of the people was not happy at all:

Oliver Finegold: 'Mr Livingstone, *Evening Standard*. How did it . . .?'

Ken Livingstone: 'Oh, how awful for you.'

OF: 'How did tonight go?'

KL: 'Have you thought of having treatment?'

OF: 'How did tonight go?'

KL: 'Have you thought of having treatment?'

OF: 'Was it a good party? What does it mean for you?'

KL: 'What did you do before? Were you a German war criminal?'

OF: 'No, I'm Jewish. I wasn't a German war criminal.'

KL: 'Ah . . . right.'

OF: 'I'm actually quite offended by that. So, how did tonight go?'

KL: 'Well you might be, but actually you are just like a concentration camp guard. You're just doing it 'cause you're paid to, aren't you?'

OF: 'Great. I've [got] you on record for that. So how did tonight go?'

KL: 'It's nothing to do with you because your paper is a load of scumbags.'

OF: 'How did tonight go?'

KL: 'It's reactionary bigots . . .'

OF: 'I'm a journalist. I'm doing my job.'

KL: '. . . and who supported fascism.'

---

lesbian navy personnel wanted to march in uniform in the main parade at the EuroPride festival in London

OF: 'I'm only asking for a simple comment. I'm only asking for a comment.'

KL: 'Well, work for a paper that isn't . . .'

OF: 'I'm only asking for a comment.'

KL: '. . . that had a record of supporting fascism.'

OF: 'You've accused me . . .'

And so ends this rather unpleasant exchange.

The ostensible point Mr Livingstone is making is that the paper 'had a record of supporting fascism', although it seems strange that he should attack this *Evening Standard* reporter with such ferocity when his principles weren't so mighty as to prevent him working for the paper as its restaurant critic. The crucial point is, though, that while the mayor is prepared to pump hundreds and thousands of pounds into his own propaganda sheets, a journalist asking a question as potent as half a pint of shandy at the end of a party to celebrate, at London taxpayers' expense, 20 years since the MP Chris Smith came out as gay is an insult worthy of a Nazi war criminal.

The mayor was suspended for this act of rudeness by the quango the Standards Board for England, but that didn't put the brakes on his ill-chosen outbursts.

The master spinner was back at it again within weeks, this time against London Jews, when he had a disagreement with property developers the Reuben brothers, who control half of the 'Olympic City' development in Stratford in the East End of London. 'If they're not happy here, they can go back to Iran and try their luck with the ayatollahs,' our champion against racism pronounced. The Reuben brothers are not, of course, Iranian but were born in India to parents of Iraqi-Jewish descent. At the time of this attack, they had never met the mayor.

This time, it has to be said, the official inquiry concluded that

It is illegal to add a new lighting point in your own home unless you are a member of the guild of qualified electricians, in which case you can issue a certificate to

his comment was proportionate and voiced with good reason, that his comments could not reasonably have been considered anti-Semitic, according to the Greater London Authority's monitoring officer, to whom the case was referred by the Standards Board for England.

But we can expect the Greater London Authority to start telling people what they can and cannot say after Ken's run-in with the Reuben brothers. A list of acceptable and banned insults is to be drawn up at City Hall following the investigation after the Standards Committee agreed to ask officials to draw up rules on the use of language by the mayor and 25 London Assembly members. In a move that is beyond parody, even our elected leaders are to be treated as children, it seems. It will be interesting, though, to see the list of acceptable insults.

'Might I say at this point, chair, that the member opposite is a dweeb of the highest order?'

'Er, yes, you may. Continue.'

Shortly after this, Mr Livingstone called the American ambassador to the UK a 'chiselling little crook' for refusing to pay the congestion-charge fees, claiming them to be a tax. He has also said that the Board of Deputies of British Jews is 'dominated by reactionaries and neo-fascists'.

In fact, in a perverse sort of way, this makes for part of the mayor's charm. Despite being a master operator, a master propagandist and a master self-publicist, it all goes towards promoting a man who is still himself. Ken Livingstone, therefore, comes across as honest in a way that most politicians don't. While he spends millions on propaganda, he's enough of a loose cannon to make you feel he is the genuine article.

The mayor proclaimed in another outburst that the Tory councillor Brian Coleman should 'win the Dr Goebbels award for propaganda' – this from the man who publishes *LondON*.

yourself for presentation to the Building Control Body

In fact, Joseph Goebbels was a strategist who wouldn't look too out of place in modern government departments. 'Think of the press as a great keyboard on which the government can play,' he said. Knowing that most press releases will get some sort of coverage, and probably not be dug into too deeply, we are living in an age where we are blasted by information on a scale that hasn't been equalled since the Second World War. We should heed Goebbels' most famous dictum: 'Tell a big lie long enough, loud enough; people will believe it.'

Addenbrooke's Hospital in Cambridge decided to hire an art curator on £37,000 days after it was criticised for cancelled operations and a poor MRSA record

Cable Street, E1.

Alison Lapper statue, with traffic jam alongside it, Trafalgar Square.

Traffic queuing in The Mall into Trafalgar Square. Here traffic lights are on green for only eight seconds, then remain on red for a minute and eight seconds.

BELOW – Buses nose to tail on the Strand.

The £400 million Holyrood Scottish Parliament building.

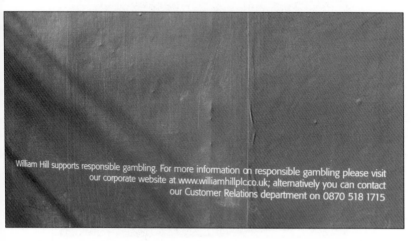

William Hill supports responsible gambling. For more information on responsible gambling please visit our corporate website at www.williamhillplc.co.uk; alternatively you can contact our Customer Relations department on 0870 518 1715

William Hill tells its online punters to 'gamble responsibly'.
(Lloyd Bradley)

Nanny remembers the ickle furry ones with Animals in
War – 'they had no choice'. (Jim Taylor)

EQUAL OPPORTUNITIES

We will not accept and will
challenge any behaviour or
language that does not respect
the differences between people
using the playground

We will respect you regardless
of your abilities, culture, race,
religion, gender or sexuality

Our aim is to make our services
available to everybody. You also
have a role to play in our equal
opportunities policy by respecting
the needs and differences between
other playground users.

Respect sign in Battersea Park, SW11.

Even schools need constant surveillance: camera signs at the
Lambeth Academy.

Cyclists can feel safer thanks to a five-yard cycle lane
on Boileau Road, SW13.

The Goodge Street two-way cycle lane that no cyclist uses because there's a perfectly decent road with a lot more room. (Jim Taylor)

Illiterate 'Please Go Slow' sign in Walworth.

'Watch Your Speed' and CCTV signs in Chestnut Grove, Balham.

TOP – 'Danger, deep drop. Do not sit on wall', Battersea. (Jim Taylor)

CENTRE – 'Be safe. Take care on the stairs', for those commuters who haven't encountered such dangers as a staircase before, Clapham Junction Station. (Jim Taylor)

LEFT – Propaganda from the mayor of London, telling us of the 'good service' on the Tube. This means normal service, which isn't very good.

The mayor warns of a £1,000 fine for not paying your fare; a far larger penalty than you'd receive for stealing another passenger's ticket.

Nanny tells us not to speed up the Embankment, where traffic normally moves at about 3 mph.

7 Strictly no ill people

Nanny oversees a mass failure of infrastructure

Bear with me on this, because this is a chapter of facts and figures, the evidence that tells us what we all suspect to be true: the nanny state is about as capable of running our services as a Pekingese is at climbing trees. It emanates from one day in early 2006 when nanny was in a particularly boastful mood about health and education – the small print was telling us, though, on a day when much of London's transport was, as usual, at a standstill, that both were in serious decline.

On this day – 19 January – the British Secretary of State for Health, Patricia Hewitt, decided to use the *Independent* newspaper for a bit of propagandising. Under the headline 'The NHS is back in business', she recalled the dark days of the National Health Service before Labour came to power, when millions were waiting months – some of them even years – for operations. She wrote of how hospitals were left without repairs and, year after year, the media showed patients on trolleys and staff struggling with queues in A&E. Now, joy of joy, thanks to the political courage of the Government in which she plays so prominent a part, we're moving ever closer to a health service *sans pareil*. 'Waiting lists are at a record low,' boasted Ms Hewitt. She went on:

In 1996/7, 283,300 people were waiting more than six months for an operation. In 2005/6 only eight people [Eight? That's what she said.] were waiting. In 1999 the NHS performed

In 2005, 20.4 per cent of the 6,900 residents of working age in Merthyr Tydfil were claiming incapacity benefits. The local council had a special car park with room for 25 disabled drivers

40,000 heart operations; by 2003/4 it was 61,800. In 1996/7 there were 4.75 million admissions into A&E – this year it is 5.5 million. The NHS is busier than ever before.

'This has not been achieved by happy accident or historical fortune,' she went on to say. 'Our extra investment is a clear expression of political values. We believe in the NHS as a tax-funded, free at the point of use, public service. We reject the idea of the NHS as a safety net for those who cannot afford to go private.'

Etc., etc., etc. This is the kind of news that politicians would love us to see every day: beautiful, shiny puffs put together by ministers and their spin doctors; the sort of thing Stalin excelled at when he showed propaganda films of smiling farmers driving combine harvesters over sun-kissed cornfields contributing to the wealth of the great socialist Russian bear. While the reality, of course, was a purge of the peasantry that killed them in their millions.

Fortunately, we aren't dependent on *Pravda* for our news bulletins. So on the same day Patricia was telling us that 'we can for the first time see what things cost in the NHS, and plan more efficiently', the headline in *The Times* was 'Hospitals shut wards as cash crisis bites'. This is a health service in which two-thirds of hospitals had closed wards and almost half of all hospital trust managers said that building and refurbishment projects were being delayed. A poll taken of 117 chief executives of NHS trusts conducted by the *Health Service Journal* suggested that health-service debts would hit £1.2 billion in 2006.

A week later, the full scale of the 'crisis facing the NHS', if you'll excuse their cliché, was revealed, with ministers admitting that 'up to' 50 trusts had lost control of their finances. Comrade Hewitt had, in fact, anticipated that something of this sort might crop up. Buried two-thirds of the way through her piece – after boasting of

Tube workers, who earn £19,000–£34,000 a year, enjoy a holiday entitlement of 52 days a year

the 681 defibrillators installed in railway stations and airports that had saved '68 lives so far' – she admitted that, 'In the short term, we have to get NHS finances under control.' A little glitch, though hardly surprising given that 'the NHS budget is comparable with the economy of a small country. It is impressive that three-quarters of local NHS organisations are spending within their budgets.'

It isn't impressive at all. This ludicrous spin barely papers over a mass failure of infrastructure. It exists in the health service and it exists in schools and transport; for every spin-doctoring politician, there is a debt-ridden hospital with huge waiting lists for operations, where if you do eventually get a bed in one of the wards that hasn't closed down, then be prepared to be hit by an MRSA (methicillin-resistant *Staphylococcus aureus*) superbug.

A week after Patricia Hewitt's reassurances that she had directed 'turnaround teams' into the '4 per cent' of NHS organisations responsible for half of the overall NHS overspend to help them balance the books, it emerged that 50 trusts had lost control of their finances.

Action was called for. The Secretary of State for Health bravely 'named and shamed' 18 NHS trusts that were in substantial deficit and revealed that they would have outside accountants imposed upon them to find millions of pounds of savings. A further 32 organisations would be given 'advice and support', while another 19 needed 'drive and focus' to meet their financial targets.

In the Never-Never Land of no-blame culture, rooted in the ideology in which radicals have, in the words of Franklin D. Roosevelt, their feet planted firmly in the air, 'drive and focus' is just the recipe to get an unaccountable, sprawling health organisation awash with bed managers and five-a-day coordinators into the black and humming along with a brisk efficiency.

'The NHS should be driven by patients' demands for better services,' wrote Ms Hewitt in a bit of spin worthy of Ken telling

Ghostbusting is to become available as a degree. Coventry University has introduced a two-year course in parapsychology

us there is room for improvement in the installation of indicators for bus arrival times. 'By unleashing patients' demands, we will go all the way to a self-improving health service with no waiting lists and services which are fair to all and personal to each. Local communities must have a strong say over local priorities and strategy.'

Here in action is the gobbledegook with which we started this book. How, pray, are patients' demands unleashed? If I get run over by a maniac in a Mondeo, I don't need a bureaucrat unleashing my demands, I need an ambulance. If I suspect I have a life-threatening cancer, I think my demands have already been unleashed. What would come in handy is more than ten minutes with a consultant in between his undertaking operations and dashing off to see his private patients.

The woman who is telling us that local communities must have a strong say over 'local priorities and strategy' is boasting of a centralised health service with a budget the size of 'the economy of a small country'. The words are simply meaningless, the lingua franca of the bureaucracies in charge of the infrastructure of the country. Strategy, in this case and in most others, is meaningless. And why is the 'local priority' for the health care in, say, Bolton different to that in Falmouth? Are we missing something? Or is the 'strategy' of the health service not to make sick people better?

The politically correct inhabit a fantasy land in which our children are getting brighter as they achieve ever-better results and our transport system, after a few more cars are bullied off the road, will be whizzing the populace across the country in record time. Once the green belt has been covered with the 640,000 new homes Comrade John Prescott decided in his role as Deputy Prime Minister were needed in the Southeast, we shall be in paradise. Well, after we've introduced a few more strategies to drive policies forward. And as long as people desist from getting themselves fat.

Eight dustcarts in the London Borough of Southwark have been emblazoned with work from local artists. 'Pairing waste collection with art is an innovative way of

The reality is that, far from crowing like this, every one of these politicians should be hanging their heads in shame.

The NHS budget has doubled since New Labour came to power in 1997 to, hold your breath, £76.4 *billion*. Patricia Hewitt boasted that the NHS budget is comparable with the economy of a small country; well, it's greater than the gross domestic product of 155 members of the United Nations. But despite this largesse, the health care in Britain ranked 9th out of 12 in a survey by a Brussels-based company designed to show how consumer-friendly health services are, with only Hungary, Italy and Poland doing worse. Criteria included rights and information (which, surprise, surprise, it did well on), waiting times, 'outcomes' and drug availability.

Needless to say, the extra billions pumped into the NHS have been soaked up by increased staff costs and pensions. So, after four years of unprecedented spending, hospital wards have been closing, and staff are being laid off and operations delayed for the maximum permitted time.

In the spring of 2006, the BBC website produced a roll call of gloom. Gloucester Health NHS Community Trust announced the close of a string of community hospitals with the possible loss of up to 500 jobs to help tackle a £38 million deficit. Pennine Acute Trust, which runs four Greater Manchester hospitals, said it might have to get rid of up to 800 jobs to help reduce a £21 million deficit. Being £14.8 million in the red prompted managers at Norfolk and Norwich University Hospital to warn that 450 jobs could be scrapped as a result. West Hertfordshire Hospitals NHS Trust said it might have to shed 500 posts because of its debts of £28.6 million. And so on.

An analysis by the King's Fund think tank in 2005 showed that hospitals and community services took the biggest share of NHS spending and received £5,086 million more than they did in 2004. Of that, only 2.4 per cent was available for new beds

getting it into the public domain,' said Councillor Columba Blango

and operations. Ten times as much – 29 per cent – went on NHS pension rebasing. The second-largest share, 27 per cent, went on pay increases for consultants, GPs and nurses, and on wages for the extra staff that had been hired.

In 2003, the Independent National Audit Commission published a report on the NHS that said the extra millions that have been poured into the NHS have been largely wasted. It revealed that in 2001 health spending rose by 11 per cent, yet health service output increased by 3 per cent.

There have been thousands of jobs created, but these have been the managers, bean-counters and administrators: people eminently qualified to unleash patient demands and introduce local priorities and strategy but not in a position to give you an injection or clean a hospital ward.

Figures from the Office of National Statistics for 2003 showed that the number of support staff in the NHS had reached 269,080 against 266,170 qualified nurses and 100,319 doctors. Since 1995, the number of senior managers had increased by almost 50 per cent, with 25 per cent more junior managers.

The cancer consultant Maurice Slevin published a paper for the Centre for Policy Studies attacking over-management in the NHS. Using government figures, he concluded that while there are eight managers for every ten nurses in the NHS, there are just under two for every ten in a comparable private hospital.

The United Kingdom is the only country in the world that has a nationalised health service – even socialist Sweden and bureaucratic France work in partnership with the private sector. Weirdly, the UK holds on to the idea that a centralised, essentially Marxist organisation – the biggest employer in the world behind the Indian railways and the Chinese army – should be some kind of a sacred cow when patently it doesn't work. It follows a myth that health care was exclusively for a few rich people who could

Motorists were stuck in an 11-mile traffic jam on the hottest July day in history in 2006 because Essex County Council decided to carry out a census during the

afford it before the great dream of health-care reform was realised in 1948.

In fact, argues James Bartholomew, author of *The Welfare State We're In*, our health service was far more impressive than most of us realise. All the great London teaching hospitals were founded before the NHS, and by the start of the twentieth century there was a vast network of hospitals across the UK treating poor and rich alike *and* making breakthroughs that are still saving lives today.

The development of penicillin, he reminds us, was supervised by Sir Howard Florey at the Dunn School in Oxford, where the work was funded by the charitable Rockefeller Foundation. The building in which they worked was funded by charity (from a bequest of Sir William Dunn, a wealthy Scottish philanthropist), as was St Mary's Hospital in London where penicillin had first been noticed 13 years previously by a Scottish farmer's son, Sir Alexander Fleming, who moved to London aged 13.

Bartholomew discusses the work of doctors such as Frederick Nattrass, who qualified in 1914 and became a consultant neurologist at the Royal Victoria Infirmary in Newcastle upon Tyne. His daughter, Anne Whittingham, is quoted: 'He went to work at the hospital in the morning, all for free, because it was a charity,' she says. 'Then, to get an income, he took private patients at our home in the afternoon. This wasn't unusual. All consultants did.'

This system of hospitals based largely on charity, with voluntary hospitals taking 60 per cent of patients needing acute care in 1936, combined with various local-authority hospitals that were a source of great civic pride, was the envy of the world before the firebrand socialist Health Secretary Aneurin Bevan introduced the NHS.

'So what did Clement Attlee and his colleagues in the Labour Party do in 1948?' asks Bartholomew in an article for the *Daily Mail*:

morning and evening rush hour at a roundabout in Laindon

They threw it all away. Eight centuries of development of British medicine was junked for an ideological socialist dream. Bevan pushed aside the passionate objections of the medical profession with all the ruthlessness of a man whose thinking was rooted in Marxism.

Looking back, what's astonishing is how little evidence he produced to discredit the old system. The Labour Party pamphlet that recommended a 'National Service for Health' in 1943 could find little to criticise.

There was mention of only one waiting list, for 'rheumatic diseases', and even this was confined to a footnote. There was no suggestion that waiting lists were a problem in any other speciality. There was not a word against the quality of care, and no claims that people were dying or incapacitated because they couldn't obtain treatment. Far from being condemned the charity hospitals were praised for having 'rendered great service'.

So why change everything? Because, the pamphlet said, a good medical service had to be 'planned as a whole'. The old system was 'unplanned' and a 'medley of public and voluntary institutions'. Never mind how effective it was – it offended the social principle of central control. It had to go.

It is extraordinary now, after the fall of the Eastern bloc and its horrendous inefficiency and failure of infrastructure, that we still hold onto this socialist ideal. By any figures you care to choose, Britain is in the bottom half of the developed world health-service table. The idea that doctors or anyone else would work for free, to do good work among the community, is anathema.

No one is suggesting that the population should be dependent on the vagaries of charities for their health care in the twenty-first century, but our modern, caring NHS is incapable of keeping

A 2006 report by Whitehall's spending watchdog, the National Audit Office, noted £31

within budget and looks after hospitals so filthy that, according to a report by the British Medical Association in February 2006, one in ten patients catches an infection. Hospitals are riddled with superbugs such as MRSA and *Clostridium difficile*, which caused 12 deaths at Stoke Mandeville Hospital, Buckinghamshire, between 2003 and 2006.

Findings from 63 NHS Trusts published in 2006 showed that 34,432 inpatients carried the killer MRSA bacteria in 2004, and deaths linked to MRSA almost doubled from 487 in 1999 to 955 in 2003. Patients are 40 times more likely to catch the superbug in socialist nirvana UK than nasty privately run hospitals on the Continent, although, of course, living in an age of scare stories and silly science, it's difficult to know quite how true these figures are.

But what is for sure is that the UK lies at the top of the hospital-bugs league table. A 2003 report for the Centre for Policy Studies claimed that 5,000 NHS patients die from infections every year. The medical professions now agree that the worst place to be for your health, if you can avoid it, is a hospital.

Quite how this could have happened is a mystery because a year earlier then Health Secretary John Reid unveiled plans to tackle the superbugs spreading across the NHS's filthy hospitals. This was after the Chief Medical Officer, Sir Liam Donaldson, had twice published 'strategies' to take on the problem. In 2002, the Government included an MRSA 'improvement grade' in hospitals' assessment ratings, but this was dropped in favour of a general mark for cleanliness and hygiene. But why should hospitals need grading in this way? Did Sir Liam really find it acceptable that hospital managers didn't know whether a hospital was clean or not without a cleanliness and hygiene mark?

When the nanny state has established why its staff are incapable of doing the most basic job of keeping our hospitals

million of taxpayers' money could be saved if the public sector handled its post better clean, it might try to discover why they are failing to teach our children.

On the same day as Patricia Hewitt was making her announcement that the NHS had never been in better shape on the front page of *The Independent*, the splash inside was how education was in 'growing turmoil'. Education Secretary Ruth Kelly was under fire because of the revelation that sex offenders had been cleared to work in schools, exam league tables revealed the Government's 'flagship academies' were among the worst-performing schools in the country and the Government's proposed school reforms, allowing independently run 'trust' schools to have more control over admissions (how dare they!), would be opposed by many of the Labour Party's backbenchers. Yet as Patricia Hewitt was hailing the UK's marvellous NHS, so ministers were claiming that schools had made 'the biggest single improvement in standards for a decade' after the proportion of students passing five good GCSEs rose by 2.6 percentage points.

The only trouble is exam passes in such subjects as cake decorating and clarinet playing have the same status as GCSEs in English and maths. A distinction in a grade-five music exam taken at school is given virtually the same value in the tables as a grade B in a traditional academic subject such as GCSE history or geography. League tables rank schools on their pupils' best results in any five subjects at grade C and above. This allowed head teachers to conceal bad performances in maths and English by disregarding those results. This meant that Selly Park Technology College for Girls in Birmingham could boast that it topped league tables for 'adding most value' to pupils aged 11 to 16, with 84 per cent of pupils achieving five A* grades (the star being a ridiculous addition, because an A can be easily enough achieved to make it meaningless). Were the school to include maths and English in its pupils' top five GCSEs, the figure would go down to 43 per cent.

The Government spends almost £650 million a year on post and sends out more than 2.5 billion items – about 10 per cent of the British market

Nationally, if maths and English were taken out of this 'biggest single improvement in standards for a decade', the proportion of pupils passing five good GCSEs would be 44.3 per cent. Take out the exam results from independent schools, which focus relentlessly on core subjects, and the percentage falls further to 42 per cent. For boys in state schools, the picture is even more dismal: only 37.8 per cent of those sitting English and maths in 2005 achieved a grade C or better.

What is even more shocking is that these pupils are going through an examination system that, despite the protestations of spin-doctoring politicians, has been dumbed down to inflate their own claims of achievement. The first question in a 1970 Cambridge Board GCE O level exam was, 'Write down any fraction between 1/11 and 1/12, giving your answer in the form m/n where m and n are integers.' The first GCSE question in 2001 was, 'Change 4 kilograms into pounds.'

In English, maths and science exams at key stages one, two and three, which are taken by seven, eleven and fourteen year olds respectively, failure is now not an option. In 2003, the Government's Qualifications and Curriculum Authority (QCA) set out guidelines to markers of state schools which told them that the 'F' for 'failure' on national tests should be substituted with an 'N' for 'nearly'. Meanwhile, maths exam answers are either 'creditworthy' or 'non-creditworthy' instead of correct or incorrect.

A QCA spokesman denied that the marking scheme blurred the distinction between passing and failing because 'the focus is on reaching level three, the lowest level targeted by the tests, so if pupils don't reach that target it does not mean that they have failed; it means they have nearly reached the target'. Isn't it gratifying to know that those in charge of our children's futures have such a clear and robust grasp of the English language themselves?

And how would the key stage two pupils fare, one wonders,

North Wales Police chief Richard Brunstrom in 2006 spent one of his days off helping to pull over 109 cars in 12 hours of blazing sunshine at Pwllheli

in a Victorian entrance exam paper for 11 year olds wanting to attend King Edward's School in Birmingham in 1898? 'Parse fully "And call the cattle home"' is the first English grammar question. A geography question asks, 'Where are silver, platinum, tin, wool, wheat, palm oil, furs and cacao got from?' In English history, the 11 year olds were asked which kings of England began to reign in 871, 1135, 1216, 1377, 1422, 1509, 1625, 1685, 1727, 1830? In maths? How about 'subtract 3.25741 from 3.3'? Or 'multiply 28.436 by 8.245'? And 'divide 0.86655 by 26.5'?

Might be a few 'Ns' there, one suspects. And that is why, by any measure, we all know that standards in education are falling in the same way we know that despite the spin, when we go into an NHS hospital after months on the waiting list, the floors are filthy and we'll get ten minutes at best with the consultant.

Despite government ministers insisting how much brighter our pupils are becoming, how is it that a survey carried out for a Channel 4 series on the monarchy in 2004 revealed that more than half of 15 to 24 year olds didn't know the British Royal Family's official name (compared to 71 per cent of all adults)? Even more shocking was that only 26 per cent knew which king was executed following the English Civil War, 16 per cent knew the first monarch to sit on the thrones of England and Scotland simultaneously, and 13 per cent which English king signed Magna Carta.

Mike Tomlinson, the former chief inspector of schools, a week before Comrade Kelly made her announcements, launched a scathing attack on the standard of A levels. *The Independent* reported that the man who headed a government inquiry into the reform of exams for 14 to 19 year olds in 2004 said the system was 'killing scholarship in almost every subject' studied in school sixth forms. In a speech to university leaders at the London Assembly, he said that even young people with four grade A passes at A level 'don't have the skills necessary to take a title and write about it'.

Fear of litigation has resulted in school trips being cut back, according to Ofsted. A teacher was jailed in 2003 for failing to prevent the death of a ten-year-old boy who

Meanwhile, *The Observer* reported in 2001 that the 'level of illiteracy among the young is above that of 1912'. A study led by Professor Loreto Todd at the University of Ulster found that 15 per cent of people aged 15 to 21 were 'functionally illiterate'. In 1912, school inspectors reported that only 2 per cent left school unable to read or write. Professor Todd also found a high level of arrogance among the 15 to 21 year olds surveyed. Seven out of ten believed they were 'pretty good' at getting words right, but when they were asked to spot fourteen mistakes in a piece of text, none was able to identify them all.

The Government's response to these figures, as was its response to health, has been to throw lots of money at the problem. It spent £1 billion on a literacy drive after Sir Michael Barber, the most senior adviser in the Education Department, said in 1997 that a major social transformation would be achieved by ensuring children left primary school with the basic skills to benefit from secondary education. He described the national literacy and numeracy strategy as the 'largest educational initiative on the planet'.

Although this was an 'initiative' and a 'strategy', as opposed to just a 'strategy', an analysis by the Institute for Public Policy Research (IPPR) in 2005 showed that despite pupils achieving much better results at the age of 11, they failed to go on to produce better GCSE results at 16.

Yet another £1 billion was spent in 2005 to try and improve struggling schools. Despite this huge investment, a report by the National Audit Office concluded that one in eight pupils in England was being denied a decent education. It said that 1,577 schools were performing poorly – representing 4 per cent of primary schools and a horrifying 23 per cent of secondaries.

But as with health, the meddling classes are viscerally attached to a politically correct ideology where the politics of victimhood are paramount. That might even be all right if the victims who had

was swept away in a river near Glenridding in Cumbria when on a school trip

talent were able to attend the grammar schools introduced by the 1944 Education Act, but these were effectively buried in the mid-1960s when the Labour Secretary of State for Education famously proclaimed he was going to 'smash every fucking grammar school in the country' and bribed local authorities to abolish these elitist institutions. Within a decade, 3,300 comprehensive schools had been created and 80 per cent of pupils were being educated in them.

What a travesty. Disgracefully, much of the objection to these institutions of excellence came not from the working classes, who would benefit so much by them, but snobbish, resentful middle-class parents who couldn't bear the fact that their little sweethearts would be forced to go to secondary moderns with the proles. And you can bet your bottom dollar that these people resented the fact that across the country grammar schools punched above their weight. Two-thirds of grammar school pupils in the early 1950s were working class, and more people from disadvantaged homes won places at Oxford and Cambridge in 1960 than they do today. Only four of the twenty-one heads of the big civil-service departments, according to ex-chief inspector of schools Chris Woodhead, were former public school pupils; the rest had attended grammars.

You would have thought that our modern political leaders, facing the fact that employers are exasperated by pupils who can't read and write and that universities are having to reintroduce tests in order to distinguish between the huge number of students with straight As at A level, might re-examine the merits of the 11-plus exam, which allowed pupils into grammars, or at least some other form of examination. Not a bit of it. Selection is privilege and the class system: the capitalist oppressor condemning the working man to a life down the mines with his tin of snap.

Even on 'mass failure of infrastructure' day, when comrade Kelly

The Government is considering a plan to weigh children at the ages of four and ten and

had the audacity to propose that schools such as her city academies should be able to be free from local-authority control and select some of its pupils, the wealthy Neil Kinnock raised his head again, saying that concept of choice being offered was 'synthetic'. 'The day was reached – which I hoped would never come – when there was an issue of such profound and lasting significance that would affect not just our generation but others, on which it was important to make my opposition known,' he told the BBC. He might have done better to ask why these academies, set up with £2 million-worth of private sponsorship and £20 million of government funding, should be among the worst performing schools.

While this posturing continues, the very people our class warriors are trying to support – the poor – are suffering. Chris Woodhead's book *Class War: The State of Education*, shows how since the '70s exams have been dumbed down, teachers drawn from the education system at the beginning of our book dismissing such things as maths and grammar as elitist, and more and more money thrown at what by anyone's standards is an atrocious state-education system. The last thing on any of the minds of the meddling classes, though, is instituting discipline in the classroom and teaching children the basics that every year, with tiring regularity, education ministers say are so essential to the good of the nation.

They could start, possibly, by asking their advisers to speak English. Mr Woodhead quotes Sir Michael Barber who says, 'For any given aspect of the curriculum . . . there are at least five different ways to approach it and these five approaches "map onto the multiple intelligences".' Well, it beats standing up with a blackboard and a piece of chalk.

As usual, when things get rough with the meddling classes, they resort to the tried-and-tested tactic of talking gibberish and blaming everyone else for their failings. The school at the bottom

to send their parents letters warning of long-term health problems if they are too fat

of the GCSE league tables, New Brompton College in Gillingham, Kent – note the self-aggrandising title of 'college' – blamed its failures on a shortage of teachers. Anti-selection campaigners said it never stood a chance because Kent still has grammar schools, which cream off what would potentially be its brightest pupils, and it served a poor neighbourhood. Still, it is some achievement that only 9 per cent of pupils obtained five A* to C grade passes: when I walk past my local secondary school, I steer my children through loud-mouthed, swearing, bad-mannered, litter-bugging nuisances, but it still manages to get 54 per cent of its pupils through to five A* to C passes.

And anyway, it wasn't always this way. There was a time when there was pride in our schools, when trendy young teachers didn't try and ingratiate themselves with the children. I remember being on holiday on the Isle of Wight when a school descended on a children's playground. Young teenagers, who gave no more regard to the terrified little ones already playing on the equipment than they did to the litter they were dropping, screeched and screamed and swore at each other. Far from hauling any of his pupils up, or even trying to have a quiet word with the ringleaders of his rabble, one of the teachers caught the eye of one of the girls and smiled. 'Are you awight, Rebeccar?' he asked in his best mockney accent.

It is patronising in the extreme to assume that the working classes want to be talked to in this way, to have their teachers ingratiate themselves with young people to whom they should be offering moral leadership and, even more importantly, hope for the future.

In Jonathan Rose's book *The Intellectual Life of the British Working Classes*, he tells a story of enthusiasm for education that is a far cry from the politically correct bleating that exposure to middle-class culture was somehow alien and boring for the lower orders.

In 1940, for example, boys were reading an average of six

A sub-postmaster who received serious head injuries as he stood up to armed robbers in Hertfordshire was asked to pay the Post Office £3,000 of the £6,695 stolen in the

books a month and girls just over seven. A 1994 survey indicates that almost half of all unskilled workers grew up in houses with 'substantial' libraries.

And the board schools, set up after the 1870 Education Act, have been condemned for their strict discipline, rote learning and gaunt buildings. But Rose's research of working-class children shows that these buildings were marvels ('sumptuous and indeed palatial beyond belief'), incorporating such wonders as running water and central heating. Chanting multiplication tables was fun and learning poetry by heart was 'pure magic'.

James Bartholomew finds the same thing in *The Welfare State We're In*. He notes that in 1860 at least 95 per cent of children attended schools for between five and seven years. The Church was funding poorer pupils, but private schools, too, were funding poorer children. For all the poverty of Victorian Britain, education was leaping ahead. In 1840, half of the women who got married in England and Wales signed the register with a mark rather than a signature. Thirty years later, it was 27 per cent and, by 1891, it was only 6.4 per cent.

Now in the nanny state, the class war continues, with middle-class children using all the material benefits they get from home to surge ahead of their poorer contemporaries under the 'prizes for all' philosophy of the nanny state.

Chancellor Gordon Brown (Kirkcaldy High and Edinburgh University) complained bitterly when he was told that Laura Spence, a pupil of Monkseaton Community High School in North Tyneside, had been turned down for a place to read medicine at Oxford. His argument was essentially that this talented student, because she was a girl and attended a state school, with the 'best A level qualifications you can have', had been rejected by an interview system 'more reminiscent of an old boy network and the old school tie than genuine justice'.

raid because he had moved away from an open parcel hatch to help a couple post a package

'I think it is wonderful that he has decided to stand up for people who don't normally go to Oxford,' chirped Laura. 'I think there has been a need for a case like mine to bring about a change in attitudes.'

But it wasn't the attitude of the college that was the problem. In fact, Laura Spence had no A level qualifications at the time (the results had yet to come in), but ten top marks at GCSE – as had the other twenty-two applicants. She did better on the interview, accounting for one quarter of the assessment, than any other part of the test, so that wasn't the problem either. And of the five who did win places, three were women, three were from ethnic minorities and two were from comprehensives (some ticked more than one box), so it wouldn't seem that that was the problem either. The problem is that top universities, thanks to the 'you're all special' philosophy of the politically correct, resulting in all their applicants getting straight As, have extreme difficulty in selecting anyone for their courses of excellence without resorting to subjective testing.

In fact, the faint whiff of nepotism that is hinted at by Mr Brown talking about an 'old boy network' becomes a rather more hollow accusation when it emerges that Laura's head teacher was American Dr Paul Kelley, who just happened that year to have been appointed to the Education and Training Export Group, a government advisory body chaired by Michael Wills. Although, astonishingly, local Labour Party activists said they had no knowledge of Dr Kelley, his school had been held up as a model of New Labour educational ideals for its innovative use of information technology. Monkseaton High had been visited by David Blunkett when he was Education Secretary and was included in the National Grid for Learning Green Paper. It also featured in the Government's *Excellence in Schools* video.

The Oxford admissions tutor, on the other hand, wasn't a flash,

---

Blackpool Council has demanded that the donkeys, which have since the nineteenth century plodded up and down the beach, bearing loads of timid toddlers and giggling

media-savvy American head teacher but did hail from Newcastle, where his mother taught in a comprehensive.

If there is prejudice to be uncovered, it isn't among the top universities, which are bending over backwards to accept more working-class students from ethnic-minority backgrounds, but in the Government first being dictated to by teachers demanding that no school can select its pupils and second by forcing universities to skew their admissions criteria to accommodate poorer students.

Naturally, there is a quango needed here, involving more meddling classes on big state salaries. This one takes the form of the Office for Fair Access (OFFA). The Government controversially decided to allow the better universities to charge £3,000-a-year fees, but in return they had to accept punishing new targets for increasing the intake of pupils from state schools and disadvantaged backgrounds.

So you work extraordinarily hard, forgo holidays abroad and live in a smaller house than you would otherwise so your children receive an education that is superior to the one offered by the state (according to their figures, the independent sector claims the ability of an 11 year old matches that of a state pupil of 14). Your child, with a solid education and probably a broader perspective than many state-school children as a result of extra-curricular activities, and will probably be extremely bright in the first place for passing the tough exams that most of the good private-sector or grammar schools require, will then actively be discriminated against because you worked so hard.

This is the bleak educational landscape of the United Kingdom more than 130 years after children gained the right to an education at least at primary level. It is one in which one in four state-school teachers admitted in an online poll carried out by the *Times Educational Supplement* (*TES*) that they would educate their children privately if they could afford to. A report on this poll

pensioners without any obvious signs of ill-treatment, should get a lunch break, have set working hours and Fridays off

in the *Sunday Times* in 2006 quoted one parent, who was also a teacher, as saying, 'My daughter has been offered a place at our last-choice school – didn't even look around it, as 18 per cent GCSE rate says it all (but it is the nearest school). Thank God she passed the exam for the nearest indie school, even if it means a remortgage for her to go there.'

'Mrs Manc and I have had to pretend to be pious Christians for Manc junior to get into our preferred single-sex "faith" high school,' another commented. 'It's big stakes. If he'd been shunted off to the nearest school with places, I would have paid for private. There's no way I want my child consorting with what is often euphemistically called a 'cross-section of society'. I only want him to experience the sector of society I approve of. Very politically incorrect. But there it is.'

Another contributor to the site, who called herself Pandora Peroxide, said she planned to use her parents' address to get her daughter into a good school. 'I'm going to play the system. I know three other families in the year group who are doing the same.'

Our politicians, meanwhile, make sure that they're above the pitiful education system they're overseeing. The Prime Minister sends his kids to posh London Oratory. The Labour MP for Hackney, Diane Abbott, who said it 'made the Labour Party look as if we do one thing and say another' when colleague Harriet Harman chose to send her son to an opted-out grammar school, could find not one school in the constituency that she represents that was good enough for offspring James, who was dispatched to City of London.

She 'doesn't remember' saying that about her friend Harriet at the time, but in the *Sunday Times* defended herself by saying sending children to private school wasn't always a problem for Labour MPs, and Harold Wilson chose to do so.

'Schools only became a conscience issue in the 1970s,' she

A report commissioned by the Government recommended that a motorist would be presumed responsible in civil proceedings for any collision involving a child in a

wrote. 'Perhaps the reason the issue is so emotive is because in England education is wrapped up with notions about class. Choosing a private school is synonymous with propagating the class system. However, like many immigrants, I see education as the most important gift I can give my son. And there are many black and Asian children at the private school I have chosen who are of the same view.'

Isn't this possibly the most noxious piece of hypocrisy you can possibly imagine? First, the representative of the people of Hackney North blames the rest of us for perpetuating a society that is wrapped up in notions about class – when it is her party who are constantly railing against class and privilege. Then she pulls out the race card, as if the colour of her skin gives her some kind of dispensation for an action that would otherwise be reprehensible.

When everyone can pass anything, and our poor children need to either get A-pluses in everything or mum and dad have to be able to cough up, it's the working classes in boroughs such as Hackney who lose out. Prime Minister Blair can afford to have tutors for his children; Cherie Blair gives her son Euan a little extra shove by passing a note to a Downing Street official to track down what relevant information can be found to help him prepare for a debate about nuclear-arms policy at school. In this way, they are not seen to be paying for their children's education, although they could well afford it and in doing so free up those places at one of the most sought-after schools in the country to some children who can't.

Meanwhile, academics urged Ruth Kelly to remove the compulsory teaching of parts of speech and syntax from the national curriculum following a study in 2005 whose results showed that teaching English grammar does not improve writing. Professor Richard Andrews of the University of York, who led a review of 100 years of research into grammar lessons, said that

residential area, even if the victim ran out into the road without looking

there was no evidence that teaching grammar helped pupils aged five to sixteen write more fluently or accurately. 'Many young people find aspects of grammar technical and an abstraction from language itself.'

Well, diddums. Many young people find helping their parents with the washing up or getting up in the morning to do a paper round an abstraction from life itself. The study simply ignores the fact that the whole purpose of grammar is to give us a key to understanding language that goes beyond class and vocabulary. Presumably Professor Andrews wouldn't care to differentiate between writing fewer lengthy academic papers or less lengthy academic papers.

So we really shouldn't be surprised that in the same year university-admission tutors warned the Government that the reputation of higher education was being put at risk by falling standards in literacy, numeracy and study skills among school leavers. Pupils were being 'spoon-fed' to pass exams instead of being encouraged to develop knowledge and understanding, according to a study by Oxford University's educational studies department and the Universities and Colleges Admissions Service. The study found that even students with top grades were likely to 'lack independent thought', 'have a fear of numbers' and 'prefer the Internet to books'.

And, it seems, go on to run our transport system. On the evening Comrade Kelly's department was boasting about how our children are brighter than ever, I was at Bank Underground station. The platform was packed far too tightly for me to open a paper and read of these triumphs in health and education. The reason was a fire alert at London Bridge. In years gone by, a couple of staff would have had a thorough look around the station and given an all-clear. But in the nanny state, there needs to be a full shutdown of the system and lots of self-important jobsworths marching up

One in ten youngsters suffers mental problems, according to the British Medical Association's Board of Science, with nearly 700,000 children affected severely

and down, talking to each other down walkie-talkies in that alfa-oscar-foxtrot tone of voice that denotes a particular kind of rather special individual who knows the general public to be imbeciles who really shouldn't be allowed the responsibility of being on a tube platform at all, let alone in a time of crisis.

Yet again my children would be in bed before I returned, yet another half-hour was wasted. Here was yet another example of the low-level aggro that is inflicted upon us whether we travel by train, plane or car.

It could have been worse. I could have been one of the poor saps who, a month later, were stuck on overcrowded tubes on the Circle Line in the middle of tunnels for two hours because of a power failure. Or perhaps I could have been on one of the seventeen buses in a row at the top of Ladbroke Grove held up by temporary traffic lights for gas works. At least on this occasion the passengers managed to persuade bus drivers to let them off despite not being at a stop. I could have been one of the passengers travelling to Bath in 2002 who arrived six hours late, in the small hours of the morning, to find themselves locked in the train station without a staff member in sight. Children were probably too exhausted by this time to enjoy watching their dads form a human battering ram to get the doors open, and like their parents none too cheered by the lack of taxis to be found when they finally escaped at 4 a.m.

This is the reality of life in the nanny state. The same sort of astronomical sums that are soaked up by health and education are poured into public-transport systems that barely work. A month after those poor people got stuck in Bath, it emerged that £33.54 billion allocated to improve Britain's shambolic rail network over ten years had been used up in a year.

Much of the blame was being laid at the door of Network Rail, the not-for-profit company set up by the Government in dubious circumstances that smacked of hatred for free enterprise to replace

enough by behavioural problems to require treatment

the collapsed Railtrack. Richard Bowker, boss of the Strategic Rail Authority (SRA), the body then in charge of overseeing the railway infrastructure, said, 'Costs are rising steeply – both on projects and operations, and this is squeezing out funding for investment. We still have a commitment for £33.5 billion of public funding secured for implementation of the first strategic plan a year ago but it now buys less than it did then.'

So much, then, for the SRA's ability to 'deliver' its first strategic plan (published at the beginning of that year on 14 January 2002):

> setting out the strategic priorities for Britain's railway over the next ten years. The SRA is responsible for delivering the Plan, within the resources available, and in particular the Government's key targets of 50 per cent growth in passenger kilometres, 80 per cent growth in freight moved, a reduction in London area overcrowding, and an improvement in punctuality and reliability.

Blah, blah, blah, deliver, strategy, peanuts, bunkum. By mid-March, figures from the Strategic Rail Authority (SRA) showed that trains were running slower. On mainline routes of South West Trains punctuality fell from 75 per cent to an abysmal 60 per cent in peak hours, while Thameslink trains fell from 80 per cent to 64 per cent.

Two years later, trains were still late despite record amounts of cash. Well, of course they were. More than 1,000 new train carriages remained stuck in sidings because delays in upgrading power supply meant there wasn't enough electricity to run them. This is because the carriages, packed with electrical systems such as air conditioning, sliding doors and computerised controls, drain more power from the system. It also means that modern trains are no more green than private cars, but we'll let that pass.

Walking was quicker in London in June 2006 than taking the bus, according to Transport *for* London's own journey planner – Trafalgar Square to Victoria took 21

In 2006, having thrown more billions of pounds at the railway system, far from increasing growth in passenger 'kilometres' – note the fuddy-duddy old miles that we all know in Britain are not good enough for our PC masters – the Government, in an effort to shave £1 billion from the extraordinary £6 billion subsidy, was cutting rail services on a scale not seen since the Beecham cuts of the '60s.

Every reason, then, to go for your own personal transport – no other people's children crying, choose your own temperature, your own music, when and where you want to stop, what time you want to travel, not having to batter down a station door at four in the morning . . .

But while the British Government is fleecing drivers with the highest taxes in Europe, it puts precious little back: only 14p from every £1 paid by drivers in fuel duty, road tax and VAT is spent on roads. In 1975, drivers paid in 2003 prices £14 billion in taxation. Most of that money, £12.5 billion, was ploughed back into roads and local transport. In the 2000–01 financial year, the tax bill for drivers was almost £38 billion, of which only £7 billion was spent on roads and local transport.

Screwing motorists means that even in London's congestion-charge zones cars are going slower than ever before. An RAC Foundation survey found that on the Strand, for example, traffic heading into Trafalgar Square moved at only 4.5 mph, and on countless other arteries it was slower than in another survey taken a year earlier. In fact, as anyone who lives in London will tell you, traffic sits at a standstill for ludicrous traffic lights that make it impossible to get from A to B by any method of motorised transport.

Of course, Ken Livingstone's propaganda machine pooh-poohed the survey. 'Driving down a street does not provide a true reflection of congestion and traffic speeds in the charging zone,'

minutes by bus and 19 on foot, Piccadilly Circus to Holborn 15 and 14 minutes respectively, and Aldwych to Piccadilly Circus 17 and 14 minutes

said a TfL spokesman. 'Many factors can affect journey times on any given day but, on average, congestion has been reduced and journey times improved since the introduction of the congestion charge . . . TfL will publish its *own findings* [my italics] which offer a true reflection of congestion in the zone.'

You can bet your bottom dollar that TfL's findings won't reflect what we all know to be true. In 2004, the *Evening Standard* surveyed traffic lights going from The Mall into the pedestrianised hell that is Trafalgar Square. The lights changed from red to green every one minute and eight seconds. The lights stayed on green for, wait for it, eight seconds each time. Drivers had to wait for an average of six minutes before passing through the lights. This has been replicated across London.

By 2003, the mayor had an extra 329 sets of traffic lights put in place across the capital. My own route from south-west London into the City has ten new sets of traffic lights. The Clapham Road, which used to be a civilised thoroughfare, is now a traffic jam.

Money is no object when it comes to saving pedestrian lives. A junction at Stockwell was 'improved' to create traffic jams that stretch for half a mile in every direction, while pedestrians, confused, cross when the lights are on green, or when they are on red while the majority of traffic is stationary, or dart in front of cars when they're on red again because by now they've assumed the traffic has simply died and given up hope of ever moving again. The cost of this: £350,000. And for the bus lanes along the Clapham Road, for the benefit of a single bus service that runs every ten minutes in rush hour, that helped turn it into a traffic jam: £150,000. And at Vauxhall Cross, works that created whole new traffic jams around a high-tech bus station through which it takes about three days for the Number 88 to pass set us back a jaw-dropping £4.5 million for the Stalinesque

Met Office employees in Devon have been issued with hard hats by Teignbridge District Council to protect them from marauding seagulls when they venture to the

structure and £20 million to bring traffic to a halt around it.

When you're building nirvana, like Patricia, Alistair, Ruth and Comrade Livingstone, you require huge amounts of our money to keep this running. In the three years to 2006, the taxes to the mayor of London increased by 29 per cent. The GLA precept in the four years running to 2006 increased by 4.7, 15.2, 29.1 and 7.5 per cent – massively ahead of inflation. In 2002, some £5,500 of our taxes was spent on Ken's taxi fares. Because although he hates the private motor car – indeed TfL documents simply ignore its very existence – he has no objection to being chauffeur-driven in a vehicle that can use the bus lanes. No one has any objection to taxis, or to the mayor using them; what they do object to is the public transport infrastructure lying in tatters while the man responsible for it spends thousands of pounds of our money bypassing it. Comrade Livingstone can look on at the chaos he's caused because taxis, according to his spokeswoman, are black cabs, and 'black cabs are public transport'.

Meanwhile, back at Transport *for* London, his acolytes prepare to soak up even more of our money on a whole variety of schemes – some worthwhile, others pie in the sky. In 2004, the mayor unveiled a £10 billion – yes, £10 billion – scheme for the capital's transport. *The Guardian* credulously wrote this up as if it were straight from the mouth of the great leader himself. There were plans that included 'further measures to cut traffic gridlock in targeted suburbs' when this 'gridlock' had been created in the first place by the mayor and his underlings. There would be 'improvements to the reliability and capacity of London Underground' and the plan would turn London into a 'low emission zone' by 2007, barring vehicles that fail to meet environmental requirements. Plans to widen the North Circular Road, though – surprise, surprise – appeared to have been 'downgraded'.

'Whether you walk, cycle or travel by bus or Tube, over the

weather station roof in Newton Abbot. An employee, David Potter, used to beat them off with a stick before the council insisted he wear the hat

next five years your journey should become safer, more reliable and more comfortable, and London will be a world leader for environmentally friendly and accessible public transport,' said Chairman Mao, sorry, Livingstone.

We might have been a bit more impressed if one thing the mayor has introduced had actually worked. Since his reign began, we are spending an unprecedented proportion of our local taxes – plus the congestion charge – on his vision. The result is congestion on an unprecedented scale, Tube lines that routinely have horrendous delays and half-empty buses stuck behind one another along the Strand and Oxford Street to the point that these roads are virtually impassable.

For that, we are paying more than 30 per cent more in taxes than we were three years ago for a town hall crammed with bureaucrats taking such meaningful jobs as 'Director: Group Equality and Inclusion' in a role that 'will create and direct equality not just internally, but externally at every customer interface'.

And all we want is the Tube to run properly.

Government quango the Health and Safety Executive has more than 4,000 employees and spends £200 million each year

8 Strictly no economies

Nanny makes sure there are jobs for the boys, or girls, regardless of race, gender and sexual orientation

What does a Secretary of State for Health do when faced with the fact that the organisation she oversees is sucking money up its publicly funded nose like a ferocious corporate cocaine addict?

Well, as you would, she splashes out more public dosh and advertises for a speechwriter on £56,000 for 18 hours' work a week – or £70 an hour, or £120,000 a year pro rata. 'In this pivotal role you will draft speeches for the Secretary of State for Health, collating material and information from senior officials, producing polished drafts within tight deadlines and ensuring every speech reflects her personal style,' reads the job advertisement. A lot of money, in other words, for writing pieces in *The Independent*, saying we 'will go all the way to a self-improving health service with no waiting lists and services which are fair to all'.

The one characteristic the meddling classes share over and above bossiness and self-righteousness is the ability to consume great pots of money. This goes into generous salaries and big final-salary pension schemes (while the rest of us must work until we drop) and relentless empire building, whereby bureaucrats increase their self-importance and salaries by employing ever-more people beneath them.

In the UK in 2006, more than half the electorate is either employed by or dependent on the Government: 15 per cent are state employees, 11 per cent are out of work and on welfare, 18

In 2005, Denbighshire County Council in North Wales paid an Olympic weightlifter £2,300 to teach bin men how to lift safely

per cent are benefit-dependent pensioners and 8 per cent are pensioners with independent means. There are 5.8 million state workers, and that leaves out anyone subcontracted to work for the Government; include them and the figure goes up to 6.8 million.

In the nanny state, there is a premium in employing, well, nannies. If you are particularly bossy, you can earn £30,000 a year as a smoking-cessation officer for Brent NHS Primary Care Trust. Oldham NHS Primary Care Trust will pay a five-a-day coordinator £27,000-plus pro rata for the important role of nagging people to eat more fruit and vegetables. Calderdale NHS Primary Care Trust drug-action team found the need to employ a criminal justice in-reach programme manager earning up to £30,571 per annum in 2003, while City and Hackney Teaching Primary Care Trust health-improvement directorate wanted a teenage pregnancy coordinator to nanny careless children who'd got themselves up the duff.

Indeed, the Department of Health itself decided in 2004 that it needed a head of research communications. The role? 'Play a strategic role in engaging effectively with audiences about research policies, programmes and outputs.' Make sense? OK, here's more: 'Communicate R&D policies and activities in a timely and effective manner.' Oh come on, you must be getting it now. No? 'Maximise use of the information sources within the directorate.' Aah, now it becomes clear . . . doesn't it? Obviously a job of such manifest importance means a sacrifice on the part of anyone qualified to take it on because there's only £74,000 on offer but, never fear, more may be available for an exceptional candidate; someone who's really made massive leaps forward in playing a strategic role in engaging effectively, obviously.

In 2004, as the Chancellor was telling the nation that he was going to cull 104,000 civil servants, so thousands of these essential jobs were being advertised across the public sector. The North West

A parent was called into a school to stick a plaster on her daughter's cut finger because teachers said they were banned from using them. Uphill Primary school near

Assembly, a vitally important unelected quango, needed a youth democracy worker to 'co-ordinate an innovative project using new technologies to ensure young people's views are mainstreamed into the policy-making process'. Greenwich Borough Council was looking for a community participation and diversity officer to 'enthuse, encourage and sustain community efforts'. The UK Passport Service was crying out for a nanny in the form of a programme support office risk coordinator to 'assist managers in developing risk registers, issue logs and produce and maintain a consolidated integrated change programme'. Well, dangerous work issuing passports. Transport *for* London was looking for a head of international and European affairs on £65,000 a year to 'promote TfL's interests overseas and influence proposed European and international policies'. He or she would probably want a bit more dosh though: TfL employed 74 managers in 2006 earning more than £100,000.

Ken Livingstone, who advocates that the workforce should reflect the society in which we live, nominates the entire board of Transport *for* London. He also picks an army of consultants at the cost to Londoners of £5 million a year. Harry Barlow, for example, gets £88,000 annually for a shortened week selling Mr Livingstone to London. He is the person, apparently, who created the cult of the personality of the mayor. Anne Kane, who campaigns against the 'oppression of women', has been appointed to research 'women in the London economy' for a modest fee of £28,000. The mayor, of course, needs environmental advice, so he hired Charles Secrett, who used to run the green pressure group Friends of the Earth, as a consultant on a £14,000 stipend to provide 'environmental advice'.

Despite the fact that the mayor's City Hall has an economics unit with 16 staff, in 2005 Ken also paid £225,000 a year to Bridget Rosewell's company, Volterra Consulting, for part-time advice

Weston-super-Mare, Somerset, had binned all plasters under safety rules in case any children were allergic to latex

from her and four colleagues. She heads a think tank that provides specialist advice and forecasting to all organisations in Ken's empire. She used it, for example, to provide a detailed rebuttal of the claim that his hated extension of the congestion charge into West London would harm business there.

Across the nation millions of pounds are being spent annually on building empires of bureaucrats speaking gobbledegook to each other. The reality of this self-importance is a quite distressing culture where phalanxes of workers hide behind the nonsense that is written in these job advertisements. While our public workforce absolutely adores going to anti-racism courses, rushing along to inclusivity meetings and, no doubt, mulling over the diversity policies of NHS trusts, no one is available to clean hospital wards or empty bedpans.

'Schools and hospitals are the only two places, with the possible exception of certain hardware stores, where you can see astonishingly good people and shockingly poor ones working side by side on identical salaries,' wrote Camilla Cavendish in *The Times* in 2005:

> I am sure this helps explain why, after so much money has been spent on these services, our individual experiences of them can differ so wildly. The doctors who delivered my baby on the NHS were superb, but my abiding memory will be of the midwives who drank tea while the agency nurse rushed around caring for the unwashed mothers and hungry babies. I could see her thinking, 'Why do I bother?'
>
> We all know how stressful it is to put up with team-mates who don't pull their weight. When the work is as hard and the stakes are as high as they are in nursing, it must be well nigh unbearable. If you don't hold poor performers to account, the good people will leave.

The Bishop of London, Richard Chartres, has declared, 'Making selfish choices such as flying on holiday or buying a large car are a symptom of sin.' The third-most senior bishop in the Church of England was talking of the release of a booklet on

She relates how a friend gave birth through an emergency Caesarean and ended up on a ward where the care was so poor that her husband had to fight his way in before visiting hours to take her to the bathroom because no nurse could be bothered. 'It's so unionised,' he said. 'Everyone knew what they wouldn't do. But no one was in charge. They apologised. They're good at that. But management by apology isn't management, is it?' It is little wonder that this should be the case with the culture of self-importance that runs through these organisations.

The journalist Julia Magnet in the *Daily Mail* recounted how a retired nurse recalled her first day on the ward in 1960, when she was not allowed to go for a coffee until she knew the name and diagnosis of every patient on the ward. The writer noted how students at the Florence Nightingale School of Nursing and Midwifery at King's College, London, now have to study 'the social context of health and health care, which considers the relevance of sociology and health policy to health care'.

Anyone visiting an NHS hospital will be familiar with the reality of what this means.

For the first time in 2003, more nurses joined the register from overseas (16,155) than from Britain (14,538). Nothing wrong with this in theory, if you're not worried by the dubious morality of recruiting nurses from poor countries so you don't have to pay to train them for three years in the UK. And the dubious morality of luring fully qualified staff from countries that have invested a huge percentage of their piffling budgets to pay for that training. Apart from this, there is also the distressing problem for our old people who find they cannot communicate with those who are meant to be looking after them.

I remember staying overnight in casualty awaiting an operation, having lacerated an artery in my arm. There was a bit of a problem in that although there was a doctor who could do the operation

environmental matters entitled *Treasures on Earth*, which also says congregations should try to walk or cycle to communion

– this was announced in a tone of voice that implied I should have been rather grateful that such a professional might be on duty in a hospital of all places – there wasn't a bed to put me in afterwards. Well, there was a whole ward that had been shut down because of lack of staff, so there were beds but not beds, as it were. I was kindly asked if there was anyone who could give me a lift to another NHS hospital, where I could present my X-rays and diagnosis, then telephoned by the doctor and reprimanded for even considering leaving a hospital with a severed artery (which I wasn't).

So it was that I spent the night in casualty on a trolley, listening to the distressing events going on behind a curtain where an old lady, also on a trolley, was unable to have a wee.

'Excuse me, dear,' I heard her call to a passing nurse.

'Yeah, wa' you want?' bellowed one of the miserable but not seemingly overworked Filipina nurses on duty.

'I'm sorry, dear, but I'm in terrible pain. Do you think you could help?'

'Wha' you wan'? I don' understand.'

'I need to relieve myself, dear.'

'Wha'? Wha' you wan'? I don' understand.'

'OK, dear, I know you're busy, but if you get a minute . . .'

And so she was left, this poor old lady at the end of her years, in agony, not wanting to complain, not wanting to be a drain, ignored by dismissive staff who not only couldn't understand her but made no effort to do so until her pain was so great she asked for help again, only for the routine to repeat itself. This, remember, not even from a hospital bed in a ward but a trolley in a noisy A&E unit.

To bring this up, you would be accused of racism. But the reality of our free-at-the-point-of-entry, helping-the-poor health service is that many medical staff are far more concerned with their place

The (unelected) East of England Development Agency wants to put £1–2 million towards Bridge of Reeds – a 177-foot-tall stainless-steel walkway suspended from three giant steel masts, featuring dozens of 160-foot free-standing steel rods – which

in its bureaucratic hierarchy than doing what they're meant to be doing. The treatment of this patient wouldn't be the nurses' fault, but that of an amorphous 'management' that was unable to administer beds properly, or the Government for not giving enough 'resources' for the ward to be open. The old lady – sweet, polite, long-suffering – was an incidental, rather unimportant piece in this bureaucratic jigsaw. We should be moved to tears.

Quite simply nothing moves in the nanny state unless there's a large drink in it for the meddling classes. This is the reality of the mass failure of infrastructure that pervades our society. The days of people being called what they are – cleaners, nurses, sisters, matrons, doctors – have been replaced by layers of coordinators, executives, professors and operatives. How many times have we visited hospital wards and watched as one hard-working nurse struggles round all the patients, is somehow the one there with the mop when there's a spillage, is making the effort to enquire of the whereabouts of a tardy doctor, while a whole gaggle of other staff sit around the central table, clipboards in hand, discussing strategies. In this atmosphere of bloated bureaucracy, the worker bee is being suffocated by the queens.

And all the time, nanny is handing out the tin for more money to improve 'services' for the disadvantaged. In 2005, the Office for National Statistics released figures that showed state workers' salaries had increased by 7.6 per cent compared with the previous year, while other workers managed just 3.4 per cent.

There is simply no limit to the amount of money that's needed to keep these well-paid professionals in bunce if we're ever to eradicate poverty in this cruel world of ours.

The voluntary sector employs the equivalent of 1.5 million staff and has an annual turnover of £46 billion – most of it, of course, tax-free. But how much *is* voluntary now is a moot point.

In the name of helping the poor and under-privileged, directors

it hopes will sway gently in the wind like fenland grasses and feature a recorded fenland soundtrack triggered by pedestrians and cyclists as they cross. The total cost of this sonic span, crossing an A road on the outskirts of Cambridge to Wickham Fen

of charities oversee vast corporate organisations in glossy office blocks and enjoy six-figure salaries. Save the Children UK employs 4,245 staff and its boss Jasmine Whitbread enjoys a salary of £110,000 a year. The NSPCC, covering similar territory, has a staff of 2,099 and Mary March, who oversees the organisation, earns £125,000.

Aren't these, surely, the people actionaid is referring to when it says that poverty is the result of 'unjust power relations'? And if not, why not? And how is it helping the people at the other end of these relations? The cleaners at the Houses of Parliament, for example, who went on strike in 2005 in protest at their wages of £5-an-hour with 12 days' paid holiday, no pension plan and no sick pay? The MPs for whom they were cleaning, by contrast, were at that time earning £59,095 a year basic, plus 12 weeks' paid holiday, plus expenses. And my, what expenses. MPs in 2004 could appoint spouses, children, parents and siblings to jobs with a salary of up to £77,534 without first advertising the position. They could use their annual housing allowance of £20,902 to buy residential property in London. A separate office allowance could be used to acquire commercial property in their constituency. The MPs, of course, keep all capital gains. Getting home is paid for, too. Members could claim £200 a month without receipts for driving to their constituency. They were also paid 57.7 pence a mile for the first 20,000 miles they drove each year. In 2003, Britain's elected representatives pocketed an average of £118,437 on top of their standard salaries. Of the 20 costliest MPs, 19 were Labour members; those committed, in other words, to a fairer and more equitable society.

In 2005, Frank Cook, the Labour member for Stockton North in Cleveland, even tried to claim nearly £1,500 expenses for landscaping the garden of his substantial London home in Camberwell. 'The place looked like a hovel,' he said. 'The work

---

owned by the National Trust, is estimated to be £8–10 million. 'I wanted the bridge to be a piece of sculpture that celebrates the natural environment, the wide skies, flocks

was such that I could not carry it out myself and take care of my duties towards my constituents.' The residents of Stockton were no doubt grateful for his devotion, but alas they were cruelly snubbed when the payments officer at the Commons, MP Myla Kelly, told him that an amount for £1,450 for the purpose of reclaiming a derelict garden was being withheld because the claim might be 'considered excessive within the spirit of the proviso "wholly necessarily and exclusively on parliamentary duties" as outlined in the Green Book Members' Guide'. Another MP claimed £22,845 in expenses by driving more than 62,000 miles in a year on 'parliamentary business', and got his money.

Lord Irvine, the former Lord Chancellor, who made headlines in 1998 by redecorating his grace-and-favour Lords apartment with wallpaper costing £300 a roll, was still doing very nicely out of the Government after his replacement in a June 2003 reshuffle, when he was awarded a £2.4 million pension, paying £100,000 a year. He claimed £32,954 for nine months and eighteen days' work in the House of Lords, including £16,032 for overnight stays in London to attend business in the Lords on 151 days and £8,016 for meals and travel. This is not to say that he was doing anything wrong or fiddling the Government. Like Frank Cook, he sees it simply as his right if he is properly to do his job of running the country and working towards a fairer society. The meddling classes always have the most honourable and selfless motivations.

Let's revisit the health service and its now ex-chief executive, Nigel Crisp. Feeling Patricia's pain, without any thought for himself, he stepped into the breach and took early retirement from his £195,000-a-year job, thereby, tacitly at least, taking some of the rap for the £620 million deficit the Government had forecast for the financial year ending in 2006. 'Not everything has gone well,' he admitted. 'I am particularly saddened by the difficulties we have had over the last few months and the financial problems

of birds and reed beds – something that everybody would recognise as special to the region and take to their hearts,' said the artist, Sara Mark

we are grappling with. As chief executive, I wish to acknowledge my accountability for problems just as I may take some credit for achievements.'

Quite what these achievements are we'll probably have to wait for Ms Hewitt's new speechwriter to make clear to us. But although they are not manifest, Prime Minister Blair obviously thought Nigel had done a superb job and immediately handed him a peerage. Neither will Sir Nigel go hungry: part of the NHS's massive debts for which he admits some responsibility will go into paying the 54 year old £100,000 a year in a pension package worth an estimated £3.2 million.

This is par for the course in the nanny state. While the little people, like the old lady next to me in A&E, have paid their taxes and worked hard all their lives aren't even offered a hospital bed, those whose careers have been built on coming to the aid of the poor pat themselves on the back and give themselves huge salaries. So 'Dame' Gill Morgan of the NHS Confederation justified 'Sir' Nigel's salary by saying, 'We need to make sure we attract the best managers.'

It's ironic, isn't it, that Patricia Hewitt's insistence on a classless society with a health service free at the point of entry for all should end up accepting the resignation of a man who will be made a peer, endorsed by a woman who is a dame?

Then again, she cut her teeth in politics under Neil Kinnock, the man, you'll recall, who was aghast at the fact that the Government was attempting to allow schools to choose the pupils they admit. This is the man who was earning a tidy £142,000 a year as a commissioner for the European Union before he retired on a pension deal that is up there in the Crisp-like regions, estimated to be worth at least £2.3 million on the open market.

But peerages and the accoutrements of wealth are very important for our modern nannies. They strut around from meeting to

The Army Medical Directorate environmental-health team has set out new guidelines telling bagpipers to wear earplugs because of fears that the military might get sued

meeting, from country to country like latter-day Prince Regents. They go to conference after conference, looking down their noses at the poor people, stuffing themselves with unhealthy food, smoking and making racist remarks to one another, and come up with ever more highfalutin ideas – smoking bans, ASBOs, healthy eating in schools initiatives – to bring them into line. While the meddling classes are obsessed with draconian legislation and the splashing out of millions of pounds in the name of equality, what they mean is equality for little people while their lifestyles are more akin to those of royalty.

When Prime Minister Blair and his idealistic band came into office in 1997, one of the first things they did was abolish hereditary peers in the House of Lords because, despite their lineage and the fact that these members were often rather more diverse in background and view than our professional politicians, they were of a class system that perpetuated the discrimination against the poor who were to be emancipated. The only trouble was our champions of democracy hadn't decided what to put in its place.

What to do with this ancient and revered House, with its over-the-top red benches and rich history? It's a problem that didn't last long. The politically correct found that the presenting of grand and archaic titles with an entrée into political debate without having to stand for election suited them rather better than they might have imagined. So, Sir Nigel Crisp, for all his magnificent efforts in running a health service that can't even keep its wards open, was rewarded with a knighthood. Well, it was the least they could do.

Prime Minister Blair has been the biggest dispenser of political patronage since life peerages were created in 1958. An investigation by *The Times* in 2005 revealed that one in ten of the life peers created by Tony Blair since he became Prime Minister was a Labour Party donor. At least twenty-five of the 292 peers he

---

by soldiers who claim that their hearing is damaged. Pipers are also to be banned from practising for more than 24 minutes a day outside and 15 minutes indoors

created since 1996 had made donations ranging from £6,000 to £13 million and two of the most generous became ministers. Paul Drayson donated £100,000 in 2001 and his company won a £32 million smallpox vaccine contract from the Government the next year. In 2004, he was made a peer and in the same year handed over £1 million. In May 2005, he was made Defence Minister. Lord Sainsbury of Turville has donated £13 million since 1994, when Tony Blair became Labour's leader, and has been a minister since 1998. He gave £2 million in 2005.

No one is suggesting any wrongdoing by any of these people, but it shows how in love our political classes are with rank and privilege. Just as Stalin and Hitler embraced their favourites, so the new establishment hands out peerages to those who please them. As Sir Walter Raleigh was knighted by Elizabeth I in 1585 and became a favoured friend, so Elizabeth II, now essentially a symbolic monarch, lays the sword upon the shoulder of Sir Paul Drayson and the rest.

All this became rather embarrassing to the people's party in 2006 when the whole question of baubles for favours came to a head after it emerged that Labour fundraisers arranged secret loans from businessmen who were then nominated for peerages. Dr Chai Patel – who runs the Priory clinic where the rich and famous go to detox – was offered a peerage within weeks of agreeing to lend Labour £1.5 million. He denounced the arrangements as a 'bazaar'.

Dr Patel emphasised that he made the loan because he was asked to and was able to and that he never expected anything in return. 'I am not ashamed of having donated to the Labour Party but have been driven to distraction by the cynicism associated with it,' he said.

Three millionaires nominated for peerages by Mr Blair in 2006, including Dr Patel, along with stockbroker Barry Townsley,

Children as young as four at Amesbury Infant School in Wiltshire have received letters from Ofsted criticising their teachers, with observations such as 'Most of your lessons are fairly good but sometimes your work is too easy!' Ofsted said

who loaned £1 million, and property tycoon Sir David Gerrard, had nominations blocked by the House of Lords Appointments Commission, which was furious at the fact the loans were concealed. Soon other lenders were brought into the fray, including Rod Aldridge, executive chairman of the technology company Capita, which in December 2005 recorded a £1.4 billion annual turnover, 53 per cent from public sector contracts. (This, by the way, is how Capita describes its important works: 'Capita is at the forefront of the evolution of business process outsourcing in the UK, focussed [*sic*] on service transformation through innovation.')

It emerged that Mr Aldridge was made chairman of Chancellor of the Exchequer Gordon Brown's £150 million youth community service scheme weeks after he lent £1 million to the Labour Party. Although again neither man had done anything wrong, and Mr Aldridge was not nominated for an honour, he resigned his Capita post after a commercial backlash to the disclosure that he was one of twelve businessmen who had made loans of £14 million to the Labour Party.

These sort of dealings are all par for the course for nanny. The Labour Party was only just recovering from the news that lawyer David Mills, the husband of Culture Secretary Tessa Jowell, was being investigated by the Italian courts for allegedly being rewarded for helping the former Italian prime minister, Silvio Berlusconi, hide various financial irregularities. Italian prosecutors had asked a judge to put Mr Mills on trial over claims that he received a £345,000 'bribe' from Mr Berlusconi for giving evidence in a corruption trial – a charge he strenuously denies. He was being investigated after he and his wife had taken a mortgage on their home to invest in a hedge fund. Ms Jowell announced she knew nothing of the investment. Then separated from him.

Again, no one is suggesting she has done anything wrong, but it

the letters were needed because pupils are not made aware of the outcome of its school inspections is another example of the world our leaders inhabit as part of their fight for a better deal for the working classes.

Silvio Berlusconi, the old rogue, is a friend of the Blairs anyway; they squeezed in, for example, a couple of days at his 27-room Sardinian hideaway in 2004, combining it with a holiday in Barbados at Cliff Richard's pad. The nation's leader and his family like to live the life of high-rollers. In 2002, they stayed in a chateau in the south of France belonging to tycoon Alain Perrin. In 1999, they stayed in Sharm-el-Sheik at the Egyptian taxpayers' expense. For this holiday, the royal flight was scrambled for 'security' reasons.

And in 2006, the Prime Minister was accused of using the *Queen's Flight* as his personal taxi when it emerged that he had spent more than £130,000 of taxpayers' money on a string of family holidays. The Prime Minister used the flight up to 60 times a year and regularly commandeered it to fly him to and from his constituency in County Durham. The Queen uses the fleet of planes, operated by 32 Squadron at RAF Northolt, around eight times a year.

This isn't too big a crime in itself. The Prime Minister is, after all, a very busy man who runs the country. But bear in mind it is he who said that global warming is the biggest threat to mankind. He leads a party that, in the name of saving the environment, has hectored and bullied we little people who have the temerity to drive cars, yet he and his high-rollers are addicted to travel, arranging conferences in faraway places that aren't Huddersfield in the name of good work.

A particularly brazen example of this pampered elite flying around the world in the name of helping the poor again involves that familiar cast member Patricia Hewitt, the woman who has berated 'snobs' for supporting an education system that turns poor people into plumbers (although how more snobbish can you be

An injured pedestrian was ticked off by a Manchester police officer when she described the motorist who hit her as 'fat'. Instead of the officer taking a note of

than to pick these tradesmen as somehow inferior) and who has overseen the mass closure of wards providing health care for the poor.

As Trade Secretary, she attended a conference on poverty in 2003. And where was this event? Well, what better place than Cancun in Mexico? To be held, say, at the five-star Fiesta Americana Grand Coral Beach Hotel, where a basic room cost £185 a night.

Ms Hewitt found, along with then Environment Secretary Margaret Beckett and Overseas Development Minister Baroness Amos, poor things, that the only way to get there was by private jet. Well, of course. Their underlings, three backbench MPs, two spin doctors and two dozen representatives from industry, unions and consumer groups, managed to struggle over there under their own steam but must have been grateful to find that the Grand Coral at least allowed them to get over their gruelling journey by resting up at the edge of its 660-foot swimming pool overlooking the Caribbean, with waiters in crisp white jackets whizzing round the sun loungers with cocktails. They must have been glad that they were on expenses, too, with those cocktails costing £12 a hit and a coffee setting you back a fiver.

Ms Hewitt could at least, if she'd had time in her busy schedule, have used the venue to get an idea of the grim effects of poverty by popping down the road and visiting Gabriela Auila, who lived with her husband and three children in a one-roomed, rat-infested shack. *The Sun* newspaper in fine tabloid tradition visited her a few days before the conference. Mrs Auila's husband, Luis, was at the time a tour guide with posh hotels such as the Grand Coral, which brought him in £30 a week: enough to pay for a fan but not a shower, or a fridge, or a lavatory, which was a hole in the ground a few hundred yards from the family's back door. That is poverty.

Although there is never enough money to pay for health, for transport or for education, whose quite shocking failure is blamed

her account, he paused and told her she could not use such language to describe an alleged offender

on lack of funds, there always seems to be something left in the pot for a conference or two, just as Robert Mugabe always seems to be able to scrape together the money from his ailing economy for a quick trip to Paris.

In 2005, four teachers from the Northeast thought it essential that they each took a week out of school during term time to attend a conference on arts and humanities. It was a terrible hardship, of course, being that it took place at the beachfront Sheraton Waikiki resort in Honolulu and being so far away from the little ones, but work's work. There was, needless to say, an initiative behind this: the Arts Council's Creative Partnerships Programme, which forked out the £7,118 it cost to send them there. 'The conference provided extraordinarily good value,' said the national director of the initiative, Paul Collard. 'It could have been in Bognor.'

Of course it could.

Almost as soon as New Labour got into power, they started spending thousands of pounds of our cash jetting around the world. By 1999, Tony Blair's Government had spent £11 million on foreign trips. The most expensive was a trip in September 1997 by the late Robin Cook, then Foreign Secretary, who took 14 officials to the Far East at a cost of £169,186.

And how can we go any further on our journey through the murky waters of nepotism and the high life without talking about our esteemed European commissioner Peter Mandelson? It was Mr Mandelson, you'll recall, who was forced to resign from the Government in December 1998 for failing to declare that he borrowed £373,000 to buy his home in Notting Hill from Paymaster General Geoffrey Robinson, himself questioned over his being the beneficiary of a Guernsey-based offshore trust. It says much for the snobbery of Mr Mandelson that he was willing to risk getting himself into trouble so he could live in trendy Notting Hill rather than spend rather less of his, let's face it, quite reasonable salary to

---

A youth who died in a car crash was sent a fake Valentine's Day card warning him to drive safely. His distraught mother opened an envelope to find a card with a picture of a crashed car and the message, 'I'm sorry, I didn't mean to kill you. I was driving too fast.

buy a place in, say, Kennington in easy reach of his place of work at the Palace of Westminster.

After his resignation, he told the press that he was going to 'normalise' his life. He said, too, that he had turned down lucrative jobs in the City to do voluntary work among the downtrodden in Africa and that he had a 'passion for compassion'.

Well, he certainly got around a bit. Since his resignation as Trade Secretary, *The Observer* kept track of his foreign junkets and revealed that he benefited from £20,000 of free travel in doing this great work and that in total he circumnavigated the world twice in business class. Some two months of his ten months on the backbenches were spent trotting around the world. Off he went to South Africa to meet ANC representatives in the run-up to the presidential election and visit a Voluntary Service Overseas project. What a morale boost to them that must have been. Another of his 13 trips took him to the luxurious Aspen Meadows resort in Colorado for a conference held by the secretive Aspen Institute, a collection of free marketers who believe globalisation can solve the world's problems. Other trips included a jaunt to Paris paid for by BP, to Madrid on the *Economist* magazine and to Corfu courtesy of Lord Rothschild.

In the same year, the Deputy Prime Minister John Prescott took on a gruelling visit to India and the Maldive Islands to lead Britain's delegation at the sixth session of the Commission on Sustainable Development, an 11-day environmental summit. Travel was first class, of course, and the six officials and businessmen who travelled with Mr Prescott stayed in £173-a-night rooms at the five-star Oberoi Towers hotel in Bombay. Mr Prescott was upgraded to the £1,358-a-night 'presidential' suite. The Indian Ministry of Defence even found a private jet to take Mr Prescott to the Taj Mahal. Well, you need a break from the arduous business of discussing policies for dealing with

I really miss you.' It was sent by the London Safety Camera Partnership as part of an initiative aimed at encouraging young drivers to slow down

air pollution and greenhouse gases. The Deputy Prime Minister magnanimously said, 'I just go where I'm told.'

Our best traveller is the Prime Minister's wife. Cherie Blair, née Booth, has a tough and demanding job as a barrister at Matrix Chambers in which she makes huge sums of money protecting the human rights of the not-so-fortunate. In 2006, for example, she defended the right of 17-year-old schoolgirl Shabina Begum – in a case that cost the taxpayer £100,000 – to wear full-length Islamic dress, despite the fact that the school, whose head was Muslim, was already prepared to allow her to wear headscarf, tunic and trousers.

Mrs Blair often bemoans life in the public eye, one of the drawbacks, of course, of being married to one of the world's most powerful men and taking on politically charged, high-profile human-rights cases. She is not so tired, though, as to be unwilling to travel the world in order to share with us the trials and tribulations of her life as a mother, a top barrister and effectively the First Lady of the United Kingdom. Off she goes, travelling the globe, explaining to the rich and powerful just how she does it. In a lecture tour of America, she was earning a reported £23,000 per speech to the likes of the New York Mercantile Exchange and the New York Board of Trade, and as star speaker at the International Futures Industry Conference in Boca Ranton, Florida. She was billed as 'Cherie Booth QC, wife of Prime Minister Tony Blair . . . a trailblazer in her professional life and dedicated wife and mother in her private life'. The blurb continued, 'Ms Booth will share her thoughts on the role of law in international business, achieving work–life balance, and the human side of a globalising industry.'

She might also have cared to talk about human rights in Malaysia, where she was flown all expenses paid in 2005 to give the annual Sultan Azlan Shah lecture, although it's not known if she received a fee for this. Her name was used to promote the opening of the

A schoolboy from County Durham repeatedly stabbed his piano teacher with a carving knife during private tuition because he had been told by a school teacher that he had

Starhill Gallery shopping complex, built by billionaire developer Francis Yeoh, who offered her a free holiday. It was a good year for talks. She'd been paid a reported £30,000 for a talk in the US as the 'First Lady of Downing Street' and is claimed to have picked up £102,000 for an Australia and New Zealand tour organised by controversial PR man Max Markson, whose PR company is called Markson Sparks.

The Prime Minister's wife also spoke of life in the Downing Street household during a talk in aid of the Children's Cancer Institute Australia. Given that the audience was granted only 30 minutes in front of the great woman, they must have been gratified to know that their money was going to a good cause. Naturally, if they felt that half an hour of her time wasn't enough, they had the option to buy a signed copy of her book, *The Goldfish Bowl: Married to the Prime Minister* – in which she discusses the pain she feels about her life married to the Prime Minister being so, er, public – for £30.

A radio interview in Auckland to promote the New Zealand part of the tour revealed that, 'One of the challenges is just making time to talk to each other as a couple. By the time you have done the children and all the jobs, there's not always enough time for each other.' Even less time if one of you is whizzing around the globe, visiting the US, Malaysia and the Antipodes, one would have thought.

But let us not be too hard on the Prime Minister's wife. She is, after all, committed to keeping up the two flats in Bristol she bought through convicted fraudster Peter Foster. And then there's the £3.5 million mortgage on the house in Belgravia to consider. Thank the Lord that they managed to get the children into the London Oratory School and don't have to pay for one of the best educations in Britain.

Property is something of an obsession for the meddling classes.

the talent to make the grade as a soccer player and resented being sent to evening music lessons

John Prescott, for example, claimed more than £70,000 in taxpayers' money to pay interest on and furnish his eight-bedroom constituency home in Hull, dubbed Prescott Towers. Mr Prescott, who heads up the socialist wing of New Labour, the man with cloth-cap values, when he's not travelling first class to India to help the environment, has property high on his agenda. His job has now been downgraded with many functions removed, but when it comes to estate management, you can see why Mr Prescott was responsible for housing policy. With his job, he got a government apartment on Admiralty Arch, which is bordered by The Mall, which leads to Buckingham Palace one way and Trafalgar Square the other. But it's a bit noisy in town, of course, so happily there was his weekend retreat, Dorneywood, a modest 21-bedroom official residence in Buckinghamshire.

But obviously good old Prezza doesn't want to lose his working-class roots. So he had use of a subsidised flat in South London from the RMT union, which he had rented at an advantageous rate for 33 years. By advantageous, we're talking £220 for a property that has a market rent estimated by local estate agents at £1,600. He didn't live there, of course, what with Dorneywood and Prescott Towers and Admiralty Arch, but his son David used it as an occasional London base.

Funnily enough, a genuine misunderstanding meant that the Deputy Prime Minister – who had overseen a 76 per cent increase in council tax since his Government took office – had omitted to pay council tax on his official London residence for nearly eight years.

Michael Meacher, who, while Minister for the Environment, told a fringe meeting at the Labour Party conference 'people like me who are privileged should not be in the position to rob other people of a home, which is a basic right', was in 2001 enjoying his basic right to 12 homes, including a large house in Wimbledon,

Judges branded compensation culture as a crippling 'evil' when the case of John Tomlinson was referred to them. Tomlinson was suing Congleton Borough Council and

a Cotswold stone retreat with swimming pool in Gloucestershire and a pied-à-terre in his Oldham constituency.

It is part of political life, though, to live in luxury locations. In 2005, as well as John Prescott, several other ministers enjoyed houses paid for by the taxpayer. Jack Straw, during his term as Foreign Secretary, had a London residence off Pall Mall and a country residence in Chevening, Kent. Geoff Hoon, then Leader of the Commons, and Margaret Beckett, then Environment Secretary, also had apartments next door to Mr Prescott in Admiralty House. David Blunkett, the disgraced Home Secretary who resigned twice after a series of events that stemmed from his having an affair with another man's wife – *The Spectator*'s Kimberly Quinn – still nonetheless had a Belgravia home worth £3 million that he'd been enjoying for the past four years.

Funnily enough, the honourable members also picked up thousands of pounds in expenses for having second homes (normally paid because of the expense of MPs needing to pay for accommodation in London as well as in their constituencies). Mr Blunkett pocketed £20,608 in 2005, while Mrs Beckett claimed £19,088 and Mr Straw £17,780. Tony Blair himself claimed £16,417 and John Prescott £14,166. MPs claimed a total of £80.8 million in expenses and staff costs, an average of £122,677.49 each and a rise of more than £23 million in three years.

These people are, quite simply, in love with the high life. The resignations of Peter Mandelson and David Blunkett stem directly from their desire to enjoy the trappings of the rich and famous. Both had the arrogance to swing their weight around, effectively proving that they were running the country and what they say goes. Peter Mandelson resigned a second time after he interfered to try and secure citizenship for the Hinduja brothers, the businessmen involved with the London Dome; likewise David Blunkett quit

Cheshire County Council after breaking his neck diving into a flooded gravel pit despite there being visible 'No Swimming' signs

after he tried to swing a visa for Kimberly Quinn's nanny and then became a director of DNA Bioscience without consulting the independent committee that advises former ministers on whether they should take up jobs.

Mark Steel in *The Independent* lampooned Blunkett's insistence that his mistake was 'only a technicality'. 'Whenever he was asked to register his interest in a company, he said "yes" when technically he meant "no",' he wrote:

> Blair said that Blunkett should stay because the only pertinent question was whether he was still capable of doing his job. What a radical step that would be if this method was introduced to all law. Judges would have to sum up by telling the jury: 'The important thing you have to decide is not whether Mr Perkins did or didn't carry out the murder, but whether he's still in good shape to drive the 249 to Tooting Broadway.'

Neither, of course, showed any remorse. Both bleated about being forced to resign through 'technicalities', having been hounded by the nasty newspapers.

What the meddling classes really want to do is get on with their (high) lives without the intrusion of the media. The snooping that is appropriate for little people in the form of millions of cameras on the streets, tracking systems for cars and the introduction of identity cards is totally inappropriate for the big people. So Ron Davies' and Mark Oaten's sexual predilections might be none of our business, but any inappropriate behaviour that's thrown up by the state watching over us is entirely acceptable.

Whenever these cases come up, the meddling classes rally round in support of each other. Margaret Beckett called the coverage of Tessa Jowell a witch-hunt. 'It really ought not to go on,' she said. So Barbara Follett extended her sympathy for Tessa and the stress

---

Police were called when two pensioners dived into a swimming pool in Erith, Kent, in contravention of new health and safety rules. They had been diving into

she was put under, saying she was finding it 'disgusting the way some people and some of the media are behaving'. Well, yes, but she does live in a very large house and we pay her a lot of money to represent her constituents and run the country, so if Mr Jowell has been a bit naughty with the family finances, we sort of have a right to know about it.

Geoffrey Robinson resigned shortly after Peter Mandelson, saying he was fed up after a 12-month campaign of 'vilification' over his business affairs. Well, just idle curiosity that he might be the beneficiary of a Guernsey-based offshore trust. And who was vilifying him? It was Neil Kinnock, who called on him to resign from the Government 'for the sake of the Party'.

Our meddling classes seem to do pretty well anyway. Peter Mandelson is back in power again, following in Mr Kinnock's footsteps as Europe's Trade Commissioner. After Ron Davies resigned in 1998 as Welsh Secretary, following his 'serious lapse of judgement' in which he met a man on Clapham Common before being mugged and dumped on a housing estate, he found himself rehabilitated as chairman of the Economic Development Committee on the Welsh Assembly (but in June 1999 quit that, too, after he was found by journalists at a beauty spot used as a homosexual pick-up point near to his constituency. He admitted afterwards that he had a compulsive disorder that caused him to seek out 'high-risk' situations).

Unlike the rest of us, these people's misdemeanours are rarely considered their fault. Because we all make mistakes, many of us may well have secrets we might not want to share: nanny uses this as a justification for its sympathy for those who have done wrong when they are rehabilitated into some other cushy job with a big salary and built-in pension. But they are stretching our sympathy. While we are taxed, hectored and let down by the mass failure of infrastructure, they bleat of

the pool for 20 years without suffering any ill effects

being treated unfairly despite taking advantage of their hugely privileged positions.

Sorry if we don't shed too many tears. Nanny is getting very rich on our enterprise and spending the money we make on empires that have the authority of Stalin and the pomp of royalty.

A parking ticket was slapped on a lorry that sunk into a North London road when a water main burst under its wheels. When the driver protested, the warden simply told him, 'You can appeal'

9 Strictly no high art

Nanny chooses appropriate culture for the masses

While the meddling classes are obsessed with bullying us onto smelly buses and trying to force us off roads we've paid for several times over, their own needs require that huge amounts of carbon emissions are sent into the atmosphere in the manufacturing of concrete, steel and glass necessary for their buildings.

Culture Secretary Tessa Jowell had certainly made up her mind that large chunks of real estate in the centre of London were essential to her part in the running of the nanny state, with conditions commensurate with the importance of her work. A report from the National Audit Office, Whitehall's spending watchdog, in 2006 revealed that taxpayers were forking out £21,000 a year to accommodate each worker at her prestige headquarters; the Culture Department paid £10,000 per worker for the nearby offices of the National Heritage Memorial Fund, a lottery quango; her offices cost more than £1,000 per square metre and gave staff nearly 20 square metres of working space each. The report said that the Culture Department spent more than £40 million a year on 95 different office buildings for its own staff and its quangos, and suites used by Ms Jowell and her 335 civil servants were being upgraded, which would add another £10 million to the bill.

Similarly, Britain's MPs just couldn't properly carry out their work without the spanking new Portcullis House, built in 1999 – complete with £450 armchairs and a £75,000 limestone front desk – overlooking the Thames by Westminster Bridge. The

A study of twins led by British scientists has concluded that people of lower socio-economic standing age seven years more quickly than their more fortunate peers

setting up of the Scottish Parliament necessitated a building with all the aesthetic merits of a silage tower at a cost of over £400 million to the British taxpayer. The National Assembly for Wales managed to construct its building for a comparatively piffling £67 million, which was still 67 per cent over the estimated budget of £40 million. Quite thrillingly, 'the juxtaposition of neighbouring buildings with great views across the Bay contrasts containment and openness. These forces are typical of the greatest urban spaces.' Eh? Something lost in the translation from the Welsh, perhaps.

Ken Livingstone naturally couldn't be left out of this display of political might. His empire is in City Hall on the south bank of the Thames, a prime piece of real estate with uninterrupted views over the river, and costs the taxpayer £4.75 million a year.

These buildings all boast of their democratic design. City Hall, designed by Norman Foster, has triple-glazed windows and an interior that features an asymmetrical ramp that twists to the building's summit. According to Jonathan Glancy of *The Guardian*, it appears to criss-cross itself, so 'that the seats around the mayor's (including a ring of 250 for the public) look up into a modern version of Guarino Guarini's breathtaking baroque vaulting at the Chapel of the Holy Shroud in Turin'. 'If debates ever get boring, (as if),' he gushes 'eyes will be drawn high into this magical space.'

Amazing that there's ever a spare seat in the house. There's nothing wrong with a fine civic edifice, but let us not forget that these buildings, in their prominent positions, are really symbols of power rather than democracy. The fact that the steps of the Welsh Assembly and London's City Hall go towards the sea and river respectively means they aren't welcoming the populace off the street but boasting to the tourists passing by. They follow in the tradition of the imperialist palaces of regimes so despised by the inhabitants of these buildings.

While our politicians spend millions of pounds on anti-racism

A 'style guide' sent to civil servants in the Department of the Environment, Transport and the Regions included a menu of phrases officers could use in their work, including 'a

and anti-sexism measures, they are in love with titled white middle-class men – 'Lord' Rogers, 'Lord' Foster, 'Sir' Terry Farrell – who massage their egos with monstrous towers of concrete, steel and glass. Their buildings soak up millions of pounds of public money and tower over our communities with a tyrannical, authoritarian aesthetic. The crumbling hospital buildings, horrific town-centre projects, depressing council estates and the quite shockingly ugly – and fittingly Stalinist – MI6 building at Vauxhall are all saying, 'Look everybody, I did that.'

It is an instinct that filters down to our regional politicians, too. How did Southwark Council think a spare £5 million they seemed to be able to get their hands on would benefit the residents of Peckham? In a thumping great big library building, that's what. The money included £1.25 million from the Single Regeneration Budget programme to 'facilitate' the regeneration of Peckham, which also included new low-rise housing – which is a mixture of owner-occupied and social housing, of course – Peckham Square and Peckham Arch, not forgetting Peckham Pulse healthy living centre (what we used to know as a swimming pool and gym).

'The library was designed to be striking, to make people curious about what lies inside, and to challenge the traditional view of libraries as a staid and serious environment,' bragged the borough.

And why shouldn't a library be a staid and serious environment? Why shouldn't they contain books and be somewhere peaceful where the residents of Peckham might want to undertake serious research to enrich themselves? Indeed, why not have a building that works in harmony with the surrounding area? Or even one that works. Within six years, the swimming pool was closed for a year to fix cracking pipes that were supplying water to the pools.

No, they have to have a great modernist edifice that bellows, 'We are Southwark Council and we are very important indeed.'

living, working countryside', 'quality homes and communities for everyone' and 'planning transport housing and business development together, not separately'

And an arch. And a square – developed by the illiterate architectural practice John McAslan and Partners who talked of the development's three 'principle [sic]' elements – where the residents of Peckham can sit and contemplate the last time politicians decided to act in the area on a grand scale and foisted upon it a ghastly red-bricked bus- and pedestrians-only high street leading down to this famous arch.

There is no part of the country, however remote, that is spared this new cultural imperialism. On Tiree in the Inner Hebrides, one of the most breathtakingly beautiful places on earth, residents were lucky enough to get a new landmark building of their own in 2003.

'At the very beginning of this collaborative project,' boasted Tiree Arts Enterprise, 'the appointed group of artists and architects resolved to create a work that would, for its audience, be unique and elemental in visual, physical and temporal terms. A work that would be totally unified (physically and conceptually) in respect of its art and architecture content; a work related to and sympathetic to the site, topography and elements of Tiree; a work of individuality, epic in scale, aesthetically beautiful and of contemporary and Scottish cultural significance.'

What was this building of such cultural significance? A town hall? Indeed, a library? Or a community theatre, perhaps? Er, no. A shelter by the ferry port.

You would have thought this would be quite a simple operation. It is, let's face it, a waiting room by the sea. Obviously there might be a few more people who want protecting from the elements than at a suburban bus stop in Solihull and, being on a beautiful bit of land, you might want it to have a little more aesthetic beauty to it. Something in sympathetic stone, perhaps, painted white, maybe backing onto the prevailing wind with a couple of benches, even a door and a heater. But not when it's set up by Tiree Arts Enterprise,

Leicestershire and Rutland Rural Community Council ordered ramblers to carry out a 'risk assessment' for a sponsored walk covering such 'risks' as rabbit holes,

a group of local and visiting artists. This was to be no ordinary waiting room but a place for contemplation as well.

The fact that a team of artists and architects wrote down a list of their collected observations of the vast sea, vast sky, etc., and these images 'fuse to make the structure striking, both at one with and in contrast to its surroundings' tells you all you need to know – it is ugly. And, at £98,000, ludicrously expensive.

The West is littered with these monstrosities. Modernism has dominated our landscape, carrying with it the weird notion that somehow they are more inclusive than the less egocentric buildings of the past. Peckham Library becomes a place where poor people will go because it's not stuffy and old-fashioned. The reality is that the middle classes – Tiree Arts Enterprise Group, or architectural partners such as John McAslan and Partners – get the material satisfaction and probably most use of the buildings, too.

At Clapham Common, nowhere is this aesthetic vandalism more blatant than the two entrances to its Tube station. On the east side is a monstrosity in concrete and glass sticking out of the pavement like a concrete molar, litter blowing around it, and about as inviting as a cold store. Across the street is one of the older entrances, with a pretty little glass dome atop its brickwork and white windows, a relic of a bygone age with dignity and, despite the grand designs of the '30s and '40s, a humility, too.

Needless to say, when it comes to their own properties, this is the architecture the meddling classes tend to buy. Bob Marshall-Andrews has his rather exceptional pad in Wales built into a grass bank, but he's an exception. For Tony Blair, it is a £3.5 million pile on Connaught Square, while most senior politicians choose tasteful and practical Victorian terraces in suburbs such as Islington.

When it comes to spending other people's money, though, they are obsessed with the building of huge great egocentric projects that stick out like sore thumbs. The Treasury levies VAT on

ploughed fields and overhanging branches

conservation but not on new building. The Government is doing everything it can to take planning controls away from the local community, so new housing estates can be built. Try and restore an old building and you're not only taxed but also up against the madness of health-and-safety regulations – the sort of rules that force retirement homes to close down because the door of an old building isn't wide enough.

Councillors in Brighton, for example, have been gasping with excitement at a proposal to build a £250-million sports and housing complex on the seafront at Hove. The futuristic complex is to be designed by Frank Gehry, the man responsible for the Guggenheim Museum in Bilbao. At its centre is a £64-million leisure centre with a roof of jagged, coloured metal panels surrounded by two towers with a crumpled, higgledy-piggledy effect that critics say will destroy the city's Regency heritage. Damn right it will, but what does that matter? The councillors say that it will turn Brighton into a 'city of this century rather than the past'.

These outré constructions are the indelible manifestation of the spread of political correctness since its ideological naissance in the second half of the last century. Old buildings with a working-class past are fondly restored – Manchester's Salford Mills, Baltic in Gateshead, Liverpool's Albert Dock, Tate Modern on the South Bank – but Lord Foster's Millennium Bridge, the pedestrian footway that links the art gallery to the more ambitious, more dignified, more distinctive, more impressive St Paul's Cathedral, is a totem of the inflated egos of the meek who have inherited the earth.

The spending of £18.2 million on the Millennium Bridge (plus another £5 million to stop Lord Foster's creation swaying, scaring the living daylights out of the pedestrians crossing it) is driven by an agenda that is as strong and pervasive as the civic linking of politics and trade epitomised by Tower Bridge a mile or so downriver. Except trade has got nothing to do with this. This is

A report passed to *The Observer* newspaper revealed that in its first three years in power the Labour Government had sanctioned the setting up of 238 task forces, ad hoc advisory

about pedestrianisation. The bridge is mildly useful perhaps to the handful of commuters and schoolchildren at City of London School who might want to cross the river, but really it is symbolic – Lord Foster's customary combination of steel and glass is telling us how magnificent it is to be *walking* over the river. Unlike Tower Bridge, which, despite its folly, was built for the convenience and benefit of Londoners, the Millennium Bridge is for tourists.

These constructions are people's constructions. The great Bankside Power Station in which the free Tate Modern art gallery is housed – free meaning paid for principally by the taxpayer – is where the proletariat can come and be inspired by modern art from around the world. In its magnificent turbine hall in 2005, for example, they could see 14,000 white polythene boxes stacked in piles by Rachel Whiteread. This is public art the meddling classes adore.

Whiteread's piece *Embankment* cost an astonishing £400,000 (thankfully, the mighty Unilever corp stepped in to assist with the dosh) and was inspired by a cardboard box that had once contained Whiteread's toys and Christmas decorations, and spurred her to think of the 'universal quality of the box'.

'I think it's going to be quite a surprise that she's chosen something as humble and throwaway as a cardboard box,' said the curator, Catherine Wood. 'Boxes have a universal quality. Everybody has used a box to pack up their belongings or shopping.'

Er, goodness. Never thought of that. Thank you so much for shedding new light on this everyday object. *Embankment* also drew on Whiteread's participation in the Cape Farewell project, which took artists to the Arctic to learn about climate change and the landscape. 'Going to the Arctic was a sublime experience and I wanted to bring a sense of that place into here,' said the artist.

Of course. Green issues are big in the arts world.

Roads around Tate Modern have been blocked off, causing terrible traffic jams on the southern side of Southwark Bridge.

groups and reviews, including one examining which statue to put on the vacant plinth at Trafalgar Square and another on how to organise national dance and drama awards

Meanwhile, on the northern side there is no longer access to the City of London. This wanton destruction of the capital's thoroughfares was supposedly instigated because of the pollution they cause. It is, however, perfectly acceptable to import concrete and steel that has been extraordinarily ungreen to source and fabricate in order to build a pedestrian bridge that has no benefit for Londoners themselves other than as a Sunday afternoon indulgence. It is completely acceptable, even desirable, too, for Rachel Whiteread to burn up a share of the earth's resources to travel thousands of miles as part of a cynical propaganda exercise to discover that the Arctic is jolly chilly and wouldn't be the Arctic if it wasn't jolly chilly. Her exhibit is put into a building, which is a massive drain on energy to light and heat, to encourage people to use up even more of the earth's natural resources to come and visit it as a tourist attraction . . . in which we're supposed to contemplate man's destruction of the planet.

Meanwhile in central London, Trafalgar Square, a symbolic place of celebration and demonstration in the United Kingdom, has under orders from Chairman Livingstone been pedestrianised. His argument was that it should not effectively be a huge roundabout, and it would therefore be greener to link it to the National Gallery and create a huge pedestrianised square instead. Unfortunately, Trafalgar Square was also one of the great throroughfares of London. By clogging it up in the name of being green, Ken and his nannies have created massive and unprecedented traffic jams, principally for the buses and taxis that have always dominated this part of London, coming into it in every direction.

In the name of helping to save the environment, these vehicles sit in monstrous queues, belching out their toxic fumes. It is impossible for someone working to the east of Trafalgar Square to travel above ground to have lunch with someone working to the west. It is impossible to catch a bus (from which ordinary people can

---

The Government in 2006 launched a 'Dad Pack' telling dads-to-be how they should behave. The pack, which cost £50,000 to produce, offered such advice as 'Bite your

find the best view of Trafalgar Square) from Charing Cross station to Oxford Street for a spot of shopping unless you are prepared to spend half the day sitting on it. The Strand, you see, is stationary at all times except between two and three in the morning when there's a full moon. As is Regent Street. As is Charing Cross Road. As is The Mall. These handsome streets have been turned into noisy diesel clouds in the name of saving the planet. Meanwhile, Trafalgar Square itself can only be viewed either by sacrificing half your day on one of the buses contributing to these clouds before they enter the square or sharing it with teenage schoolchildren showing off to one another and, if you're particularly unlucky at the weekend, a Livingstone apparatchik bellowing down a microphone, introducing some suitably proletarian entertainment laid on by his boss. The rumble of buses and taxis that used to travel around this great landmark are nothing to the noise and irritation of these cultural pursuits.

Summer in the Square 2005 was 'an exciting programme of events and performances taking place in the summer months'. They 'can be enjoyed by people of all ages, Londoners or visitors to the capital, on their way from work and after school or simply passing through the area', whinnied the wordy, self-evident, patronising blurb for this gross intrusion on Londoners' right to walk across and enjoy this great cultural landmark unfettered by some noisy propagandist nonsense laid on to keep us amused.

And what was there to enjoy during Summer in the Square that was so preferable to simply enjoying it for what it is? Well, BikeFest, of course, 'where you will discover that there is a pedal-powered answer to almost all of our green energy needs'. Disappointingly, this did not mean turning the turbine hall at Tate Modern back into a turbine with hundreds of cyclists pedalling like fury to provide enough power to heat and light the building and surrounding streets. There was 'fun stuff too, from a giant

lip, not your partner, when she is ratty,' and also explained, 'Raising children costs money, which can be tough'

cycle sculpture to choreographed street dance on bikes'. Makes you glad to be alive, doesn't it?

And, of course, a public square wouldn't be a public square without some healthy green propaganda. Then NSEW A 360° View of Climate Change feature, was a thought-provoking photographic exhibition 'Highlighting the impact of global warming and climate change, the exhibition, film and associated campaign seeks to communicate, educate and inspire'. Note the sickly use of transitive verbs intransitively. Inspire whom, exactly? Still, you could maybe nip round the corner and make a contribution of your own by taking a picture of Ken's traffic jams and sticking it up with the rest of the work.

There's London Pride, of course, and Children's Art Day, Jazz on the Streets (and how about jazz in jazz clubs for those who want to see it?), Bollywood Steps performing a dance, a celebration of London Mele, Saraswati Academy of Indian Dance with music by Strings, Roma culture and, of course, Producciones Imperdibles dancing on a transparent stage.

You'll note there's not much British stuff going on in the centre of the capital of the United Kingdom, but we are a nation that was, let's remember, a nasty exploitative oppressor, so far better to have a St Patrick's Day parade (Ken turned down any money for St George's Day) or some Afghan kite fliers, as featured in 2002's Summer in the Square.

'Nasser Omar is a refugee who has shared one of Afghanistan's best-loved traditions with thousands of people across Europe,' explained the mayor. 'His work is a powerful reminder of the power of art to bring people from different backgrounds and cultures together through shared experiences.' Didn't exactly work in Kabul, though, Ken, did it? In fact, English democracy and the rule of law has done rather more to bring people together, but that is anathema.

On one not untypical day in London in 2003, the Northern Line had severe delays in both directions due to 'closed sections' of the line, the Hammersmith and City Line had delays

There is nothing wrong with any of these events. Anyone is free to promote any of them and good luck to them. But why is it that huge wads of taxpayers' money is spent on forcing them upon us whether we want them or not?

Because the nanny state is in charge, that's why. 'It's the Regent Street Festival!' nanny shouts. 'Regent Street, the curviest street in the West End, is dressing up for a party: the "Mile of Style" is banishing cars, sprouting a lawn and inviting people to its international themed festival.' As Snoopy used to say, 'Bleeurggh.'

The reason that these events are principally staged by public bodies is because there are only limited numbers of people prepared to pay to be hectored and lectured to like this. In the neo-classical National Gallery that looks proudly over Trafalgar Square are works by some of the finest artists in the world – Constable, Van Gogh, Monet, Seurat, Turner, Raphael, Vermeer – who reward our contemplation with genuine inspiration: you are enriched by spending some time in front of them.

Outside it's enforced fun that nearly always has some underlying message that we should all take on board underwritten by a group of politically correct commissars who decide on what and what isn't good for us.

So we have *Alison Lapper Pregnant*, an 11-ft 6-in. 13-ton statue by Marc Quinn of an artist with no arms or legs who, in this sculpture, is eight and a half months pregnant. Mr Quinn won a £160,000 commission to make his sculpture. It was funded by the Greater London Authority and the Arts Council (who will get their money back if and when he sells it) as part of a project to select sculptures to rest on an empty plinth in Trafalgar Square, erected in 1841 to accommodate a statue of King William IV on horseback but which remained empty when the money ran out.

'Nelson's Column is the epitome of a phallic male monument

and I felt that the square needed some femininity, linking Boudicca near the Houses of Parliament,' said the artist.

Why? Surely the principal criterion of a sculpture in Trafalgar Square is that the person has done major good for the country. The one thing Nelson's column is not is phallic. It is a celebration of a man who, at the age of 48, sacrificed his life for Great Britain during a brave and brilliantly planned battle that prevented the nation being overrun by a nasty, arrogant autocrat. Alison Lapper might be disabled and courageous. And we can also find much to admire in the statue. She has not, however, sacrificed herself for the good of the nation. In fact, you can argue that it is thanks to Nelson that we have a democracy in which she can participate.

This sculpture was selected by the Fourth Plinth commission, a team of contemporary art lovers (selected by the mayor, of course) from a shortlist that also featured a Ford Fiesta splattered with pigeon droppings and two wooden life-size replicas of Tomahawk cruise missiles. Its replacement is *Hotel for the Birds* by the German artist Thomas Schütte, which resembles a giant asymmetric Meccano set. Then the competition starts all over again.

The GLA, in its normal boastful mood, said that Quinn's statue 'considered questions of idealism, heroism, femininity, prejudice and humanity'. Translated, this means that you might not like it very much, it might make any member of the public over the age of 50 extremely uncomfortable, but it's good for you. Nanny is lecturing us, saying, effectively, that if we are not to be prejudiced, this is the art we need.

The nation, though, doesn't really care for this sort of thing. When the public voted for the greatest painting in Britain, the winner was *The Fighting Temeraire*, which pictures a steam tug towing the ship of the same name to be scrapped. Turner painted it in 1839, and it is free for all to see in the National Gallery that overlooks Trafalgar Square and the statue of Alison Lapper.

That same day, the Bakerloo Line had no service between Queens Park Station and Harrow Station due to a defective train, Queensway Station on the Central Line

It, too, relates directly to Nelson's Column: 'The 98-gun ship *Temeraire* played a distinguished role in Nelson's victory at the Battle of Trafalgar in 1805, after which she was known as the "Fighting Temeraire",' explains the National Gallery's blurb. 'The ship remained in service until 1838 when she was decommissioned and towed from Sheerness to Rotherhithe to be broken up.

'The painting was thought to represent the decline of Britain's naval power. The ship is shown travelling east, away from the sunset, even though Rotherhithe is west of Sheerness, but Turner's main concern was to evoke a sense of loss, rather than to give an exact recording of the event.'

All this in one painting, and we have not even gone on to consider its aesthetic merits or the symbolism of steam heralding a new industrial age. And inside those walls are probably a hundred others or more by which you could be similarly inspired, and contemplate and discuss aspects of our collective history and culture. Rachel Whiteread's boxes are OK for a bit of a laugh before you meet some friends for a cup of coffee by the river, but very few of the exhibits in Tate Modern, unless there really is a hidden depth to someone having an orgasm in front of a video camera, come close to the discipline and rigour and imagination that combine to produce truly great work.

The promotion of our culture now has been reduced to a politically motivated sham funded by ever-more initiatives by an ever-increasing number of bodies seeking public funding.

It is epitomised by the Dome in south-east London, opened with a great fanfare and put together by Peter Mandelson when he wasn't securing loans for his new flat ten miles away in fashionable West London, far away from this 'regeneration' he was sponsoring. This white elephant was to have been the modern equivalent of the National Exhibition, a symbol of national pride, to celebrate two millennia of achievement. In the end, the politicians charged

was closed due to maintenance work and Bermondsey Station on the Jubilee Line eastbound was closed due to defective platform equipment

with running the Dome filled it with soppy, vacuous, inclusive, quasi-educational nonsense, such as its centrepiece, the giant Body Zone.

> The human body is the most complex object in the world which up until recently has undergone no significant evolutionary change since Homo Erectus became Homo Sapiens up to 150,000 years ago.
>
> Now, scientists believe that diet, exercise and technological developments over the past 100 years have helped to transform our bodies and lives.
>
> Today we can run faster and jump higher. We are stronger, taller and live longer. But we are also balder and more prone to cancer and allergic conditions.
>
> The exhibition will show how we can affect our own future and the world around us

was the inane justification for this ludicrous centrepiece of an enterprise that cost the nation more than £800 million and for which it was still forking out £250,000 a month after it had closed as an exhibition due to lack of interest at the start of 2001.

In 2005, meanwhile, the nanny state was ensuring that the people of Shetland, not having access to these great white elephants of the capital, were getting the benefit of the meddling classes' cultural ambitions with *A Shetland Odyssey*. Supported by – take a deep breath – Shetland Arts Trust, Calouste Gulbenkian Foundation, PRS Foundation, Hinrichsen Foundation, Britten Pears Foundation and friends of Tête à Tête, 'Pioneering opera company Tête à Tête teams up with Shetland Islanders to launch a truly ground-breaking new work combining opera, knitting and spinning to portray the adventures of Odysseus.'

It is patently far too obvious to offer Shetland Islanders a straight, dramatic interpretation of this epic journey. Without using people knitting and spinning to help bring Odysseus's journey to life, they presumably wouldn't be intelligent enough to understand this great work.

This particular 'Odyssey' [geddit?] began with an introduction in 2003 from the revolutionary On the Edge project at Gray's School of Art, Aberdeen, which pioneers new lines of attack for the visual arts in remote rural areas. Since then, the company has met well over 100 knitters and spinners in Shetland, plus many leading members of the Shetland arts scene, to see how they might collaborate with this unique group of artists.

The result is the development of a highly intriguing new work that will incorporate knitting and spinning, words and music, singing and playing, involving Shetlanders as professional performers and their craft as inspiration.

Of course, Odysseus was a 'war criminal, mercenary, compulsive liar, opportunist, fantasist', but rather than our having the intelligence to work this out for ourselves from the text, and acknowledging that Homer might too have had this in mind when he wrote *The Odyssey*, thus its enduring appeal, these smart arses are going to spell it out for us with the aid of six singers, seven instrumentalists and five Shetland knitters and spinners.

In order to produce this great work, Tête à Tête commissioned composer Julian Grant and librettist Hattie Naylor to write *A Shetland Odyssey*. Of course, the story is a 'natural vehicle for the merging of opera and knitting/spinning'. Uncannily, Hattie Naylor's previous adaptation incorporated six knitters representing the Fates.

Just as great science makes the complicated seem simple and politically correct science makes the simple complicated,

to stem the flow of illegal immigrants into the UK

so great art – such as *The Odyssey* – makes sense of our complicated emotions, while politically correct art complicates simple ones.

The Turner Prize epitomises this pretentious strutting around. Finalists in the 2005 competition included a work by Simon Starling, from Epsom, Surrey, who dismantled a shed, turned it into a boat that was paddled down the Rhine, then turned it back into a shed. His work was called *Shedboatshed*, and he described it as 'the physical manifestation of a thought process'. He was up against *Split Endz* by musician and DJ Jim Lambie, which was made up of belts and training shoes spilling out of a bright pink wardrobe, and *If I Had You* by Darren Almond, a video installation focusing on his widowed grandmother's personal memories. There was, however, great excitement because for the first time in five years a painter – a painter, would you credit it? – Gillian Carnegie, was nominated. Starling, though, walked away with the £25,000 first prize.

Nanny has deemed that this is what is good for us. This is culture as sanctioned by the new establishment: to bring in the grants and attract the attention of the meddling classes, it has to be non-sexist, non-racist, break down cultural barriers – displays of Gypsy art at the University of Greenwich (formerly Thames Polytechnic) anyone? – take work back to the people, be inclusive.

So the Barbican theatre in London in 2006 hosted Grupo Cultural AfroReggae, which was 'founded out of tragedy'. After police gunned down 21 innocents in a violent *favela*, Vigário Geral, in Rio, a local promoter, José Junior, started to run music and dance workshops for local 'kids', and AfroReggae was born. It offered an escape route for 'countless favela kids' and so this 'explosive mix of rap and percussion' ends up in the arts centres of the world. Of course, AfroReggae also ran workshops in London, Oxford and Manchester (where they also played), introducing

British teachers have been trained to deliver 'happiness classes' to 2,000 secondary-school pupils in an experiment in South Tyneside, Manchester and a rural location

their unique philosophy to excluded young people and bringing their own message of 'empowerment and belonging'.

Maybe they'd like to visit the London Urban Collective, an initiative sponsored by, inter alia, the London boroughs of Camden, Islington, Lambeth and Southwark, the Arts Council of England, Job Centre 'New Deal', FX, The Play Centre, Munister, Freeport Records, Downside Fisher Youth Club and, surprisingly, the LSO, which gives money for young musicians and DJs to cut records. The Urban Collective project gives 30 young people from areas in need of urban regeneration the chance to write, record and promote their own album with the help of music industry mentors, guest artists and producers. 'The results are taking the public and the music industry by storm.'

Isn't this complete folly? The one thing we are awash with is aspiring musicians. What the sponsors are saying to these presumably disadvantaged young people is that they should enter an arena where no amount of grants but huge amounts of talent, drive and having a thick skin might just lead to success.

It is surely misguided. What the meddling classes should be telling these young people is that if they have the drive and talent, give it a go, but what the country really needs is engineers, accountants, mechanics and plumbers. They should be giving them an education that takes them into the mainstream, that will offer them a future that will lead them out of the council estates, rather than one that in all probability will lead them not to the bling jewellery and four-wheel drives of their heroes but back home poorer than before. They should be telling them they can try and get an education and still explore their musical talents, and if they're good enough, they have the same chance of reaching the top.

But that's no fun for the meddling classes. That means working hard themselves and starting to teach these poor estate kids

to combat a rise in depression, self-harm and antisocial behaviour among young people

what they might not want to learn. It means undoing the woeful educational policies of the past and teaching them to read and write rather than kowtowing to a youth culture that might be fun and exciting but – look at the rise of gun culture and pregnant teenagers – is also misguided and naive.

The free market, anyway, is happy to cater for the 'kids'.

On a Sunday in November 2005, Trafalgar Square was turned over to a snowboarding arena (sponsored by the energy drink Red Bull), with 8,000 watching snowboarders. Residents of south-west London know to give Clapham Common a miss every summer during the weekend when it hosts the Urban Games (sponsored in the past by Coca-Cola and Sony), where BMX riders and skateboarders compete for prizes announced by gobby DJs playing loud music.

But this, too, is a marginal part of our culture. For most of us, of all ages, culture is something that we devise for ourselves. Those 'kids' developed skate culture long before Coca-Cola and Sony saw an opportunity in sponsoring it. Our culture might include going and having a giggle at the ridiculous artworks at Tate Modern and contemplating the emperor's-new-clothes mentality that allows us to marvel at a pile of old steel. But it is also about sitting down with a good book, about racing a sailing boat on the local reservoir, about Sunday lunch with friends, about going to see pop concerts by groups who've managed to play music without the aid of a local initiative. Our culture is about Sunday football and watching Leyton Orient, it's about bingo and bacon sandwiches, rowing early on Saturday mornings, fiddling around with a vintage motorbike or pottering around in the garden. It's about showing off your marrows and helping out with the Scout group. It's about playing in the darts team. It's about church on Sundays and rock music on Friday nights.

This culture has been celebrated, lampooned and criticised for

The Sentencing Guidelines Council (SGC) has said that 'peer group pressure' is one of the mitigating factors that can reduce the sentence of young offenders

centuries by artists from Chaucer to Shakespeare to The Beatles. The whole point is it didn't have a bureaucrat schooled in socialist realism interceding and demanding it be non-racist or inclusive.

Strangely, as those artists challenged the establishment of the Church, the Government and the cultural elite, so the Church, the politically correct government and the cultural elite of today has turned its back on those great patrons of the Victorian museums, the university presses and plays by Shakespeare and Ibsen. It is the nanny state that has become the establishment that our contemporaries could do well to lampoon.

In a strange twist of words, BBC Radio 4 controller Mark Damazer told the Broadcasting Press Guild in 2005 that his radio station must challenge political correctness to satisfy an audience that no longer 'wears tweeds and plays golf'.

This meant, of course, that there was room for sex and violence and that we should get ready for swearing on the station.

'Dissent must be one of the qualities of Radio 4,' he said. 'There should be a lack of political correctness and a willingness to challenge the foundations of political ideas. We won't be afraid of the politically unorthodox. Sex and strong language is not something for Radio 4 to be frightened of.'

What he was saying, in fact, was the exact opposite. Sex and strong language is the lingua franca of political correctness. He was really telling us that he was putting Radio 4 into the heart of the new political orthodoxy. There's nothing the new establishment likes more than a bit of swearing and sex, a few gay relationships and hopefully some racial issues too. Our new young radicals will probably start demanding some P.G. Wodehouse.

Yoof broadcasters such as Janet Street-Porter and Wahid (now Lord) Ali are now at the centre of the politically correct establishment. The precedents they have set mean that no television programme dares to have a middle-class English voice,

---

– although ringleaders can have sentences increased – under new guidelines issued in 2006

especially one with clear diction. The fear of being elitist means a regional accent is de rigueur. Patrick Barwise, of the London Business School, was probably decidedly anti-establishment when he criticised CBBC for 'crass' presentation and 'tastelessness and cruelty' in some of its programmes. He cited the common use of 'ain't' and 'you was' as examples. The governors retorted that it is important that presenters such as Dick and Dom 'use a vernacular that children can understand and identify with' [they mean 'children can understand and *with which* they can identify'].

Far from lacking a 'willingness to challenge' ideas, as Mark Damazer has it, we are awash with a culture that challenges them. Jacqueline Wilson, the children's author, revealed on *The South Bank Show* that she railed against Enid Blyton's books because they 'leave out everything in real life'. So she's vowed to serve us up an oeuvre that presents real life as an ordeal of the new step-dad, bullying, abuse, redundancy and repossession. Jacqueline Wilson is an author for our age: this is a celebration of victim culture.

Her grim roll-call of real-life incidences of divorce and Great-Gran going into hospital is somehow deemed to be more radical than the world of Enid Blyton, where children climb the magic tree and with strange alien friends such as Moonface and Saucepan Man explore weird countries hidden in the clouds that this tree stretches into; or climb onto a wishing chair that sprouts wings and takes children on flights of fancy to magical and sometimes dangerous lands.

Whereas Jacqueline Wilson's children are victims, dependent on the actions of adults for their happiness, Blyton's characters have no contact with their parents beyond asking them if they can go out for the day and being told that they have to do their chores first. While Jacqueline Wilson's characters have a best friend with whom to share their woes, Blyton's youngsters go out and take responsibility for their actions, bound across fields unfettered by

Research from Virgin Money in 2003 found that three-quarters of women were using alternative therapies such as yoga, acupuncture and massage to combat stress

the detritus of modern life. By being children, they are unwittingly becoming young adults as they learn to cope with the obstacles that inevitably come their way. Jacqueline Wilson's, on the other hand, are treated as adults and become perpetual children as their lives are a reaction to events for which they aren't responsible.

For all the radicalism that is promulgated by the politically correct, there is a rather depressing ordinariness characterising the work that nanny feels it important we learn about.

Tracey Emin's illiterate ramblings, for example, far from being radical, or informative, or inspiring, are, like Jacqueline Wilson's novels, rather prosaic. Once you have marvelled at how daring it is to call your work *Fuck You Eddy*, say, a childish misspelt riposte to some boyfriend, or *Tracey Emin C.V. Cunt Vernacular*, her great work from 1997, or the frightfully witty *Is Anal Sex Legal* and *Is Legal Sex Anal* in Tate Britain, you simply recognise it as making a big deal of the banal. She is an artist for our times: an adult child dependent on the amoral culture that nanny is insisting is good for us.

Real culture, inspiring culture, is to be found in other salons, created by artists working within far more restrictive moral codes (without the meddling classes, such as Tête à Tête, pouring thousands of pounds into their conception), yet producing work that soars; work that is witty, sad, clever, radical, complicated, deep, gay; work that you can take your children to.

What, on the other hand, do you tell them they can read into *Fuck You Eddy*?

Norfolk and Norwich University Hospital announced in 2006 that it was having to spend £40,000 on equipment including beds, hoists, armchairs and commodes to cater for very fat patients

10 Strictly no thinking for yourself

Nanny treats us all as children

Why, when you're unveiling a statue – of a naked, pregnant, disabled woman such as Alison Lapper, say – is it necessary to wear a hard hat?

Since it weighs 13 tons, if Marc Quinn's icon came crashing off its plinth, the hat, let's face it, is not going to do a whole lot of good; workers would still end up looking like pizza. Or perhaps there are hidden dangers in the pulling off of the substantial tarpaulin to reveal this great work. The wind could blow it out of the workmen's hands, its tethers might wrap around their legs and, with an extra violent gust, drag the poor men across Trafalgar Square, smashing them into one of the lions. Before they know what to do with themselves, it could blow them upwards and, just as they get level with Nelson's nose, drop again, plummeting them to the ground. Well, if that happened, then the helmets could be a lifesaver.

Otherwise, a hard hat for unveiling a statue is about as much use as a bonnet for a commando. But we now live in hard-hat culture, so hard hats there must be however remote the possibility of injury.

Kevin McLeod on his television programme *Grand Designs* dons one as soon as he gets within a mile of a building site that so far consists of a pile of mud and a pipe; hard hats are a must for politicians visiting new hospital buildings that are complete bar one last roofing tile; even the crew of the Isle of Wight car ferry wear very fetching hard hats, although one would have thought

---

Nearby James Paget Hospital at Gorleston, near Lowestoft, was forced to buy a specialist bed to take a patient weighing up to 71 stone and two operating tables

that they would offer little protection should a Volvo estate with a family of five plus the dog crash from one deck to another on top of the hapless worker.

Since it was popularised by Village People, only the most curmudgeonly wouldn't admit that it has improved immensely the look of men on building sites. One wouldn't be surprised even if the Government made the wearing of them compulsory on aesthetic grounds. But the reality is that the hard hat is just one of the most visible manifestations of those two words with which nanny is obsessed, which hover like a black cloud over any activity we decide to embark upon – *health* and *safety*.

In the early 1970s, as the politically correct were making the move from the corridors of academia to the corridors of power, an insidious development was taking place where, by making it compulsory to wear a helment when riding on a motorcycle, for the first time in our history, politicians felt it morally acceptable to enact laws protecting us from ourselves. It seems so long ago now, 1973, when it became illegal for mods and rockers to feel the wind in their hair, when Grandma stopped getting on the back of Grandpa's Ariel Square Four to pop down to the club because her blue rinse would get flattened.

What a small price to pay, it seemed at the time, for the fringe benefit of saving so many teenage lives. This was surely a tiny liberty that would be missed by no one (until they went on holiday to Greece and revelled in the freedom of cruising over the mountains on a rented Honda 90 without a great big lump of plastic on their head). It was, though, the start of an era when politicians were not only starting to feel they had the right to dictate what we were able to say, but also what decisions we were able to make for ourselves.

The nanny state was not only going to stop us being rude to each other, but, armed with erroneous statistics and a statute

that can take people weighing up to 50 stone

book, it was going to tighten the bars of our playpen. Never had we been more secure in our history, never before had we such advanced medicines at our disposal, never had transportation been so safe; now our comrades from our right-on university courses were going to prove that they could save millions of lives. One of their weapons was what we now recognise as the health-and-safety inspectors who stalk our everyday actions like inverted grim reapers, wearing not hoods but hard hats and bearing not scythes but clipboards.

Like the grim reaper, there is no one who can escape their maw.

Lawyers hover over us, twenty-first-century angels waiting to swoop to earth with scrolls of litigation should we trip over a paving stone and our right to walk along the pavement in safety be violated by the local council. The two moral codes of health and safety and human rights have inexorably ratcheted each other up a notch, so as one sues, so the other puts a heavier restriction on our lives lest we should sue again.

The only possibility of escaping this claustrophobic cycle is by claiming a victim status that elevates your needs above the rest of the population. So, in 1973, in what, looking back, was a prescient move, the Sikh community demanded that their right to wear a turban was not to be taken away from them should they want to hop on a motorcycle and visit their mates on the other side of town (and who could blame them?). So, in the name of protecting their rights, they were allowed to put their faith in God rather than Her Majesty's Government to keep them safe.

Even such a minor concession from nanny now is unthinkable. Since that fateful point in our political history, as politicians nodded and agreed that more should be done to protect individual members of society, year by year the state has drawn in the limits of personal freedom to the point where on a housing estate in

Scotland's fire service has distributed posters in gay bars and clubs across the country

Brighton, officials have given themselves the right to arrest you for swearing.

This might seem reasonable. Residents of the 3,500 homes on the Hollingdean estate were no doubt so sick of the behaviour of the yobs who committed an average of 34 car crimes a week that the drawing up of an agreement where residents pledge not to play music, or drive recklessly and swear, might be seen as a godsend. As would the £5 million – yes, £5 million – that the Government pumped into the area in 2002 as part of a ten-year regeneration programme.

But is it not a symptom of our age that we have become so immature that the individuals in our society are incapable of policing themselves without having ASBOs imposed on them, as our youths exercise their right to enjoy nicking cars and throwing them into handbrake turns at two o'clock in the morning? What nanny has effectively been doing over the past 30 years is tolerating abhorrent behaviour on the grounds that miscreants are victims, while creating ever more crimes that are obeyed effectively by those sections of society who are willing to be policed.

In the name of protecting ourselves from ourselves, it didn't take long before it became law to wear seatbelts in the front of a car. Then the back. On the grounds of health and safety, smoking is banned in public places because of the harm this is alleged to do to innocents. There are laws ready to be put in place to restrict the amount of salt in food. And it will soon become a legal requirement in the UK, following recommendations from nanny's Food Standards Agency, for folic acid to be added to flour, and therefore bread, because 'experts' believe that if it is eaten by pregnant women, it will reduce the number of cases of spina bifida and other defects by 40 per cent. The vitamin also reduces miscarriages and 'may' help to combat strokes, heart disease and bone disorders in adults.

---

as part of an equality campaign and an attempt to shed its 'macho' image

There is, of course, no law to prevent a pregnant woman, who by definition will be in contact with her doctor and a raft of other health workers, from making the decision to take folic acid herself without its being imposed on the nation.

This isn't good enough for the meddling classes, though. It isn't expansive enough, expensive enough or important enough. All these heavy-handed, anti-libertarian laws are made on the basis that if nanny looks after we toddlers properly, if we are sufficiently cosseted, then we shall live for ever.

We've mentioned already that Japan, which has the third highest rate of smoking in the world, has the second-longest life expectancy. But not only that, it was in the top 20, along with Kenya, India, Sri Lanka and Kyrgyzstan, when it came to the highest incidence of road injuries in 2001. The facts, in other words, tell us that a) there are rather more reasons for our deaths than nanny believes; b) we're going to die anyway; c) we can make our own decisions as to how best to live our lives, i.e. non-smoking restaurants and pubs were proliferating before the meddling classes insisted on interfering.

And these restrictions, even if you are in agreement with nanny so far and haven't as yet tried to escape the nursery, are only going to get tighter.

John Smith, president of the Royal College of Surgeons of Edinburgh, proposed in 2005 a restriction on how much we should be able to drink. 'The legislation to ban smoking in public places is very welcome [of course] and it is a major step forward,' he said. 'The logical thing to recognise now is that smoking is bad for you, as is alcohol.

'Should we now limit the amount of drink that can be served in pubs? If, as a nation, we are serious about trying to prevent illnesses associated with social habits, then this is something that must be considered seriously. I think for the Government to follow

---

Enid Blyton's Famous Five and Secret Seven stories have been altered so that 'I say' has been replaced by 'hey', and 'queer' with 'odd', while in The Faraway Tree Stories

the American model of saying, for the benefit of each patron, we will provide three drinks only, would be very interesting to look at.'

Indeed it would if you are serious about treating the population as five year olds. The city council in Santa Monica, California, has powers to impose a three-drink ban on bars, while voluntary schemes operate in Virginia, Oregon and Massachusetts. And if that still seems perfectly reasonable, consider the fact that in Texas nanny can send the goons into bars and arrest drinkers on the basis that they *might* commit an offence. Undercover agents from the Texas Alcoholic Beverage Commission can arrest drunk people who have committed no crime but obviously look a bit tasty.

In an operation in a Dallas suburb in 2006, agents visited 36 bars and arrested 30 people for intoxication. Carolyn Beck, the commission's spokeswoman, said the arrests were designed to detain drunks before they misbehaved. 'There are lots of dangerous and stupid things people do when they're intoxicated,' she said. 'People walk out into traffic and get run over. People jump off balconies trying to reach a swimming pool and miss.'

Quite. And they stagger home happy and a little tipsy, a little more at one with the world, their troubles rather further away than before they sipped that first beer. Surely this is a better alternative to lying around at home with cans of Bud, fistfuls of prescription drugs, a bowl of pretzels and an X-rated video game. Not, it seems, for nanny.

Research in the medical journal *The Lancet* suggested that obesity accelerates the ageing of human DNA by 9 years and smoking by only 4.6. So, if smokers should be vilified, it stands to reason that fatties are next. Like the illiterate warnings on cigarette packets ('Smokers die younger'. How can I die younger? Younger than what?), are we to see similar entreaties on packets of doughnuts? 'Eating this will make you repulsive, then dead,' suggested Tim

the characters Fanny and Dick have been changed to Frannie and Rick

Luckhurst in *The Times*. And what about the risk of secondary eating? Munching away on a cream bun will cause envy among fellow diners and encourage them to overeat, surely. Shouldn't our politicians be considering far more stringent labels, such as 'Eating doughnuts harms you and those around you'?

Already Sainsbury's is treating us as cretins with its 'Wheel of Health' labelling system introduced in January 2005. The contribution of five key nutrients are shown on certain foods – salt, fat, saturated fat, added sugars and the number of calories per serving and then colour coded as 'red' – think; 'orange' – OK; 'green' – go. These are what the supermarket believes must be included to enable customers to make an informed choice and reduce the threat of an obesity epidemic.

But surely customers – who amazingly have learnt to walk, talk and in some cases drive motor cars – are already making an informed choice. They are deciding that the joy of eating huge quantities of pizza with lashings of lager is worth the spots, not being able to play park football as well as you'd like and, frankly, kissing goodbye your chances of ever marrying Jennifer Aniston.

Needless to say, nanny doesn't see it that way. This is a call to arms, a call to action, and our chubby little wrists have to be smacked. In 2004, a House of Commons select committee issued a report on obesity, which it declared to be a 'devastating epidemic' that was costing the economy £7 billion a year and the National Health Service £3.5 billion. Sir John Krebs, at the time head of the Food Standards Agency, wrote that people on low incomes are more likely to suffer from diet-related diseases. 'Poverty limits both choice and the motivation to make healthier choices,' he said.

Here we go again, the plebs going and ruining their health with no thought for the distress it might cause the meddling classes. And here's nanny again to bring these obscene fat people into line and whip them into shape. No matter, of course, that the nanny state is made up of the same people who have campaigned against competitive sport, sold off school playing fields and deemed school field trips too risky to undertake lest a poor little waif trips over and decides to sue teacher.

Hysteria has become the bedrock of modern political action to the point where Professor Ian Gilmore, chairman of the Royal College of Physicians' alcohol committee, in supporting John Smith's suggestion that alcohol should be restricted, said, 'Not allowing people to consume more than three drinks in a pub is a wonderful solution if it was practical. We need to change our culture.'

Why do we need to change our culture? And why is it up to Professor Gilmore to decide what is and what isn't legitimate culture? And what if gluttony – unlikely given the proportion of the population that is so vain it is prepared to sacrifice high living for health spas – does become part of legitimate culture? Enforced rehab that operates along the same lines as the USSR's mental hospitals to cure people of anti-revolutionary thinking?

Well, Scotland's nannies have with their smoking ban introduced de facto censorship that is worthy of the Eastern bloc. By extending the ban to smoking in the workplace, and the workplace including a television studio, no one can be seen smoking on television. The Scottish Parliament thinks this is a good thing because smoking, although legal, is akin to a crime and therefore shouldn't be shown on television on the basis it encourages others to smoke.

Logically this means rape, murder, prostitution and taking hard drugs should also be barred from our screens. *Hamlet*? Sorry, guv, multiple murder and corruption. *The Sopranos*? Don't even ask. But logic is a bit-player in this kind of thinking, so full-on sex can be shown, of course, as can buggery, but the protagonists enjoying a recuperative cigarette afterwards will have Plod marching the producers down to the station.

2006 World Cup because they might offend other nationalities

Censorship, the embodiment of the totalitarian state, then, is welcomed back by the Scottish Parliament, who find it perfectly acceptable that this will contribute to the discrimination of a minority of some 30 per cent of the country's population despite the fact that they have done nothing illegal.

Inevitably it will make some people happy, like Sue Tsoucalas, who was troubled by the smoking on stage at various theatre productions. 'I have recently had the misfortune to see three plays during which the actors smoked on stage, and in none of the cases did this appear to have any relevance to the play,' she wrote to *The Times*. She went on:

> Neither, without smoking, would it have 'compromised the artistic integrity for the work in question'. What it did compromise, however, was my asthma.
>
> During one play I had to rush out of the auditorium and was unable to return. During the other two I was able to remain, albeit with sufficient coughing to have probably spoilt the enjoyment of the people around me.

Hers is a letter of our times. How poor her health must have been for this whiff of cigarette smoke that wafted down from the stage to have caused such agony. God forbid she should ever get downwind of a barbecue. How could she have ever survived the past century when smoking wasn't just a luxury but de rigueur in every household? A country pub with a log fire must be a pleasure never experienced. How grateful we should be that she had the good grace to restrict herself to ruining the enjoyment of her fellow audience members (and probably put the cast off sufficiently to mar their performance, too) rather than suing the theatre for such inconsideration.

In the nanny state, adults are ready to cry foul for the slightest

---

Members of the Scottish Women's Rural Institutes have proposed changing the name of their Housewives' Committee and Housewife Proficiency Tests to Homecraft

misdemeanour, and there is no shortage of lawyers who are more than happy to fight for the rights of Ms Tsoucalas, or anyone else who might have fallen victim to such hazards.

In 2005, for example, a hospital consultant who was fired after claiming her boss had told her she would not succeed because she was a black woman (despite the fact that this discrimination didn't stop her attaining the post in the first place) was awarded £1.6 million in compensation after she was fired for 'gross personal misconduct' following an inquiry that resulted from three years of clashes with other senior staff. In one of these, a consultant raised his voice and, wait for it, shouted at her.

We don't know all the facts of the case, and no doubt the award must have been merited. But like Ms Tsoucalas, this consultant is effectively rattling her bars and shouting for nanny to come and help because 'LIFE'S NOT FAIR!' Although one, if stretched, is willing to believe that this tiny whiff of cigarette smoke wafting into a smoke-free auditorium might have had Ms Tsoucalas coughing like a tramp, and it could indeed be racism that led to our consultant's dismissal, why do they merit ruining first the enjoyment of others and second going to court? Well, it's their rights, innit?

How lawyers must have salivated when in the UK in 2000 the Human Rights Act was introduced. It offered the following: 'right to free elections; right to liberty; right to a fair trial; respect for private and family life; freedom of thought, conscience and religion; freedom of expression; freedom of assembly, association and to join a trade union; prohibition of discrimination.'

Um, hang on, didn't we have these rights anyway?

Well, yes we did. In fact, surprise, surprise, in the years since the Human Rights Act was introduced, the right to liberty has been taken away from fox hunters wanting to pursue a tradition that had lasted hundreds of years; respect for family life has been seriously

Committee and Homecraft Exams and Displays

undermined by legislation putting the traditional family set-up of husband, wife and children at a financial disadvantage; the right of assembly has been denied to those who wanted to protest against the Iraq war near the Houses of Parliament; the Prevention of Terrorism Act has resulted in citizens being held for months under control orders imposed by the Home Secretary without being arrested, let alone charged or receiving a trial; freedom of expression has been severely curtailed under the Religious Hatred Bill, which has made it an offence to say what you think about organised religion; prohibition of discrimination does not apply to smokers – indeed discrimination against smokers has been encouraged; the right to liberty is only exercised on the condition that the state can follow you with state-of-the-art video cameras; the people of Britain are to be forced to carry identity cards.

The Act – 'You'll probably never need it. But it's nice to know it's there' ran the advert accompanying the launch – in other words, isn't worth the paper it is written on.

These rights are totally arbitrary, decided upon by politicians who, far from allowing us to pursue our own interests unfettered, are obsessed with forcing their values upon us whether we agree with them or not.

What rights were there, for example, for Brian Hasker, who seven days a week for sixteen years served up traditional English fare at his café at St Nicholas Park in Warwick? Council officials refused to renew his lease because, they claimed, he was not, horror of horrors, selling trendy healthier foods (even though these weren't what his customers wanted). Mr Hasker, 63, who had hoped to retire and pass the business on to his son, was left claiming benefits.

The lease was handed to former communications worker Terry Griffin, who was understandably bewildered to be caught up in the local controversy. He, too, was offering up the chips and burgers

A Christian reform scheme run at Dartmoor jail, helping prisoners leave their lives of crime, has been forced to close because it does not support gay relationships and

but had pasta, salads and baked potatoes on the menu too, which is what led to the council awarding him the lease.

'The council has a healthy-eating policy which says that people using our facilities should provide a healthy option for the punters,' said parks manager Nigel Bishop.

So sod off, Mr Hasker. Perhaps he should spend his new-found spare time as an unemployed man by taking long walks in the countryside before going home to a nice healthy supper of pasta. Nanny is quite happy to intercede, you see, on behalf of your rights as long as they are the correct ones.

The British Government introduced 'right to roam' legislation with the Countryside Agency in 2001, publishing maps of areas to be opened to walkers. This was doubly attractive in that generally it would inconvenience landowners and toffs – farmers who shut out walkers were 'medieval', said Alun Michael, the Government's Minister for the countryside, no doubt seeking to pour calming waters over any anger they might express about people in loud cagoules having the right to march over their land. On the other hand, would Mr Michael be 'medieval' were he to intercede as hosts of ramblers trotted across his garden because it happened to be part of a rather scenic bit of countryside?

How far is nanny prepared to go to protect our rights and oversee our safety? Under the maxim if it saves just one life it will be worth it – well, it won't actually, not worth it at all – surely striding across the Yorkshire Moors or the Peak District or even worse the Cairngorms should carry risks that are unacceptable to our political masters. We read weekly of walkers and climbers being brought down dead from mountain ranges across the world, of skiers dying after getting caught out for venturing off-piste, but these, because they're pursuits of which nanny approves, are acceptable. And quite right, too. Those who gorge themselves in front of the television with a packet of pretzels and a few cans of

officials were worried that it may discriminate against prisoners from non-Christian faiths

lager, who aren't engaged in such wholesome activities but with life chances probably statistically better than for a group of mountain climbers, deserve the full wrath of our rulers.

Indeed, quite preposterously, nanny is taking all the right steps to make those climbers less rather than more likely to be able to fend for themselves.

A lifeguard instructor and her husband, a health-and-safety officer – you could say, elite members of the meddling classes – were told by staff at Sedgemoor Splash in Bridgwater, Somerset, that they couldn't take their children aged five, two and one for a swim in the pool. The reason? Health-and-safety rules, which dictate there has to be one adult per child under five; never mind that they were going to use a separate toddler's pool with a depth of 2 ft 6 in. and the obvious abilities of the parents. But anyway, why should this matter? Why should Sedgemoor District Council dictate what we can and can't do with our children?

Because nanny has said so, that's why, which means that anyone with three children has to enlist the help of an adult if they want to teach them to swim and ultimately become more able to look after themselves.

Our children, certainly, have been barred from any sort of outdoor activity that might result in so much as a scratched knee, so scared are schools of parents exercising their 'rights' to sue. Schools have outlawed skipping, British bulldog, tag, tree swings, even running and conkers on the grounds that they could cause accidents and injuries. Research by Sarah Thomson of Keele University in a survey of the playground pursuits of 1,000 children in Staffordshire, Shropshire and Lancashire found that schools had banned conkers, for example, as 'offensive weapons' and schools were terrified of litigation from parents. And so they might be. A Mori poll showed that 57 per cent of parents would

---

A Cambridgeshire schoolgirl was in 2006 taken to court for common assault after she 'pinged' a classmate's bra, even though she had been punished by the school.

seek compensation if their child suffered an injury at school that they felt could have been prevented.

A 15-year-old boy who was expelled for allegedly taking a knife into school was in 2005 awarded £11,000 in compensation – £6,000 of it towards his home tuition and the other £5,000 for his 'hurt feelings'. It wasn't as if the boy, who had behavioural problems, didn't have form. He was initially suspended for five days when he was thirteen for fighting. A month later, he was suspended again for three days for the same offence. Three months later, he was given a two-day suspension for using a knife from the school's technology department to rip pages from a classmate's book. Then in May 2003, he was finally expelled for taking a knife into school and passing it to a friend.

His mother complained to the Local Government Ombudsman, who said, 'This is a very depressing story of a boy who is reasonably able academically and is not receiving the education which he needs and to which he has a right. This is partly because of his own behaviour difficulties and partly because of the council's failure to provide him with an education which meets his needs.'

What were these needs, exactly? The right to write his essays in blood?

The message the ruling gives is that even the most yobbish, thuggish of children have 'rights', however bad their behaviour. Our schools are plagued by gangs of feral, illiterate children who feel they are immune to any moral imperatives other than those they select.

They are made to feel that their opinions, however ill-formed, carry the same weight as those of adults. Teenage gangs roam our streets, safe in the knowledge that if any member of the public dares to restrain them, they have 'rights' that, should they be considerate enough not to knife them, they can fall back on. It is their right to choose how obnoxious or not they are because they have been told

She was told to pay the victim £20 in compensation

time and time again by nanny that their feelings count. In other words, the message they're hearing is that they are simply smaller versions of adults and have every right to think of themselves as such, even if they don't have any adult responsibilities.

So important have our children become that England now has a Children's Commissioner to look after their rights as part of its 'Every Child Matters: Change for Children' quango.

'Over the next few years, every local authority will be working with its partners, through children's trusts, to find out what works best for children and young people in its area and act on it,' it boasts. 'They will need to involve children and young people in this process, and when inspectors assess how local areas are doing, they will listen especially to the views of children and young people themselves.'

This is another chance for the meddling classes to group together and talk simpering nonsense to each other. In Manchester in 2004, a joint children's unit was established in response to the Every Child Matters Green Paper to:

- Work with stakeholders to develop and maintain a shared diagnosis of the barriers to improving outcomes and the actions required to overcome them;
- Contribute to, and ensure the coordination of, strategic developments across all issues relevant to children, young people and families;
- Provide a focal point for the interpretation of Government requirements and new initiatives in the context of local aspirations and strategies and help make and plan appropriate responses.

And so on and so on and so on, with other measures that will 'identify mainstream evidenced-based good practice'.

Eleven mental-health patients, deemed 'incurables', threatened to sue Broadmoor Hospital because the windows in a new £36-million secure unit violated their

London Mayor Ken Livingstone, nanny-in-chief of the capital, couldn't, of course, be left out if there was some spending public money and talking gobbledegook to be done and established his own 'strategy for children', even though he has no direct powers in relation to children's services. He created a children and young people's unit to help 'fulfil the strategy's goals', which are 'placing children and young people's interests at the heart of policy-making, tackling child poverty and social exclusion, and giving voice to their opinions and concerns'. Nicky Gavron, the deputy mayor, said, 'It is important for me to listen to young people and children, not because they will be adults tomorrow but because they are children today.' Whatever the hell that means.

In fact, these children are not becoming adults tomorrow, anyway. At the core of society's malaise is the fact that the meddling classes have treated children as adults and adults as children. In the words of Richard D. North in his book *Rich is Beautiful*, 'We are watching people grow old without developing. We are watching the middle-aged become botoxed without becoming civilised.'

He writes of emotional incontinence such as Olympic athletes weeping at each success or failure; language inflation – a flood in which no one is killed or injured is 'devastating', and we could add here the word 'tragedy' attributed to death, however it is caused; the blame culture, where nothing is an accident but people rather are victims of heartless officialdom or greedy capitalists; a praise culture, where everyone expects to be told how well they are doing, and is entitled to whatever they want, and where not getting it is 'unfair'.

'Infantilised non-adults cannot govern themselves, and are hard to govern for two reasons,' North continues:

> They will not submit to the wider needs of society, and they
> do not understand the value of the elitist institutions by which

human rights by letting in draughts

society mediates competing needs. Childlike adults could not be expected to see the merit of representative democracy and stern professions, nor to value compromise. They are bound to be attracted by glamorous campaigners led by shrill, intemperate and petulant stars.

We will need to reassert adulthood before we can expect to see the institutions of politics regain their former respect and value.

There's little sign of that so far. As the nanny state has developed, so we have come to blame nanny for our failings and misdemeanours. Indeed, the state has become so powerful that it is now, in threatening to take obese children into care, even prepared to take over the role of parenthood. We are at the stage where it can override the role of parents and send a 'supernanny' into the houses of problem children. After a pilot scheme in Dundee, politicians agreed that especially trained social workers could be sent into the homes of troublesome families to receive 24-hour supervision and counselling – including classes in anger management. And how cross would that make you?

And what, pray, are these problems? And if they are problems, why are these people not breaking the law, and why is the law not protecting the public?

Charles Clarke, former Home Secretary, launched a 'Respect' agenda to cope with the antisocial behaviour that is afflicting modern society. This is a bit rich, considering that the police are under government orders to follow a politically correct agenda and have responded by hounding motorists and policing those of us who aren't members of the criminal community, while leaving the proponents of antisocial behaviour to behave as they wish. But Charles Clarke is an elected politician, and he knew that at some

A bronze statue in Bristol of Isambard Kingdom Brunel shows the engineer without his customary cigar, even though he smoked 40 a day and was never seen without one

point someone was going to call him to account, so he had to do something. Or at any rate be seen to be doing something.

Closer examination of the Government's 'Respect Action Plan,' in fact, reveals that we get more of the same, with professional nannies interceding on behalf of infantile adults who are no longer deemed responsible enough to run their own affairs. The stick, in this Respect agenda, is a new house-closure order temporarily sealing properties that are the constant focus of antisocial behaviour, and the right of a school to apply for parenting orders against unruly children.

After that, it's nanny on the march, as an 'Action Plan' includes funding of 'up to' £28 million to set up a network of intensive family-support schemes and provide parenting help. Also included in the plan are proposals to establish a national parenting academy to train staff to help families where 'kids' are at risk of getting involved in antisocial behaviour. And, wait for it, there will be 'Face the People' community meetings to allow residents to hold to account officials responsible for community-safety issues and raise issues of concern.

We all know what this spin amounts to: nothing. It will be administered by the likes of the Manchester joint children's unit with people who 'work with stakeholders to develop and maintain a shared diagnosis of the barriers to improving outcomes and the actions required to overcome them'. They have not so far helped the Hollingdean estate. Nor will nanny help by this ludicrous piece of nonsense.

For how can there be a respect agenda when the power of adults to act as adults has been eviscerated by the Human Rights Act? Even by using the word respect, Charles Clarke was pandering to the parlance of disaffected inner-city youth constantly telling each other to 'respeck ma space', 'respeck my rights', 'respeck my woman or I'll mash your face'.

Youth-centre staff of the sport and youth development team in Derby have been asked to wear hoodies to 'challenge the stereotype' that all hoodie wearers are thugs

Respect is not a verb that works unconditionally, such as 'to see' or 'to hear'. Respect can be accorded only to those who earn it, not those who demand it. In a world where soppy sentimentalism dominates political thought and bogus rights are bandied around the playground and Parliament alike, the chances of earning it become slimmer rather than greater. For nanny has created a dumb world, in many areas bereft of manners, discipline or intellectual rigour, thus pride and, ultimately, contentment. If you tell children they are all special, then no one is. If you tell children they have rights without having earned them, they will naturally grow up to expect their right to have a job, a car, a phone, a house. If happiness doesn't follow as a result, then they will look not to themselves but others for the answer.

There is a desperation to this culture. The Western world has become dumber, fatter and more self-obsessed, but nanny won't let anyone say it. Instead, the meddling classes insist that we blame nasty old capitalist fashion houses for putting their clothes on slim models and therefore cause untold distress to the spotty, fat adolescents who aspire to buy them. Why can't our girls' role models, bleated parents in a survey commissioned by a skincare brand Dove, look like Charlotte Church? Three-quarters of them disliked some part of their body by the age of 12, the survey revealed. Of course they did. They are 12. But look around at these heavily made-up girls waddling around with their iPods: are they really so traumatised at being a stone or so overweight? Traumatised enough to eat a bit less? And anyway, if they are so influenced by these skinny models, why are they all not anorexic? But of course, they are victims, just as they are victims of an education system that can't make learning 'fun'.

It seems incredible to us now that in *Swallows and Amazons*, published in 1930, a group of children led by their 12-year-old eldest brother could sail off without life jackets in a dinghy that

A £224 million Children's Index recording lives of all 12 million children living in England and Wales will, among other things, record whether a child's parents are

would sink should it capsize, camp overnight on an island in the Lake District and seek adventures with a pair of girls of a similar age remarkably untraumatised by role models, who at that time were pretty much all slim. Their mother raised a little concern at letting them go off like this, but their father, in the navy, simply wrote back: 'Better drowned than duffers, if not duffers won't drown.' And so starts a great adventure in which these children learn to take responsibility, to look after each other, to stretch their skills and their imagination, to have fun beyond belief and ultimately equip themselves to become responsible adults. If nanny discovered such behaviour in a parent now, the children would be taken into a care home where they could learn instead to steal, fight and fail their exams.

In 2006, a motorist, Simon Thompson, made a middle-finger curse when he spotted a mobile speed camera while driving home from work. He wasn't speeding but was nonetheless issued with an £80 fine. He claims he made the gesture at the camera. The policemen claimed it was at them. Not that they were worried, of course, being brave, burly upholders of the law who have seen it all. Their concern was that a member of the public could have glanced that way at the same moment. The 'offence particulars' section of his penalty notice – brace yourself – read: 'Used offensive hand gestures towards police in full view of passing public for 3–4 seconds.' Shocking crime, wouldn't you agree? This was contrary to the Public Order Act 1994.

Mr Thompson, not entirely unreasonably, said, 'A teacher gets attacked by thugs and by the time the police get there they've all scarpered. Yet they pursue me to my own front door for making a gesture at an inanimate object.'

Doesn't this tell us, in a nutshell, the depths to which our society has sunk? It tells us, certainly, how unpleasant life has become under the nanny state, how far the meddling classes' influence is

providing a 'positive role model' and even whether they are eating the recommended daily number of fruit and vegetables

now stretching, and how petty and controlling they are prepared to be. There is the po-faced self-righteousness of the penalty notice, intimating that although the big, tough, seen-it-all-before police officers were immune to such a shocking display of rudeness, the public – the kidults whom the nanny state has charged them with looking after – could be traumatised by such behaviour.

It reveals, too, that in a civilised society the state can take close-up photographs of us like this. And that, in a civilised society, the obnoxious middle-finger curse has become the vulgar signature of our daily behaviour. The two go hand in hand: the uncalled-for intrusion into our daily lives and spoilt, unpleasant, rude, self-righteous behaviour, like using the one-finger salute, that is a manifestation of the immaturity of the population living at the beginning of the twenty-first century.

Surely it would be better if nanny went and took a long, long holiday. Then we might all grow up.

The local council in Rockdale, Australia, blasted boy racers with Barry Manilow songs at full volume from speakers in the streets to stop them congregating. Unfortunately, residents couldn't abide the music either